I0822978

WINGS OF PARADISE

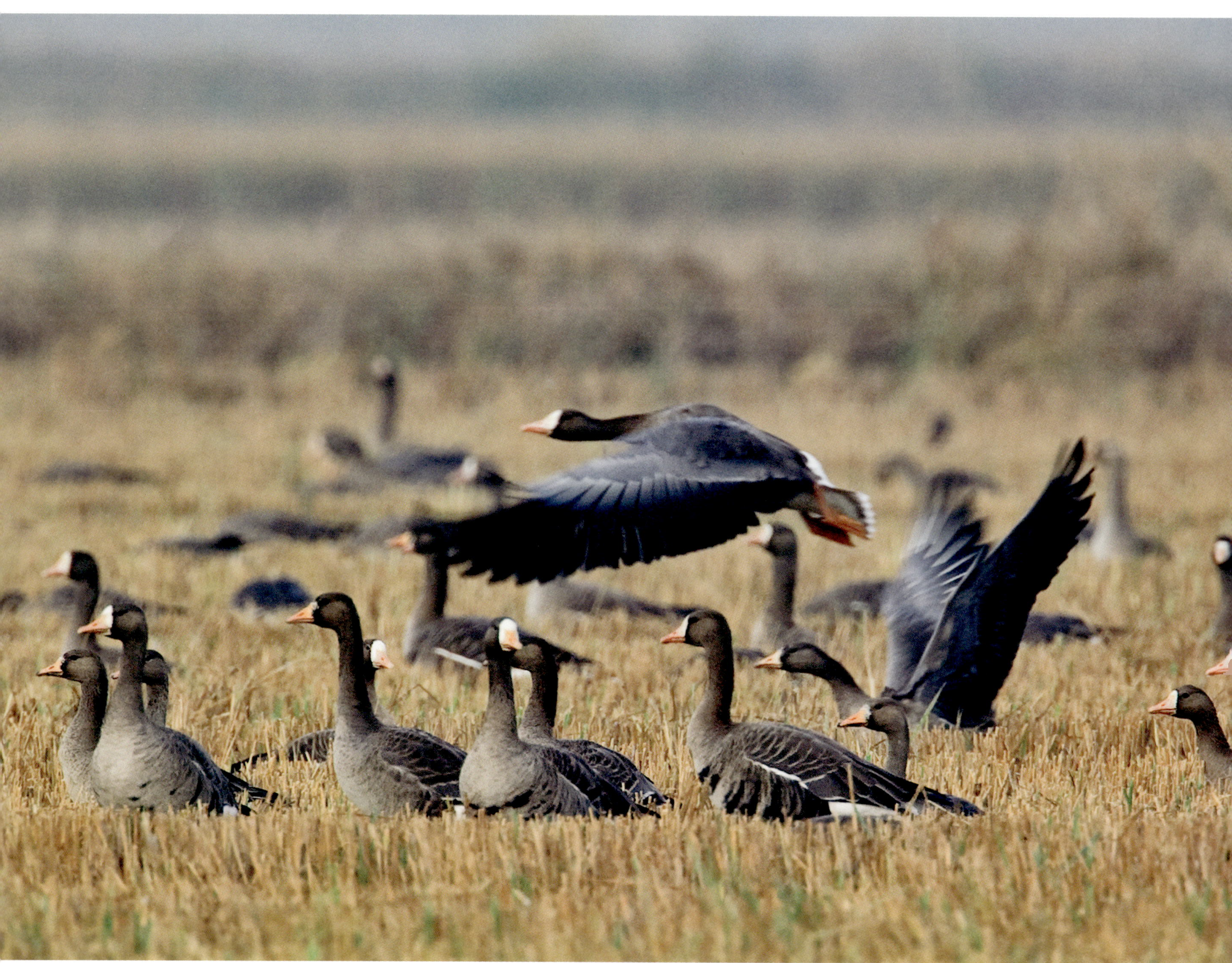

WINGS OF PARADISE

BIRDS OF THE LOUISIANA WETLANDS

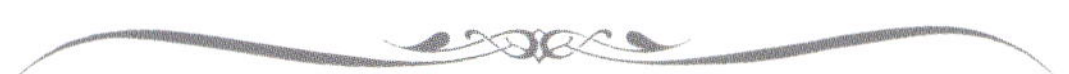

CHARLIE HOHORST, JR., *with* MARCELLE BIENVENU

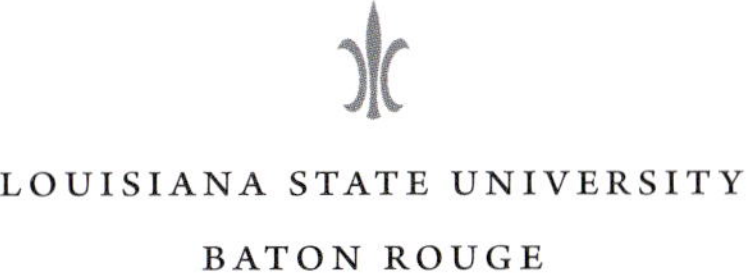

LOUISIANA STATE UNIVERSITY

BATON ROUGE

Published by Louisiana State University Press

Manufactured in China
SECOND PRINTING

DESIGNER: Barbara Neely Bourgoyne
TYPEFACES: Centaur and Gotham, display; Arno Pro, text
PRINTER AND BINDER: C&C Offset Printing Co., Ltd.

LIBRARY OF CONGRESS CATALOGING-IN-PUBLICATION DATA
Hohorst, Charlie, 1940–
Wings of paradise : birds of the Louisiana wetlands / Charlie Hohorst, Jr., with Marcelle Bienvenu.
p. cm.
Includes index.
ISBN 978-0-8071-3450-4 (cloth : alk. paper)
1. Wetland birds—Louisiana. 2. Wetland birds—Louisiana—Pictorial works. I. Bienvenu, Marcelle. II. Title.
QL684.L8H64 2009
598'.176909763—dc22
2008053876

The paper in this book meets the guidelines for permanence and durability of the Committee on Production Guidelines for Book Longevity of the Council on Library Resources. ♾

I dedicate this book in memory of my father, who introduced me to the outdoors at a very early age, and to my grandson Charlie IV, who I hope also experiences being one with nature.—C. H.

While working on this book, I thought often of my late father Marcel M. "Blackie" Bienvenu. An avid sportsman, he loved nothing better than spending time with his buddies in the marshes hunting ducks and geese. It was he who taught me to love and appreciate the great outdoors, and it was from him I learned to prepare perfectly roasted mallards, baked teals, and a superb goose and oyster gumbo. Here's to you Papa!—M. B.

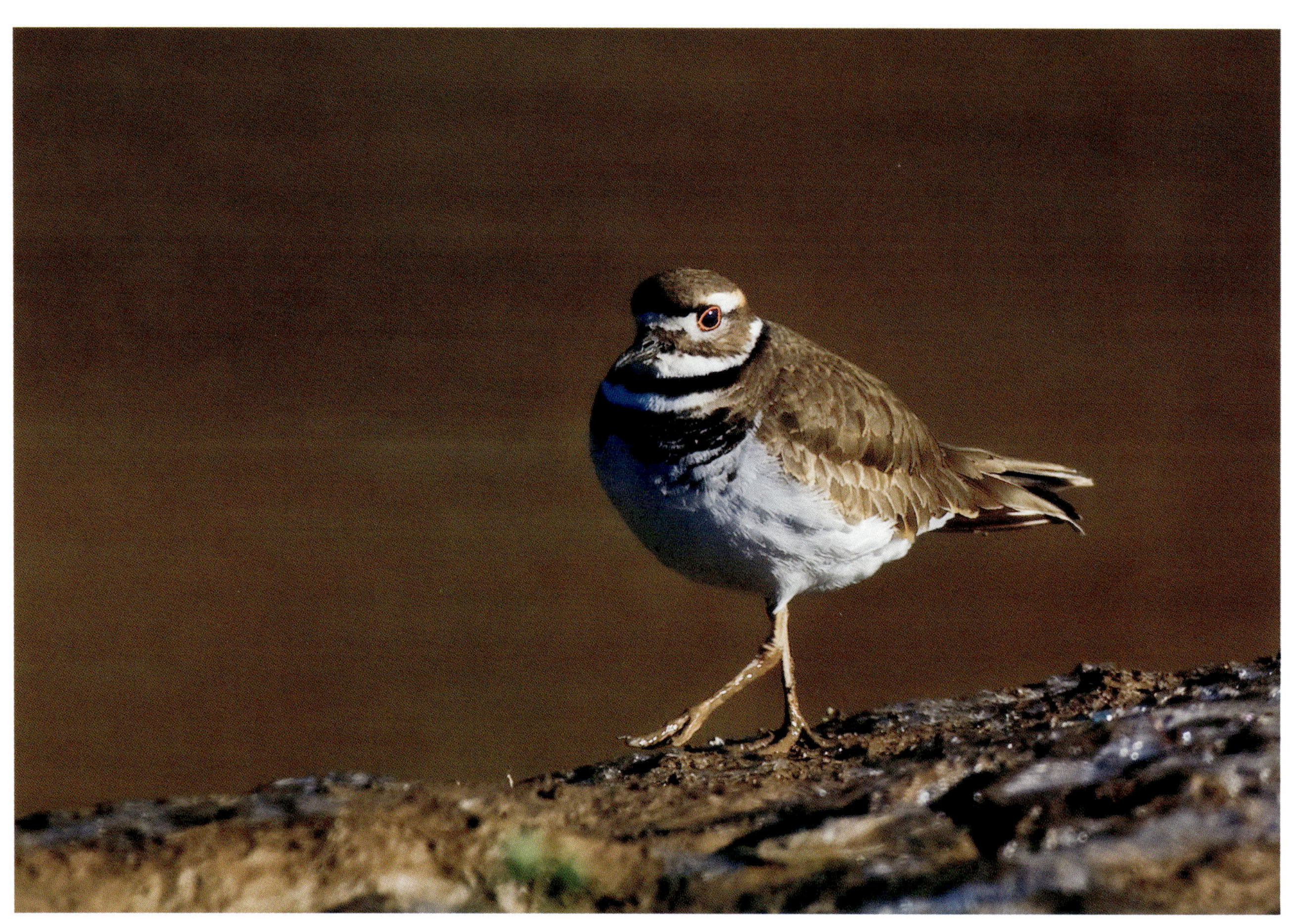

CONTENTS

FOREWORD

I have always been an admirer of wildlife photography, especially images of waterfowl in their undisturbed moments. A flock of pintail ducks descending into a pristine marsh pond with nothing more on their minds than a good meal or a little romance captures that mental image for me. It truly takes an artistic eye and a steady hand to do these moments justice. Charlie Hohorst, Jr., rises to the occasion time after time, taking incredible photographs that make us wonder how he could have been so ready at just the right moment.

I first met Charlie many years ago when he was working in the men's clothing business in Lafayette, Louisiana, and it did not take us long to realize that we both shared a passion for duck hunting. For both of us, time spent in the field pursuing that passion was quality time indeed! What I did not discover until many years later, was his intense passion for shooting wildlife with the camera as well.

I had not run into Charlie for quite a while when one day, a couple of years ago, I received an e-mail from one of my hunting buddies that included waterfowl photographs which Charlie had taken in the marshes of south Louisiana. Charlie was capturing incredible images of ducks and geese over and over again in a way that I had never seen except in wildlife books and magazines. I immediately fired off an e-mail to Charlie asking him to include me on his distribution list, and he responded that he would.

I began to look forward to Charlie's e-mails with great anticipation and was in turn sending each one via e-mail to a long list of my friends and hunting companions. Every time that I sent a collection of Charlie's photos to my friends, I received a flood of responses ranging from "this guy is incredible" to "these are so good that they can't be real!" Some of these comments came from guys who were pretty good amateur photographers, and they were so amazed by what Charlie was capturing with his camera. That was when I began to see that Charlie possessed a special gift in the world of wildlife photography.

About a year ago, I contacted Charlie to see if he would be interested in taking some wildlife/waterfowl photographs at the Florence Club, which is a hunting lodge that my family owns south of Gueydan, Louisiana. The Florence Club was founded in 1911, and its mature agricultural fields and untouched marshes have always served as a haven for ducks and geese, as well as many other forms of wildlife. Charlie jumped at the opportunity and we arranged a time for him to be inserted into "the nest."

I was there that day at 5:30 a.m. when Charlie was preparing his equipment, and I immediately observed two things. First, he was jacked up for the photo shoot like a 7-year-old waiting for Santa, and second, the man was totally committed and completely focused on what he was about to do. Drop him in the field before daylight, pick him up after dark. That is how Charlie operates.

Charlie traveled to the Florence Club several more times after that first shoot and assembled an astonishing portfolio of photographs that still has me shaking my head in amazement. Beyond the incredible waterfowl photos, he took pictures of a baby owl sticking its head out of a wood duck box, a majestic hawk holding a mouse in its mouth by the tail, and a blue heron reflected in the water that one has to see to believe.

I continued to send many of these photos snapped at the Florence Club to my friends, and the responses that I received confirmed my belief that it was time for Charlie's photographs to be published. When I called Charlie and asked him what he thought about doing a book, he sounded a little bit surprised and a great deal honored. His first question to me was, "It sounds great, but how do we do it?" I suggested that he put together a portfolio of his photographs and then contact Louisiana State University Press, which has been in the publishing business since 1935. Since the majority of Charlie's work was done in the state of Louisiana it seemed natural that LSU Press would be the first choice as a publisher.

Charlie contacted Marcelle Bienvenu, who is a well-know author living in Louisiana, and asked her if she would be interested in writing the narrative for his book. Marcelle happily agreed, and together they pitched the book idea to LSU Press.

Well, the rest is history, and I am so pleased that Charlie is able to share his passion for wildlife photography with the world, so those admirers of great photography everywhere will be able to enjoy his work. What's so great for me is that for years to come, even in the summer heat of Louisiana, I can look at the beautiful images of ducks and geese that Charlie captured with his lens, and in my mind's eye I will be sitting in my favorite duck blind on opening day!

WILLIAM W. "BILLY" RUCKS IV

ACKNOWLEDGMENTS

First, I want to thank William W. "Billy" Rucks IV. Because of him, this book has become a reality. It was he who suggested that the photographs needed to be shared with present and future nature enthusiasts.

And thanks to Tommy Guilbeau and his late wife, Dottie, who purchased my first print and showed continued interest in my photography throughout the years.

I also must thank my friend Danny Dobbs for never hesitating to help me with identification requests and for getting me interested in the smaller birds like the warblers and neo-tropicals.

To all the landowners and farmers all over south Louisiana who allowed me the opportunity to photograph on their property, I say thanks. They share with me a deep appreciation for the wonderful world of nature.

I am also grateful to my son, Charles III, who encouraged me and gave me the flexibility to pursue my passion. I must also thank my daughter, Meagan, and my daughter-in-law, Ashley, who are always supportive in my endeavors.

I want to express my gratitude and appreciation to Juliet Thibeaux for her constant support. She never makes demands on my quest for photographing nature just about every day of my life.

Marcelle Bienvenu also deserves my thanks for her dedication to the project. She joins me in thanking all those who contributed their recipes for the book.

And most of all our sincere thanks to LSU Press and to Margaret Hart, our editor, who was always patient and supportive.

CHARLES HOHORST, JR.
www.CharliehPhotography.com

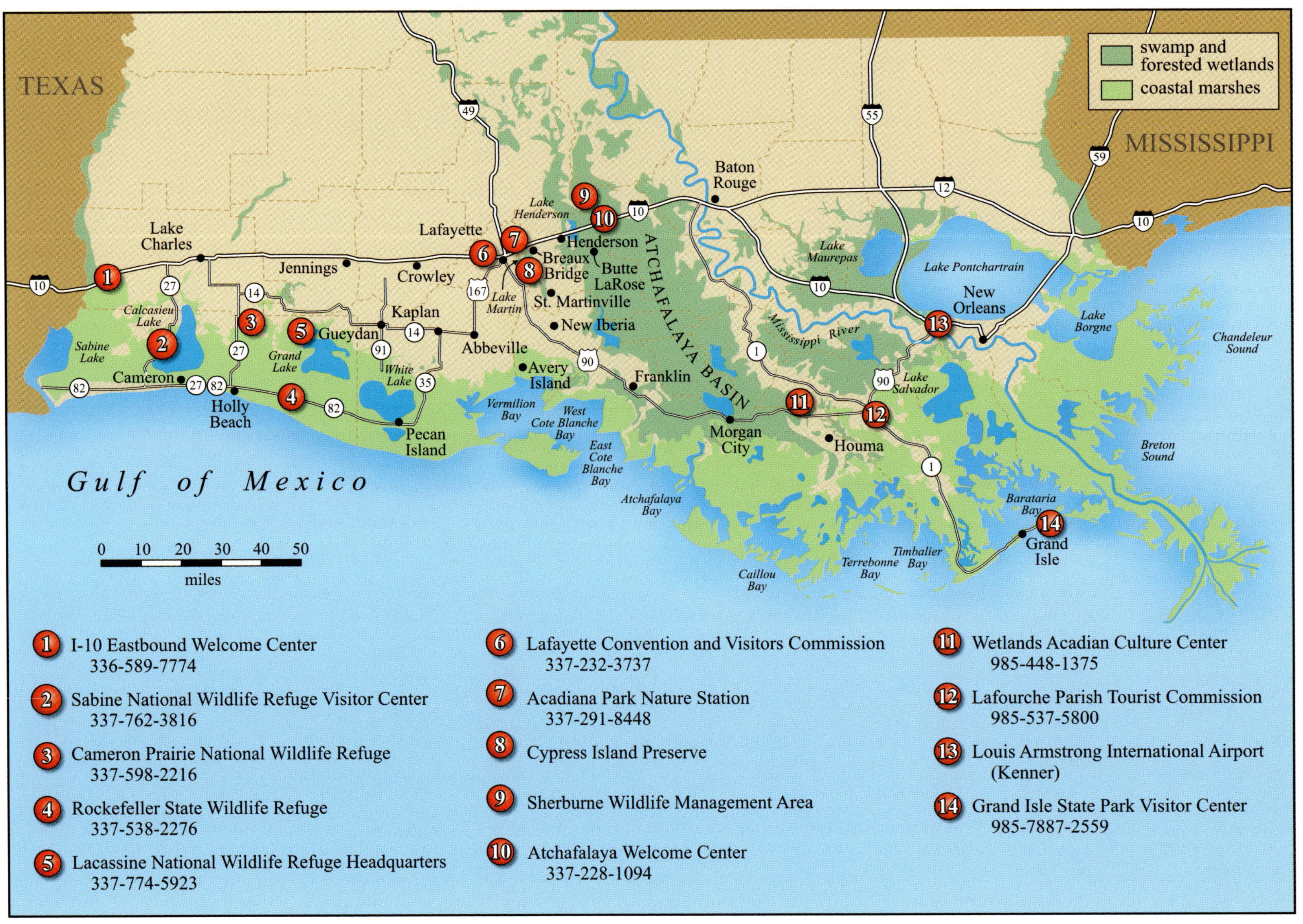

1 I-10 Eastbound Welcome Center
336-589-7774

2 Sabine National Wildlife Refuge Visitor Center
337-762-3816

3 Cameron Prairie National Wildlife Refuge
337-598-2216

4 Rockefeller State Wildlife Refuge
337-538-2276

5 Lacassine National Wildlife Refuge Headquarters
337-774-5923

6 Lafayette Convention and Visitors Commission
337-232-3737

7 Acadiana Park Nature Station
337-291-8448

8 Cypress Island Preserve

9 Sherburne Wildlife Management Area

10 Atchafalaya Welcome Center
337-228-1094

11 Wetlands Acadian Culture Center
985-448-1375

12 Lafourche Parish Tourist Commission
985-537-5800

13 Louis Armstrong International Airport (Kenner)

14 Grand Isle State Park Visitor Center
985-7887-2559

I

BIRDS OF THE LOUISIANA WETLANDS

CHARLIE HOHORST, JR.

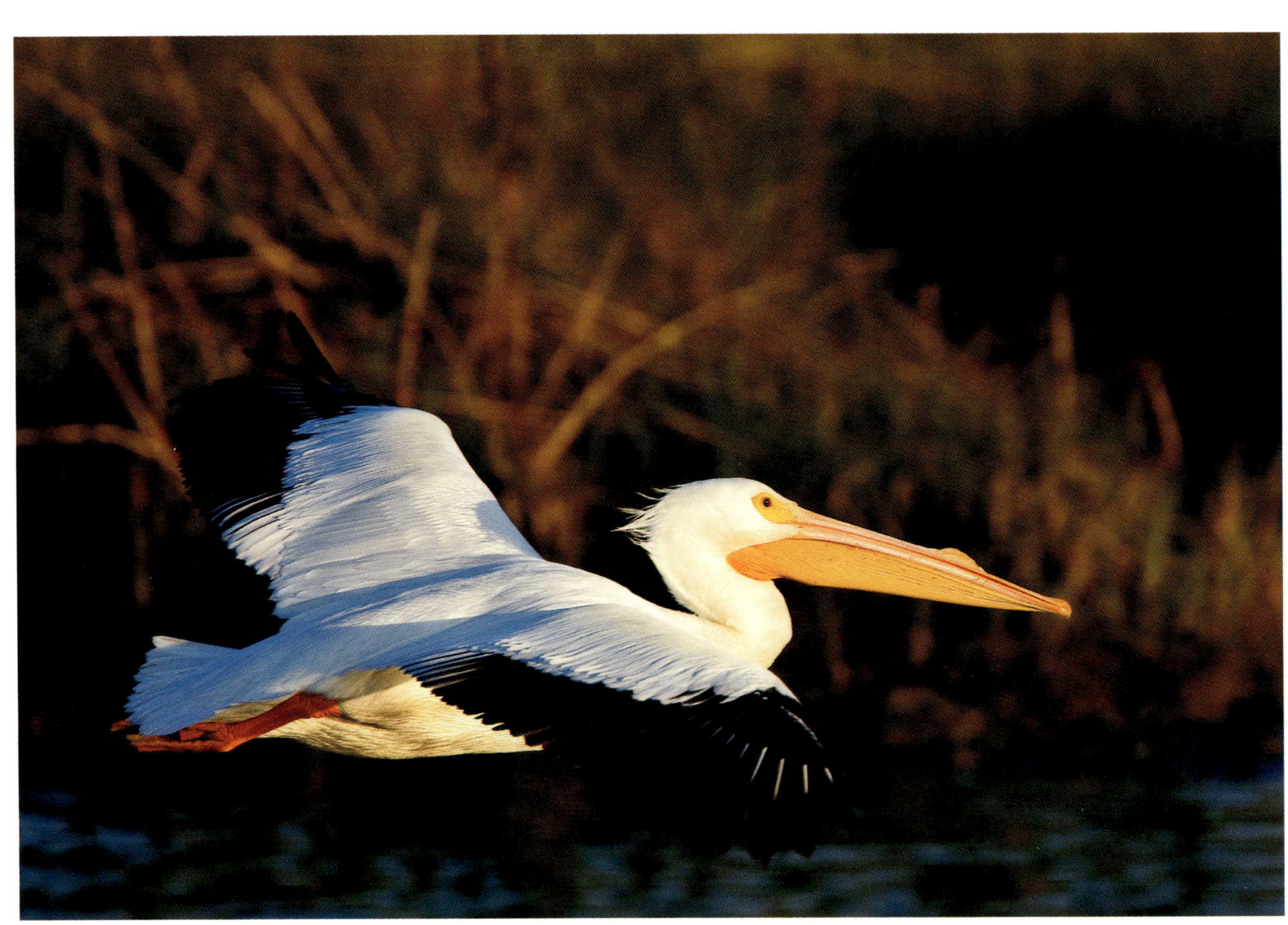

I became interested in nature photography as a young man but didn't get serious until sometime in 2000 when I saw a photo by Tom Mangelsen, one of the premier nature photographers in the world. The photo showed a side view of a brown bear sitting atop a twelve-foot waterfall in Brooks, Alaska. Mangelsen was able to capture the bear with its mouth wide open, about to snatch a salmon as it jumped up the falls. The salmon, as it went upstream to spawn, was briefly suspended within the open jaws of this bear. What a moment to witness in nature! I was hooked!

Having no formal education in photography I taught myself by reading all the technical and esthetic books about nature photography I could get my hands on. I couldn't get enough of the work of Art Wolfe, George Lepp, John Shaw, Art Morris, Moose Peterson, Frantz Lanting, and, of course, Mangelsen.

I have been an avid duck and dove hunter for over fifty years and have long been drawn to the beauty and flight of ducks in the marshes and lowlands of south Louisiana. I vividly remember my first hunt in a rice field near Andrew, Louisiana. I was twelve years old and recall running neck and neck with a black lab to retrieve a green-headed mallard I had just brought down with my single-shot 20-gauge shotgun. Even then I was intrigued by how the ducks and geese maneuvered into a spread of decoys, each giving a variety of wing positions as they approached, then landed.

Back in the 1950s I hunted and fished according to the season at Lake Martin but never really bothered with the other wildlife in this pristine area, which was a short ride from my hometown of Lafayette, Louisiana. But in the mid-90s I discovered the wonders of the Lake Martin Rookery. I spent many early morning hours there watching and photographing a menagerie of wildlife, particularly herons, egrets, roseate spoonbills, ibises, woodpeckers, raptors, wood ducks, and what I came to call my "tweety" birds—passerines that included a great number of songbirds.

The more I photographed, the more I wanted to capture the birds in different perspectives—in flight, coming in to land, in their nests. But, in the beginning, I couldn't seem to get what I wanted because the camera and lens required for action photography lacked a responsive autofocus, plus the equipment was extremely heavy and bulky. Later the technical advances of both cameras and lenses allowed me to capture what I always envisioned. I began photographing seriously with the professional Nikon F5 camera and a used Nikon manual focus 400mm f/3.5 lens (even to this day it's still considered a great piece of glass), and Fuji Velvia 50 and 100 were my film of choice. Along the way I added the following Nikon lenses: 20mm, 50mm, 105mm, and the 200mm, plus extension tubes, remote cord, flash, teleconveters, tripods, polarizers, warming filters, and a light meter.

Most of my images in the beginning were macro or static—nonmoving. I tried birds in flight but could not manually focus fast enough. The camera and lens combination weighed a ton, which also restricted my panning technique—very tiresome. I kept waiting for Nikon to catch up with the autofocus advances Canon had made with both their cameras and lenses so I could do birds in flight. I was particularly interested in the image stabilization feature they brought to their big lenses—the 400, 500, and 600mm. This feature gives the photographer two to three more stops (shutter speeds), which were beneficial in early morning or late evening light.

After seeing a great many flight images of birds using Canon equipment, I sold, or rather gave away, my Nikon equipment and jumped over to Canon. Today I photograph nature using EOS-1D Mark 3, EOS-1D Mark 2n, EOS-5D Mark 2, and EOS-50 D. Lenses include EF 16-35mm f/2.8L USM, EF 17-40mm f/4L USM, EF 24-70mm f/2.81 USM, EF 70-200mm f/2.8L IS USM, EF 400 mm f/4 DO IS USM, EF 500mm f/4L IS USM, and EF 600 mm f/4L IS USM. Extenders include the EF 1.4x 11 and EF 2x 11 and Extension Tubes EF 12 11 and EF 25 11 (for macro: EF 180 f/3.5L Macro USM).

Having gone on big-game hunting trips out West in the 1970s and 80s, I had visions of hunting brown bear, goats, and sheep in Alaska, and even a trip to Africa. But now, rather than shooting animals, I am committed to photographing them in their natural environment. My trips find me photographing brown bear and eagles in Alaska and many other animals in Yellowstone National Park, Grand Teton National Park, and Bosque del Apache in New Mexico. In 2008 I traveled to Botswana where I photographed leopards, brown lions, herds of elephants, giraffes, zebras, and an incredible array of wild birds I had never seen before. Another journey was to Jasper National Park in Canada to photograph elk, sheep, and rams.

I have been very fortunate to travel with several wildlife photographers who have a deep appreciation for being one with nature. At times I find a deep spiritual connection, which is rejuvenating to the soul, spirit, and body.

"It's all about being there."

ALONG THE SHORE

Along the shoreline of Louisiana, where the waters of the Gulf of Mexico meet the coastal marshes, lies one of the largest natural aviaries for waterfowl, wading birds, shorebirds, and songbirds. Tens of thousands of birds—gulls, terns, pelicans, skimmers, plovers, rails, and wrens—are permanent residents that share the lush region with millions of transient birds that make their stopovers during seasonal migrations.

Many days throughout the year you'll find me at the jetties at Grand Isle on the eastern edge of the Louisiana coast as well as the mud flats near the Texas-Louisiana border. There, in the early morning when the air is as thick as our Louisiana gumbos, and in the late afternoon when the sun makes its descent into the horizon, are the best times, in my opinion, to observe and photograph the shorebirds as they swoop, skim, plunge, and meander along the seashore.

The lapping of the waves and the smell of the salty sea air, mixed with the sounds of the hoarse, squawking brown pelicans, the constantly chattering seagulls, and the loud, rolling *keer-reet* of the royal terns, is a remarkable experience of nature at its best.

During the spring and summer months, wading birds—roseate spoonbills, herons, egrets, and bitterns—fill the sky with flapping wings as they return from the south to breed in the marshes, swamps, lagoons, lakes, bayous, and bays that border the southern rim of the Bayou State. At that time of year I spend quite a bit of time at the Cypress Island Preserve, which includes Lake Martin, situated between Breaux Bridge and Lafayette, Louisiana. There, thousands of egrets, roseate spoonbills, and herons come to nest in the bald cypresses and tupelos.

Not far to the east is the Atchafalaya Basin, the largest swamp in the United States. It is a combination of wetlands and river delta where the Atchafalaya River and the Gulf of Mexico converge, making it an ideal location to observe ibises, wood storks, herons, and a plethora of other birds.

Surrounded by these great wildlife areas, I often have a hard time deciding where I'll spend my day, but no matter which choice I make, I know I'll not be disappointed. Wherever there is water—swamps, marshes, bayous, lakes, rice fields, and crawfish ponds—you'll find wetland flyers such as cormorants, anhingas, gallinules, rails, and coots. The large, black cormorants dive majestically into the water to catch a fish or a snake for a meal. Similar to cormorants are anhingas, a dark-feathered fish-eater with a very long neck that resembles a snake. Although I occasionally observe them over open water along the coastline, I see them most often in wooded wetlands like the Atchafalaya Basin. The busy common moorhens are more like ducks and forage on vegetation at areas like Lake Martin. Usually I see the brightly-colored purple gallinules tiptoeing among lily pads and other lush, wet vegetation. The less colorful rails and coots are rather secretive, and I happen upon them most often while photographing other birds.

SHOREBIRDS, GULLS, SKIMMERS, AND MORE

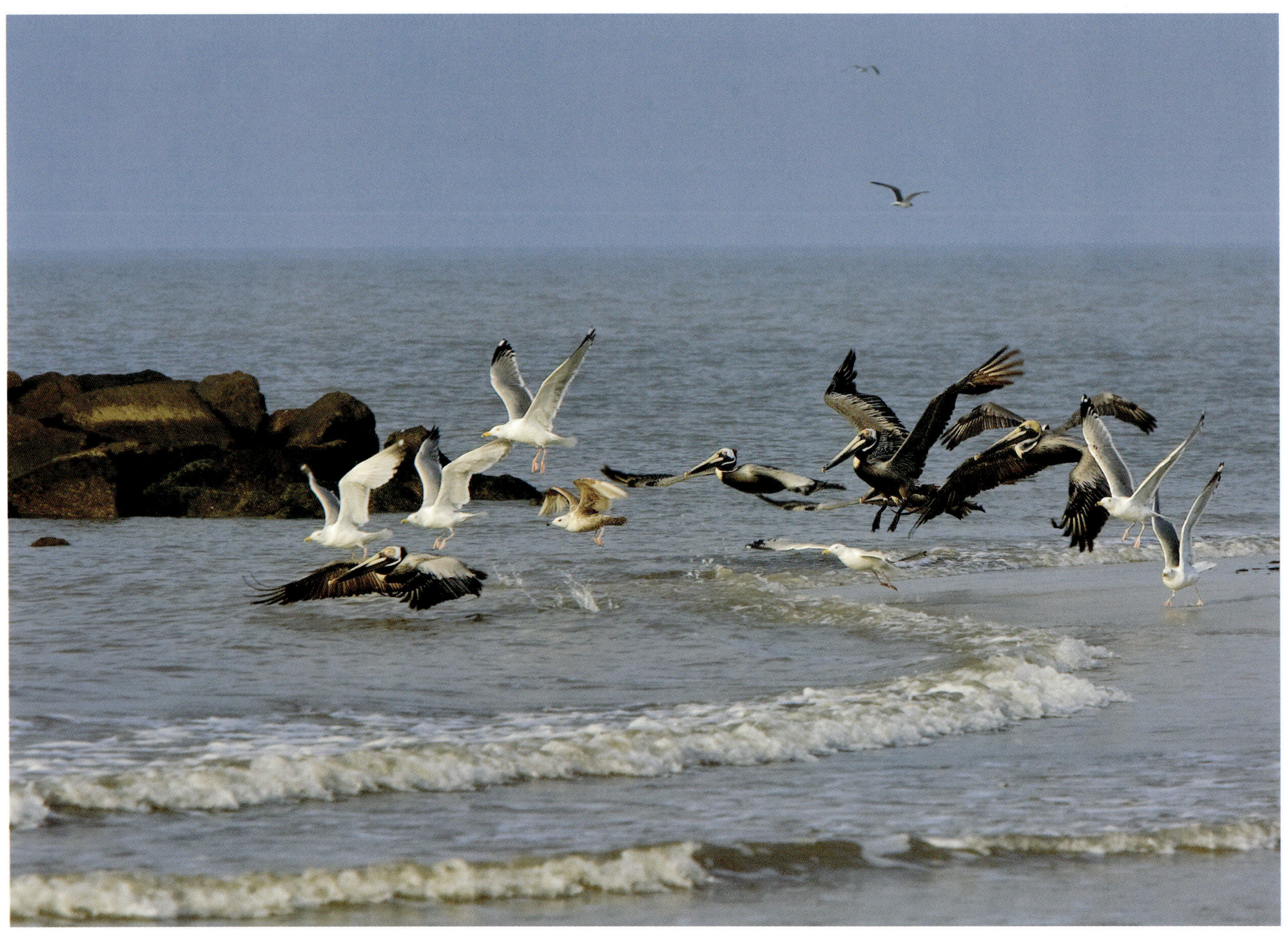

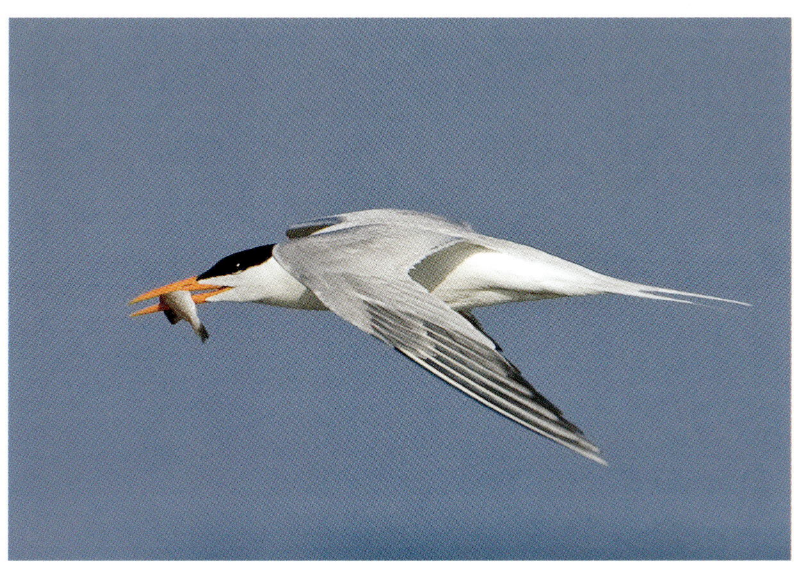

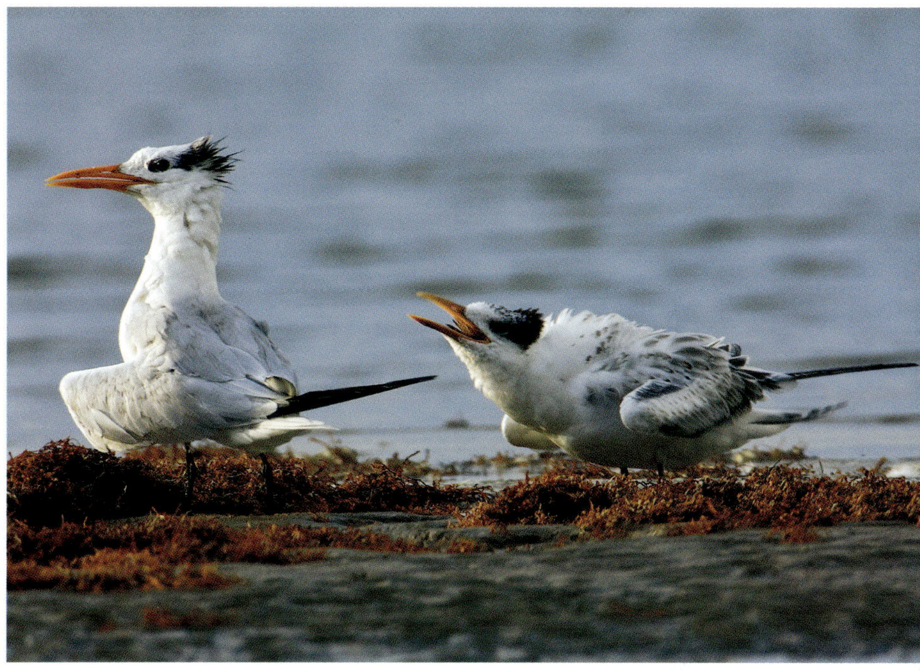

Above, left: On the beach at Cameron this royal tern took off with a fish in its beak. (April 16, 2005)

This pair of royal terns (*above, right*) seems to be having a domestic dispute on the shore at Holly Beach. Nag, nag, nag! I can watch them for hours as they plunge along the shoreline for food. Royal Terns are very defensive of their nests and young. (July 30, 2006)

Facing page: On a hazy, cool morning near the jetties at Cameron in the southwestern part of Louisiana, I watched these gulls and brown pelicans in a feeding frenzy. The sound of their squawking was almost deafening as they swooped, plunged, and fought over the fish in the shallow water. (April 9, 2005)

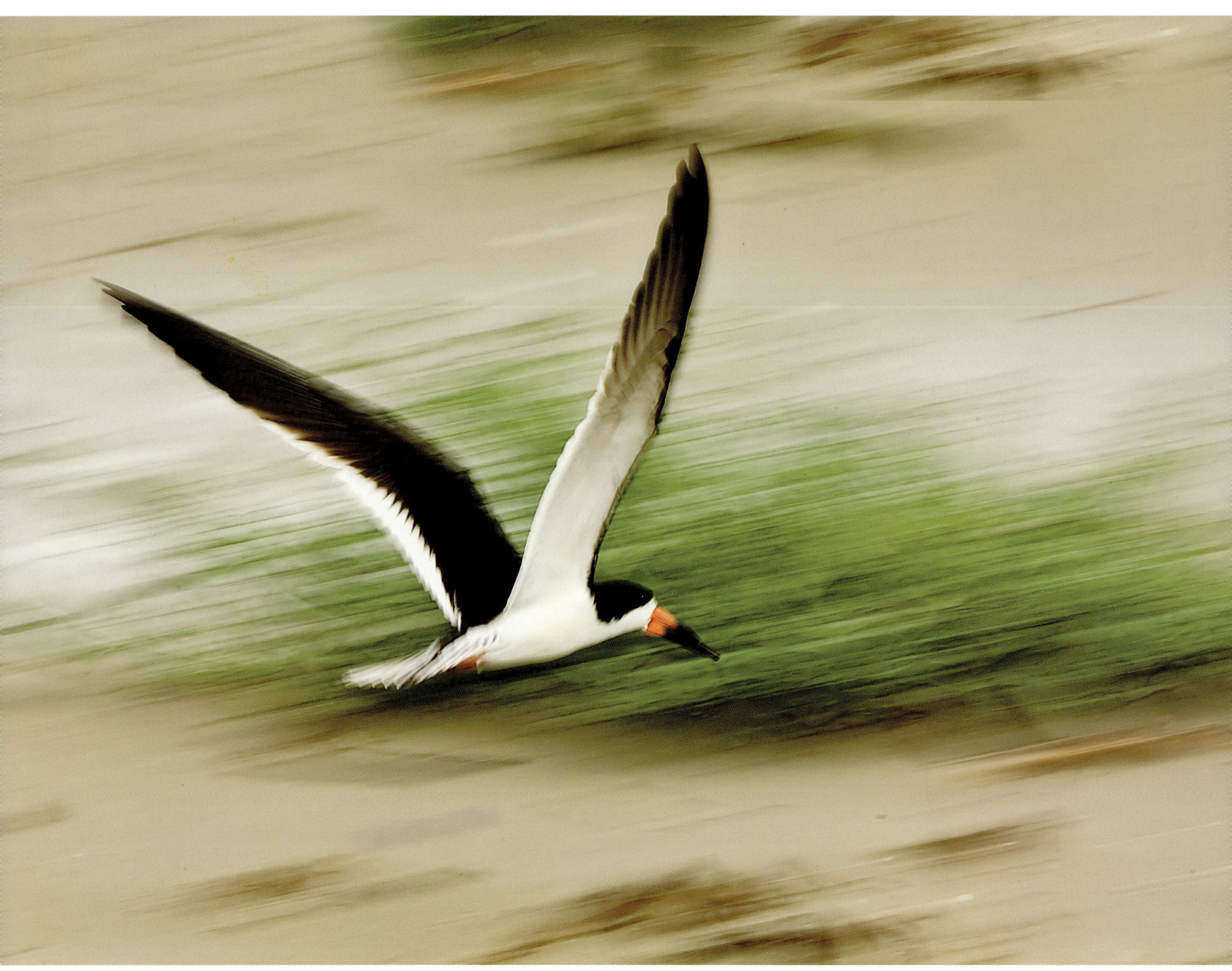

Right: This young, solitary sandpiper is very dainty. Notice the tiny white spots on the feathers—reminds me of tiny snowflakes. I see them usually in December and found this one standing in a small pool near the shore at Cameron, Louisiana. They can migrate from as far away as Alaska. (December 15, 2008)

Wilson's snipe (*below, right*) likes to probe damp soil in grassy habitats for insects. This one was having quite a day in a rice field near Kaplan, Louisiana. (December 10, 2005)

Facing page: Soaring black skimmers are amazing to watch as they gracefully glide along the surface of the water. The lower half of the bright orange beak, which is the greater in length, skims just below the surface of the water to find small fish—then SNAP, and the bird seizes whatever it has found. These shots were taken at Holly Beach along the southwestern Louisiana coast a couple of months before Hurricane Rita ravaged the area. (July 9, 2005)

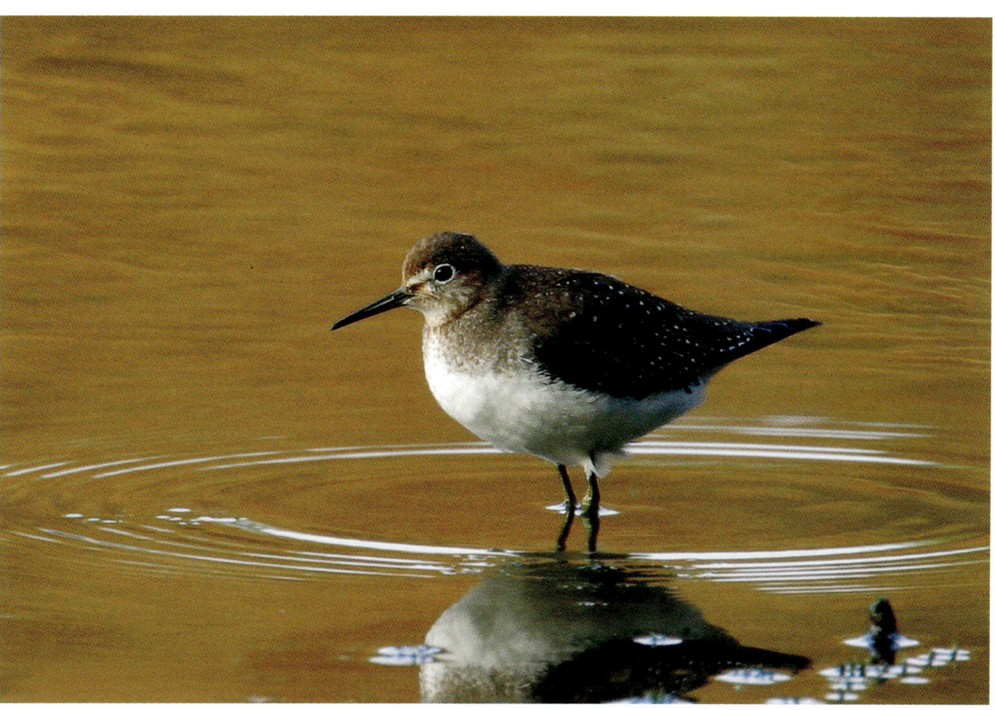

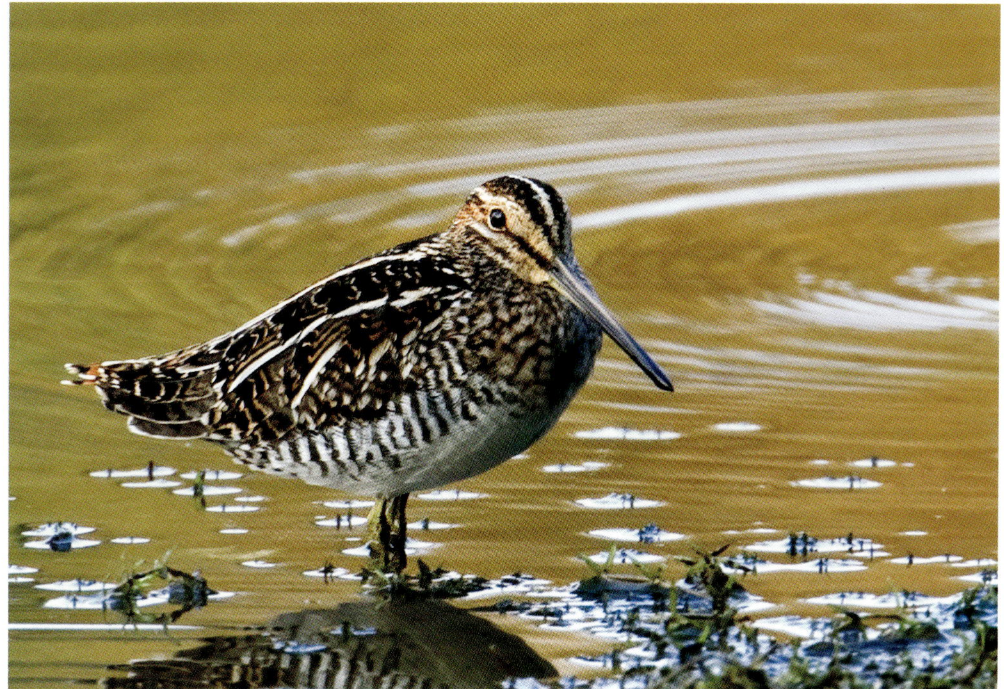

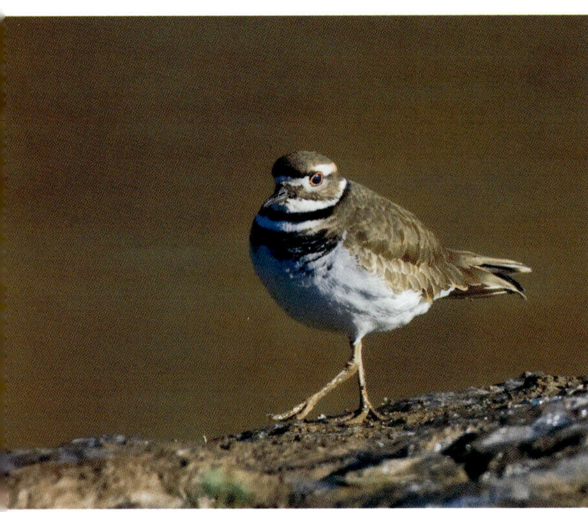

Above: The killdeer, also known as a banded plover because of the black rings around its neck, is both handsome and smart. It can fake a wounded wing to lure away intruders from its nest. I found this one pecking around a rice field near Kaplan, Louisiana. (January 2, 2008)

Right: A pair of black-necked stilts, with their thin, pink legs, remind me of long-legged ballerinas. Those legs are ideal for these waders, who are very active along the coast of Louisiana where they peck vigorously for snails, crustaceans, and insects. (March 21, 2008)

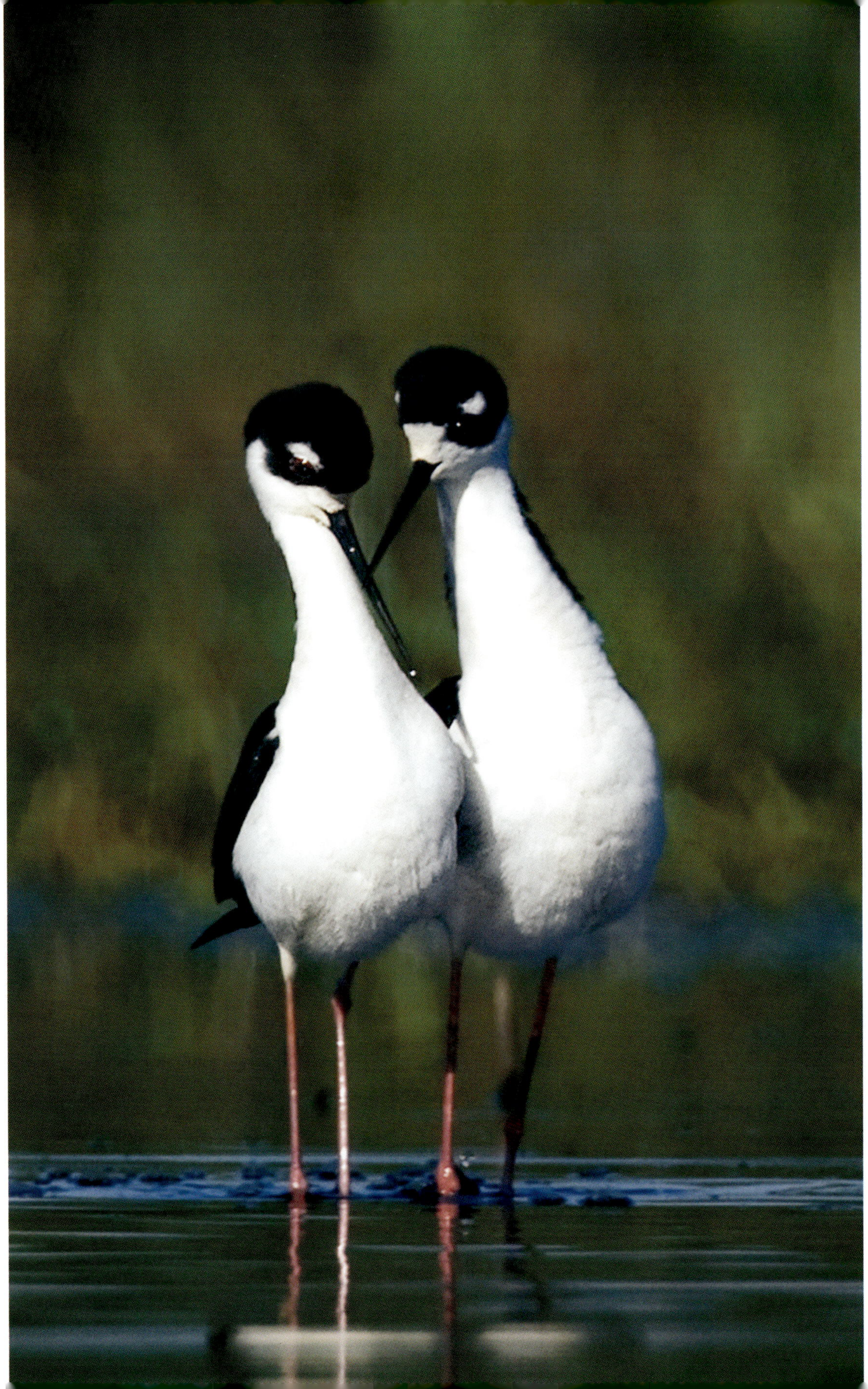

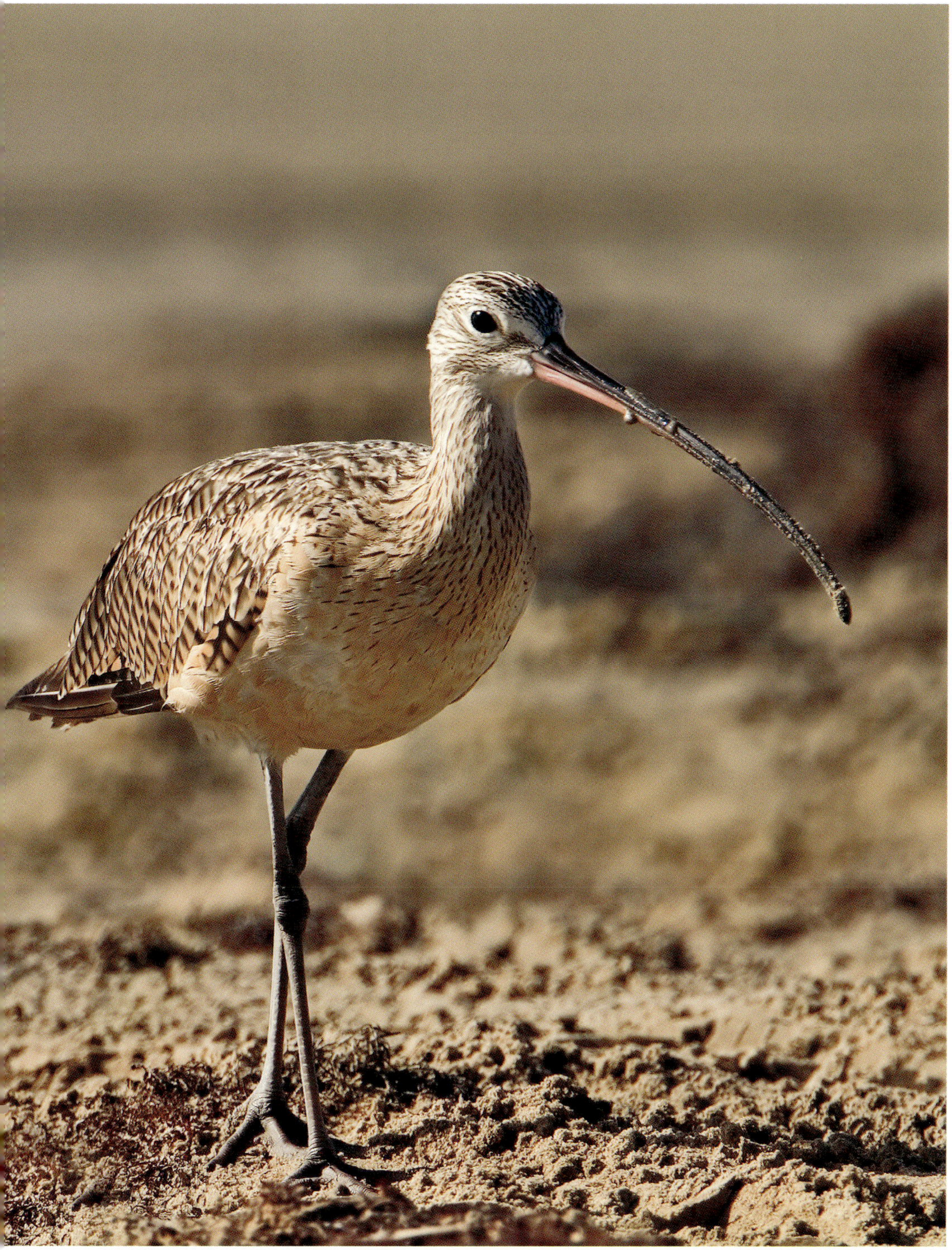

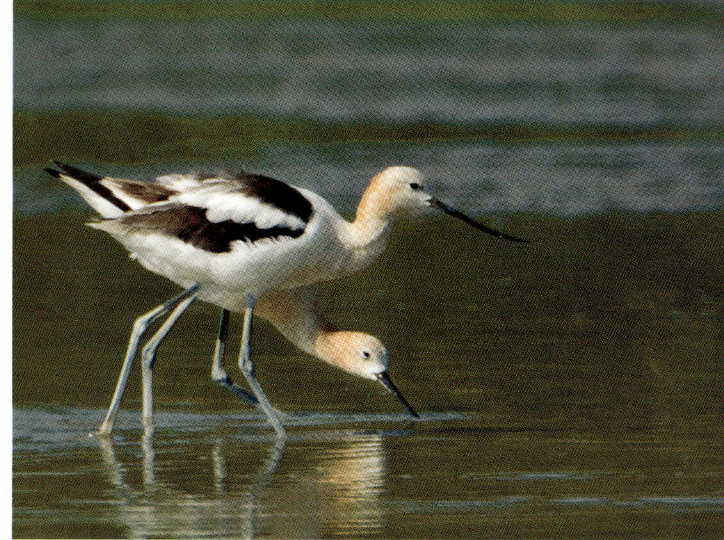

Above: When I came across these American avocets pecking away on the mudflats near Pecan Island, I watched them swishing their curved bills back and forth to churn up water insects, small crustaceans, and worms for their supper. (February 19, 2004)

Left: Morning on Holly Beach. A long-billed curlew with its long, slender down-curved bill searches for crabs and worms. (July 30, 2006)

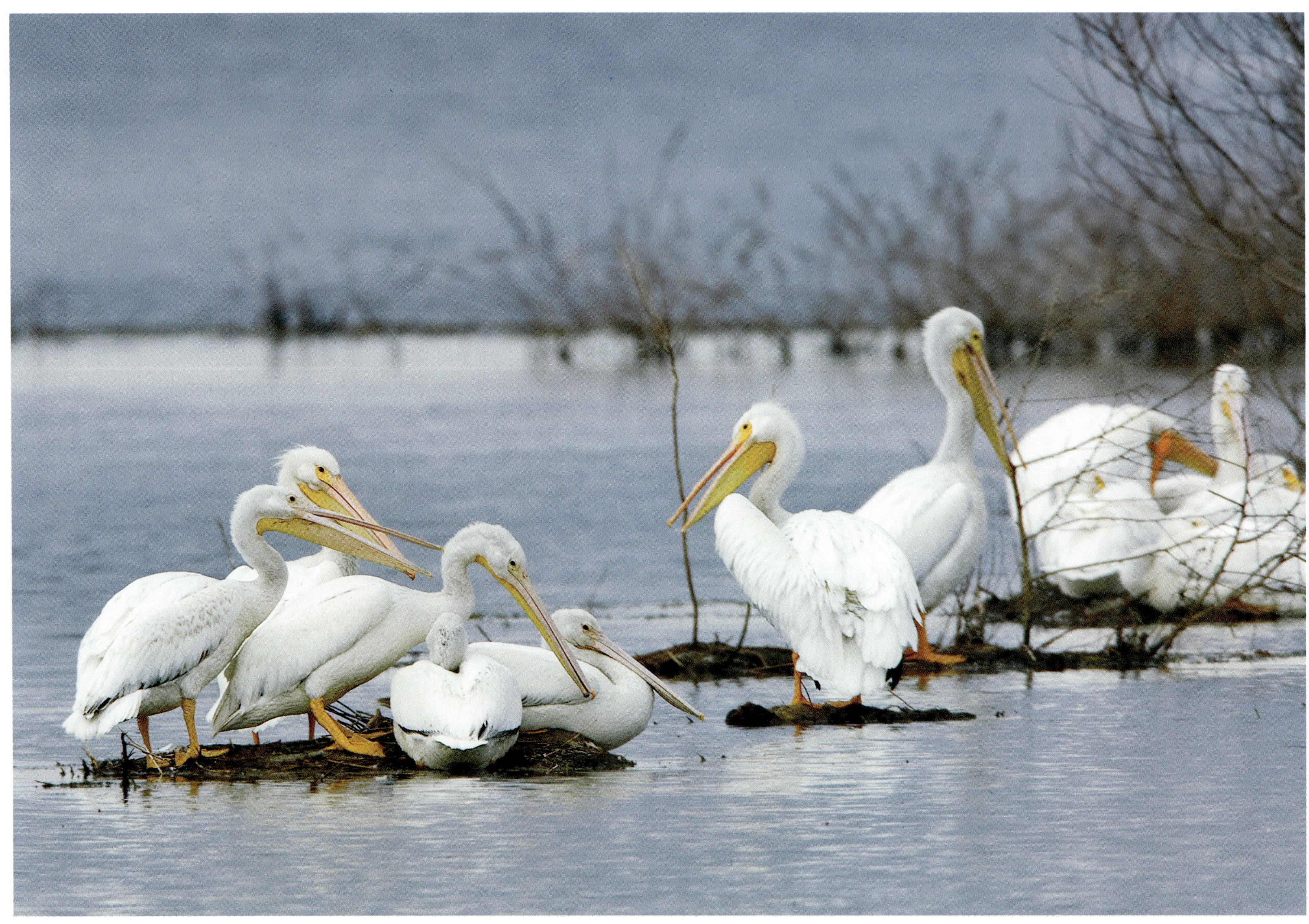

Unlike the brown pelican, the American white pelican does not dive for its food. Instead it practices cooperative fishing, which means a flock will gather where schools of fish are running, close in, and scoop them up in their large bills to carry away. This group of white pelicans was having its afternoon rest period. These large white birds with their black-tipped wings are incredibly graceful in flight. (February 21, 2005)

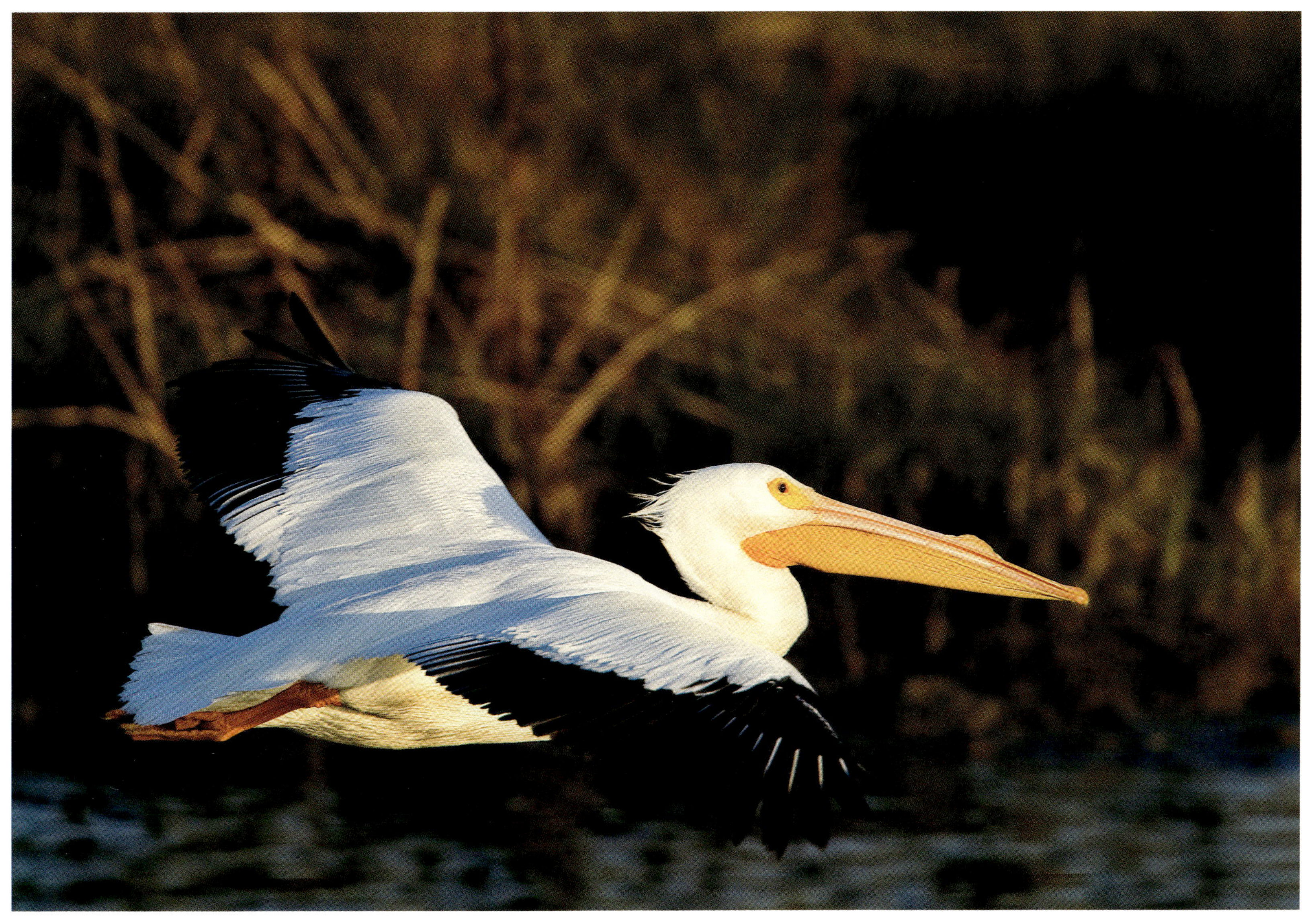

A white pelican working the bay at Grand Isle. (February 9, 2008)

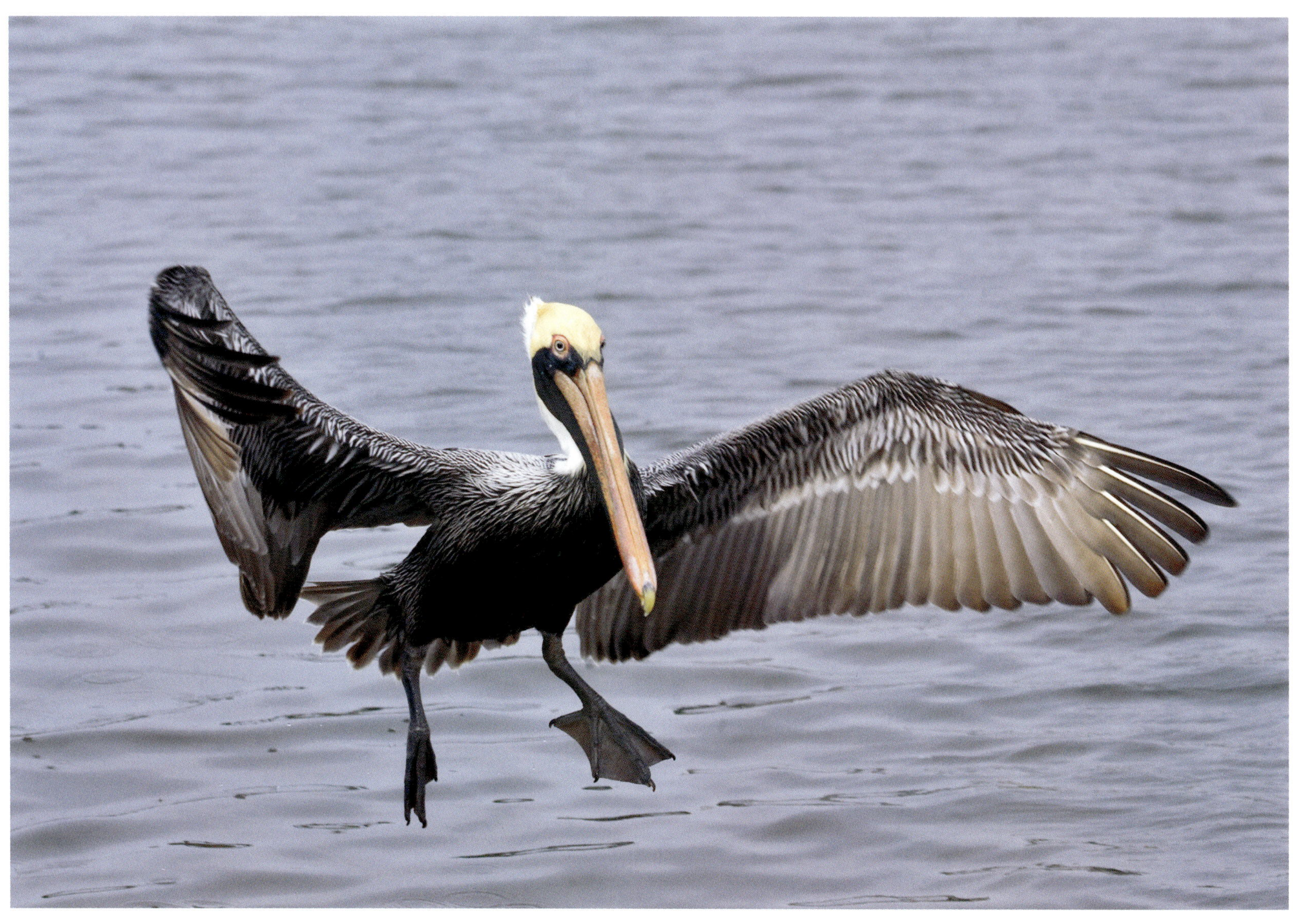

The brown pelican is Louisiana's state bird. As large as these birds are, they are the smallest of the eight species of pelicans. They can plunge from as much as seventy feet above the water to pluck up small fish along the shoreline of the northern rim of the Gulf of Mexico. (February 26, 2005)

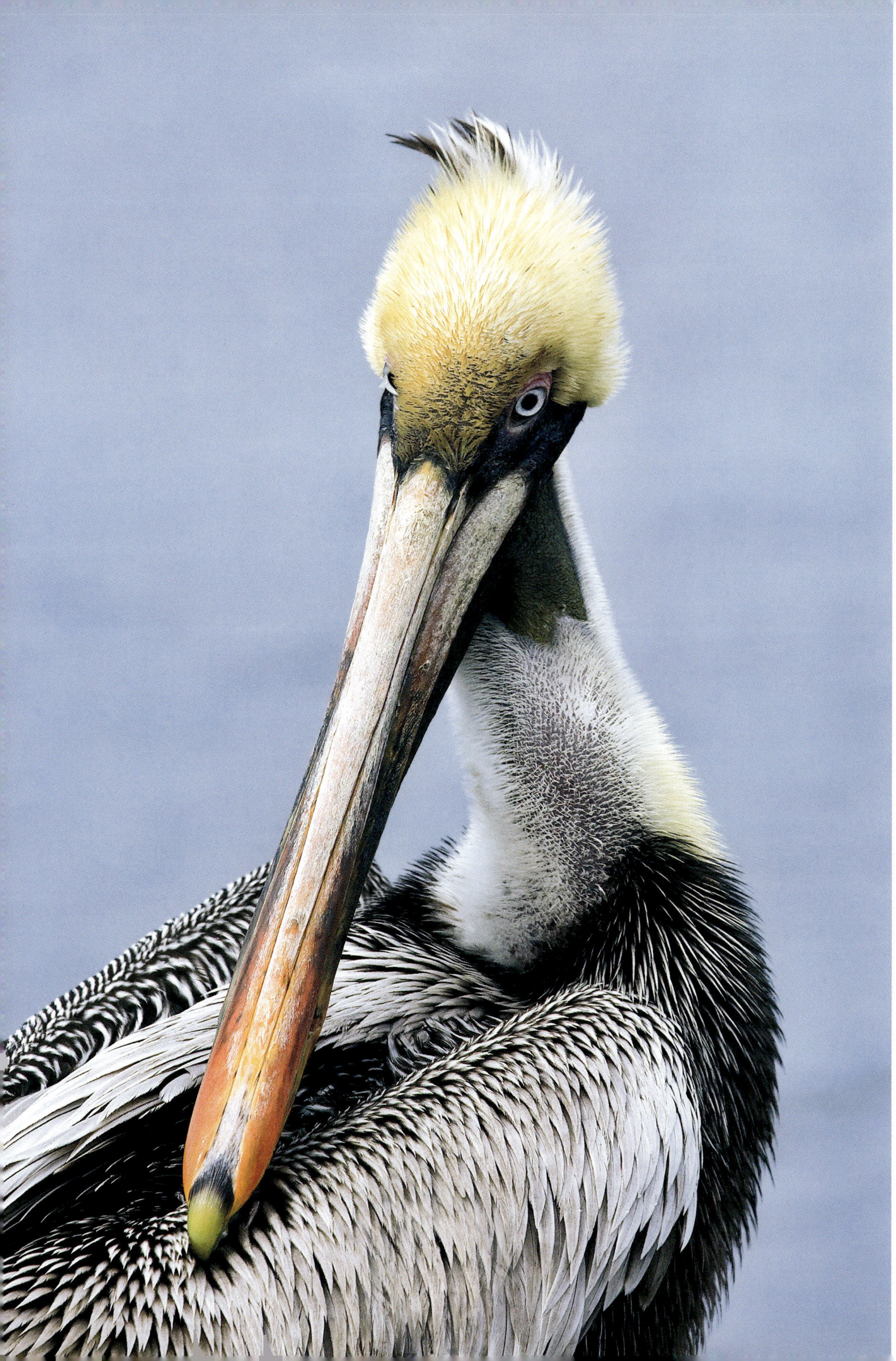

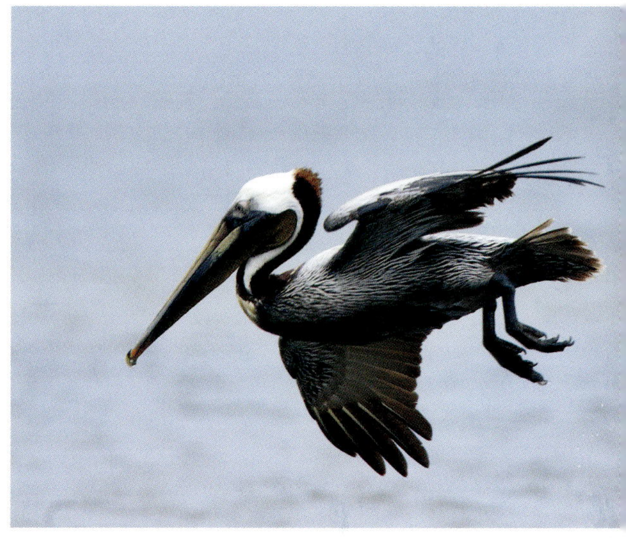

Above: This profile image of a brown pelican as it pushes off over the Gulf of Mexico shows the classic markings—the long hooked bill, the gular pouch that can expand to scoop prey, the short and stout legs, the webbed feet, and the white head and neck with a black stripe on top and a yellowish-red crown. These pelican photographs were taken along the southwest coast of Louisiana. (April 25, 2007)

Left: Him and me—nose-to-nose. His quizzical stare seems to be asking, "What's up? Take my photograph and get on with it!" (February 26, 2005)

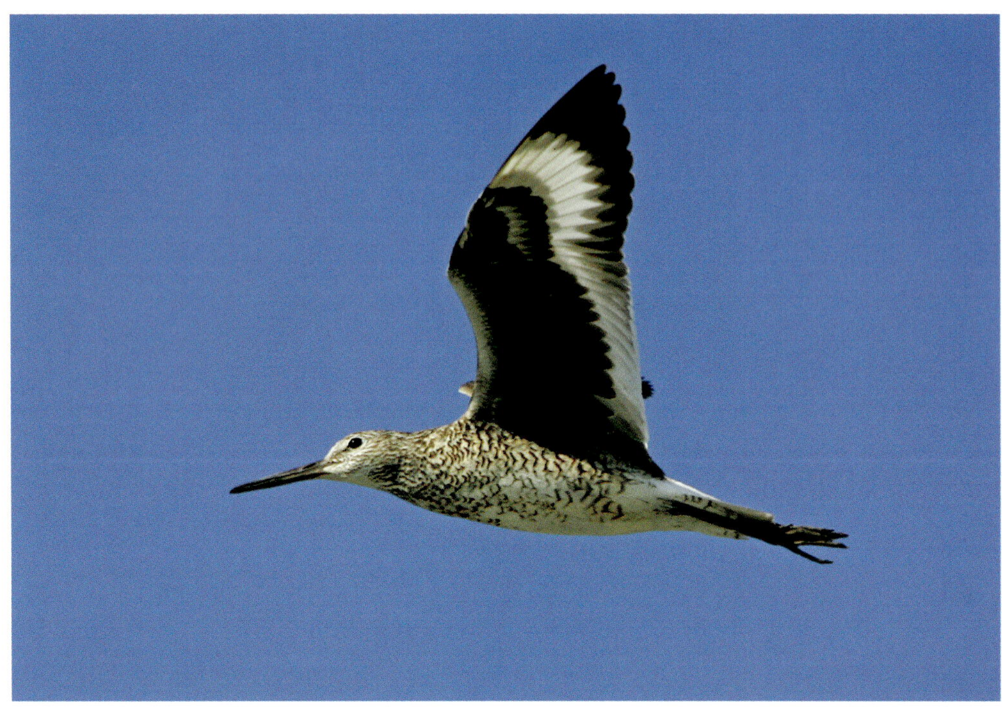

Left: I witnessed this Willet, a large sandpiper, soaring along the Gulf of Mexico shoreline at Lacassine National Wildlife Refuge at Lake Arthur, Louisiana. Note the striking black-and-white wing pattern. (April 9, 2005)

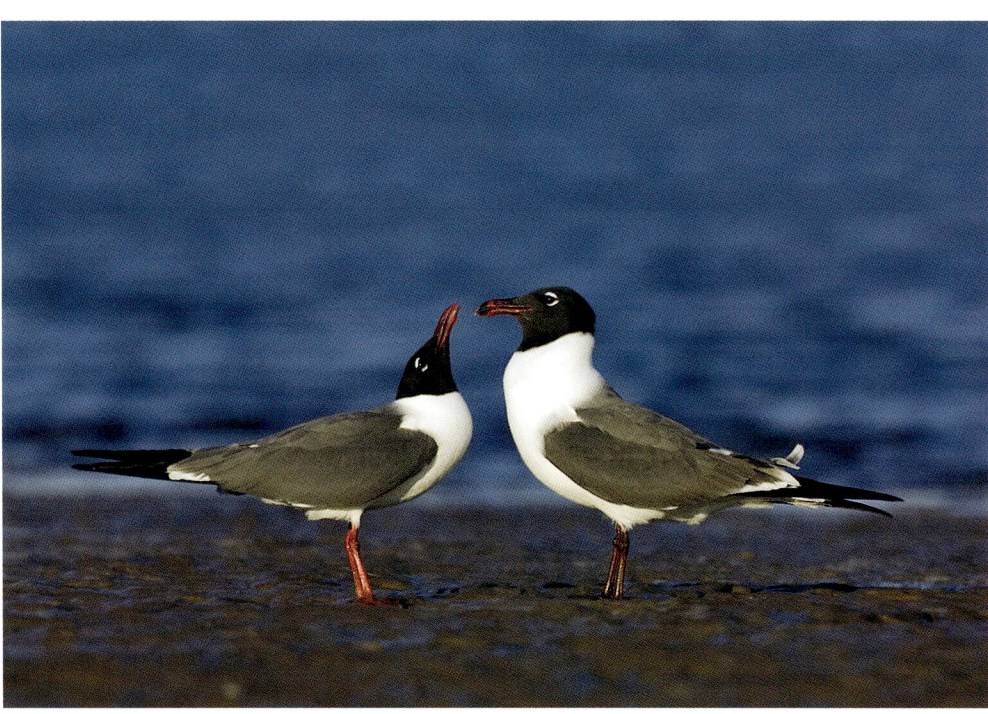

Below, left: A pair of laughing gulls romancing at Grand Isle, Louisiana. Dark-hooded gulls, they are often referred to as the "parking lot variety" along the Atlantic and Gulf of Mexico coasts because they are so plentiful. Busy birds, they feed on insects and small crustaceans in the sand. (April 16, 2005)

Facing page: Some find the common ring-billed gull very boring. I, on the other hand, like to watch them scavenging in crawfish ponds as this one is doing one morning near Kaplan, Louisiana. (December 10, 2005)

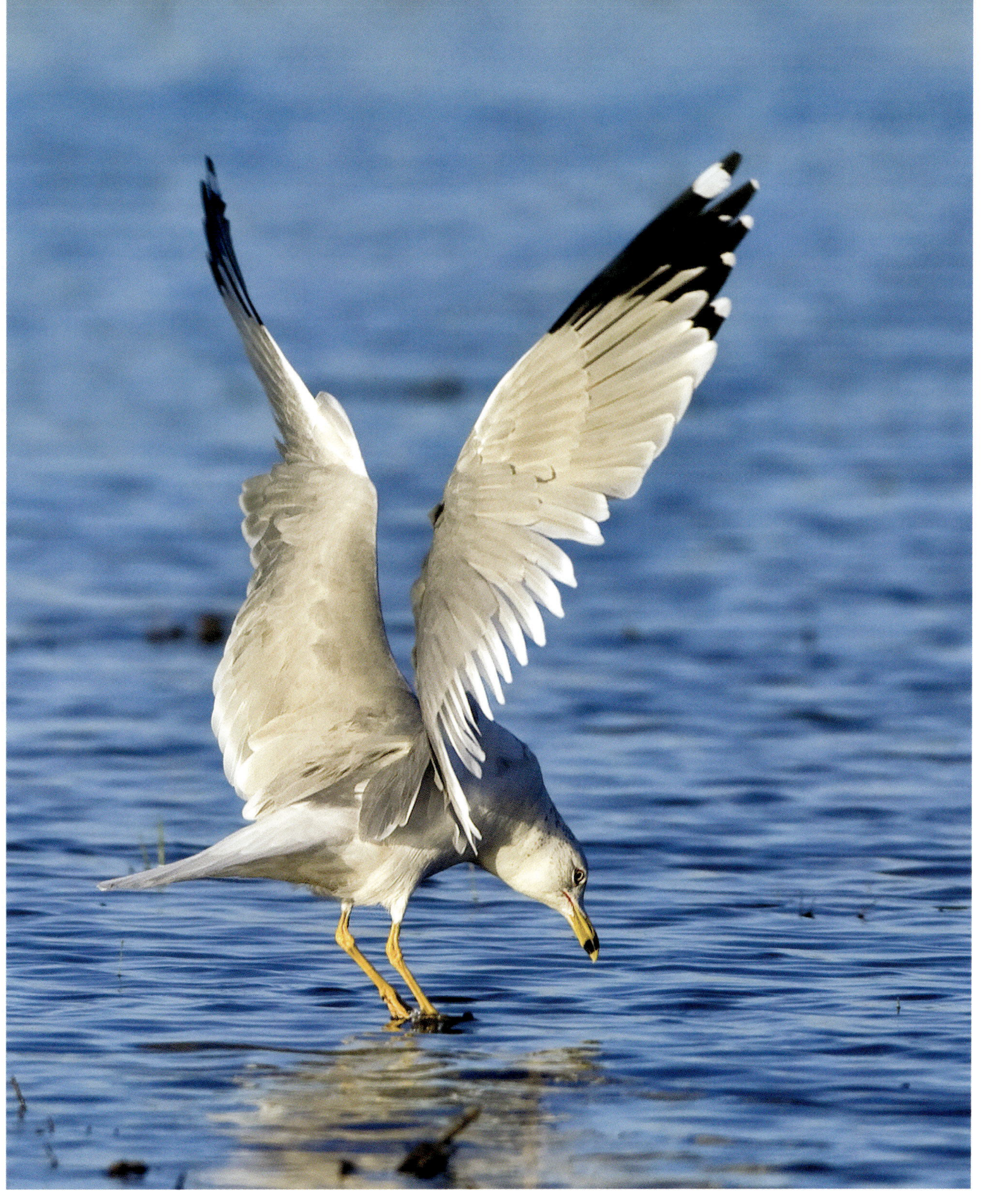

WADERS

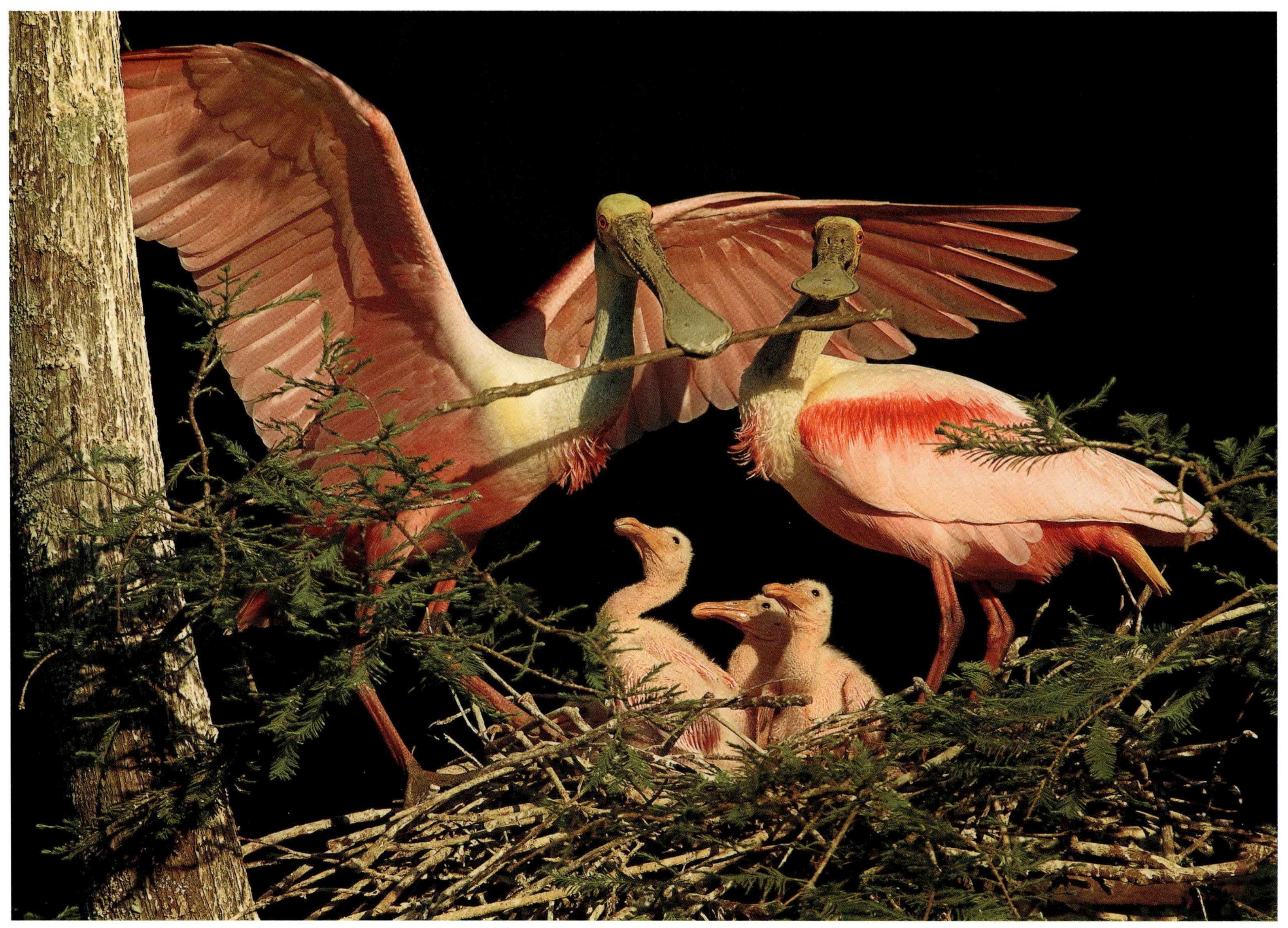

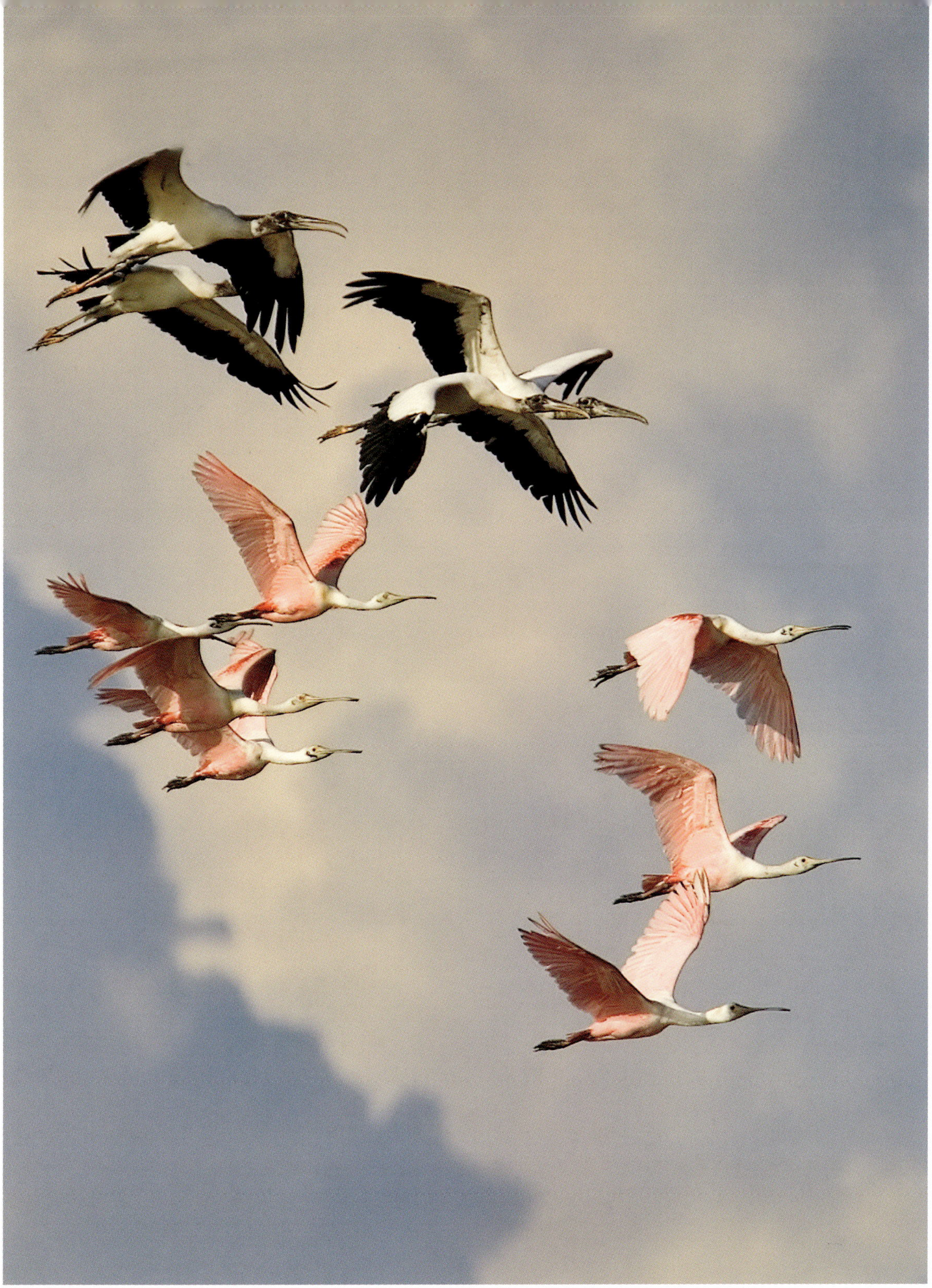

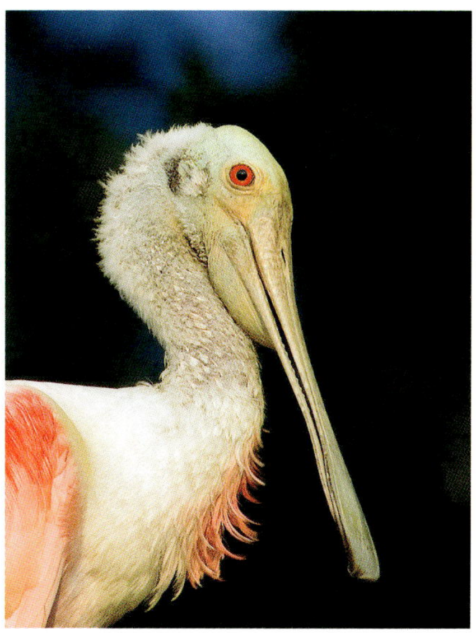

My first introduction to these flamboyant roseate spoonbills was at the rookery at Lake Martin in 2005, and I immediately fell head-over-heels in love with the pink, showy birds. Like a teenage boy with a crush, I photographed them from early in the morning until late in the afternoon. They can usually be observed along the coast from Cameron Parish to St. Mary Parish in south Louisiana. However, in recent years, they are appearing more and more on inland waters in Louisiana because of the food sources in crawfish ponds and flooded rice fields. (Spring 2005)

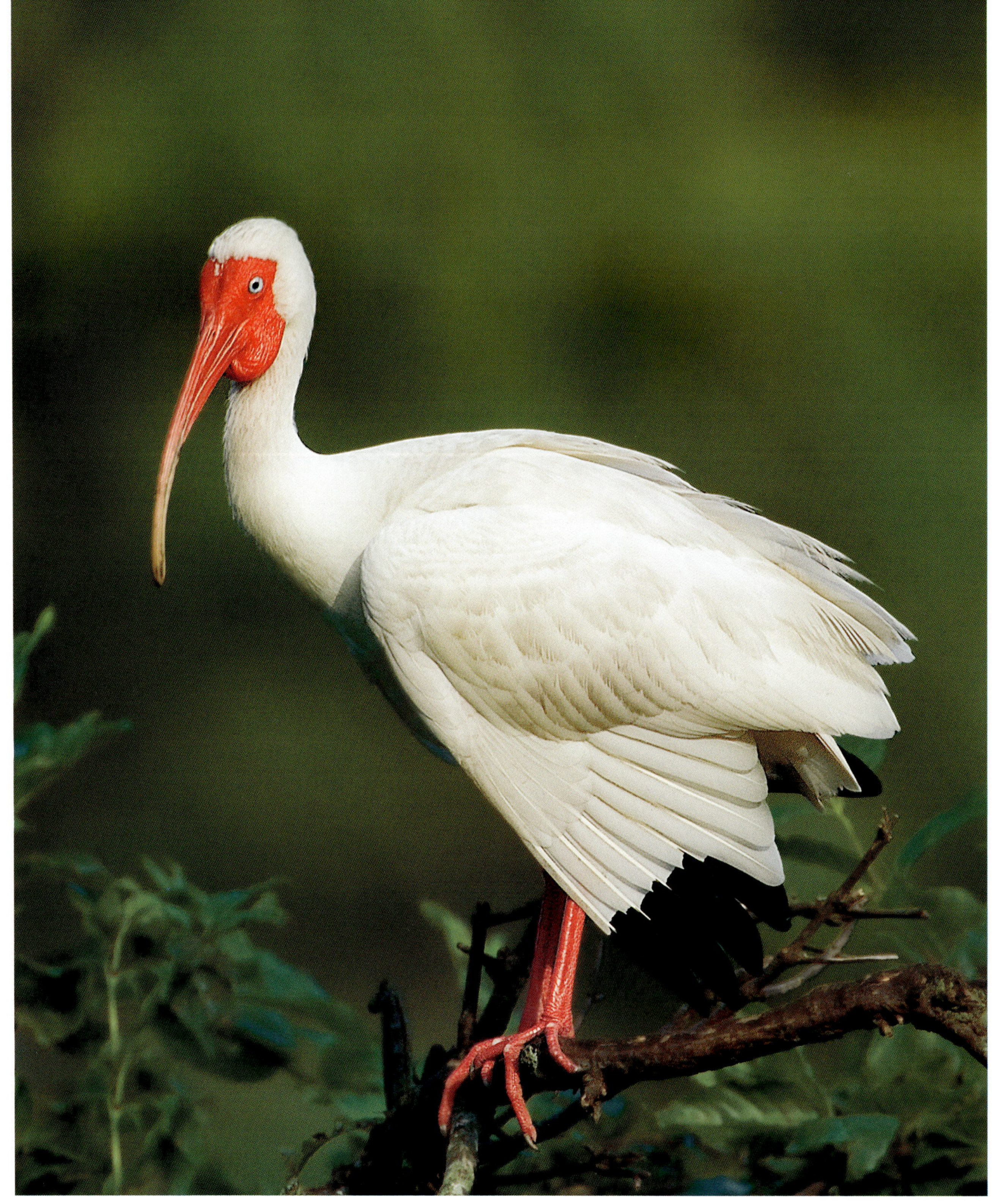

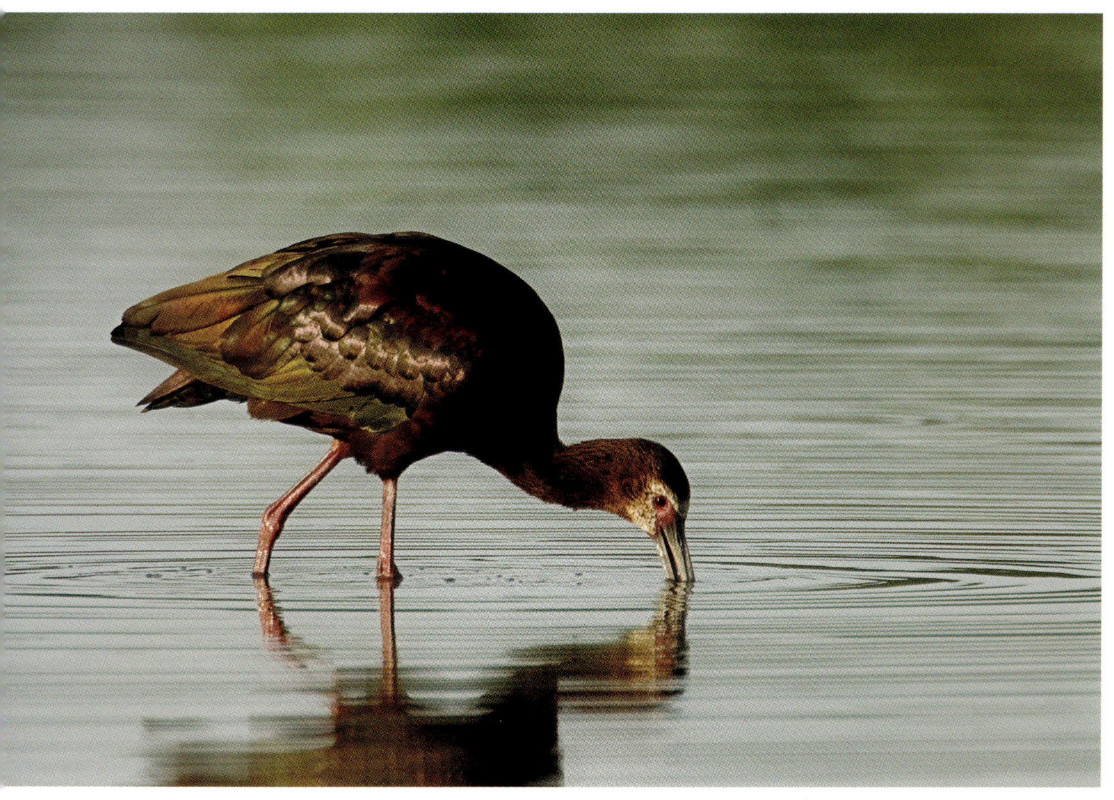

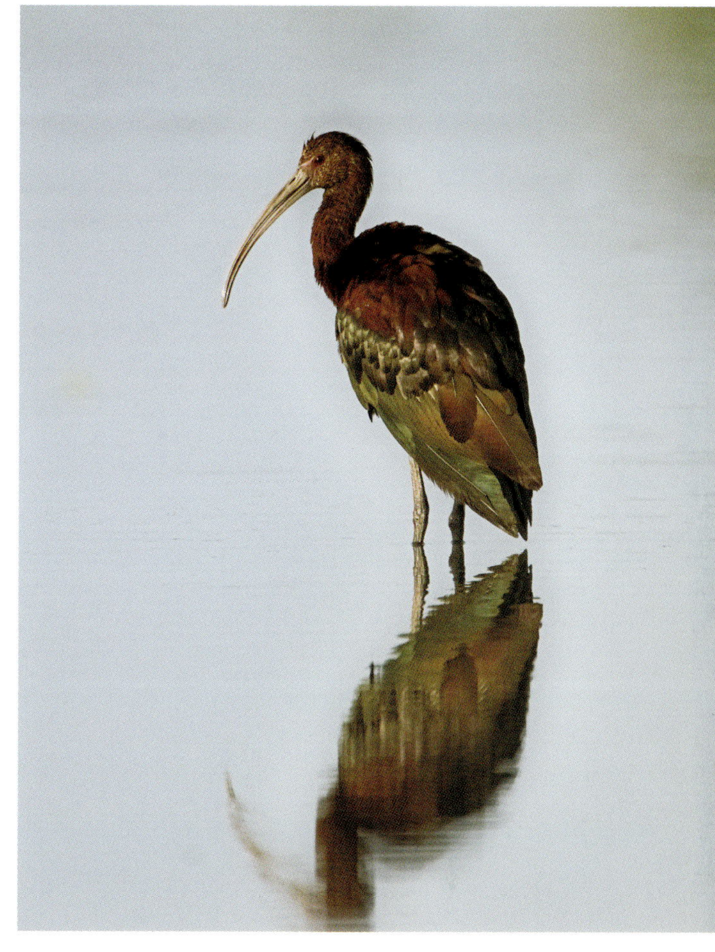

Facing page: I observed this white male ibis, with its bright red legs and beak, in mating mode at Lake Martin in midsummer. White ibis stand about two feet tall and have a wing span of about three feet. They sweep their long, curved bill from side to side searching for food. Since these waders forage in wetlands, I often see them feeding on crustaceans such as crabs and crawfish in freshwater marshes. They are also partial to insects, frogs, and small fish. (July 2, 2005)

Above left: Very similar in appearance to the glossy ibis, the white-faced ibis can be distinguished by its red eyes, red legs, and red facial skin with a white border that is of even width and encircles the eye. It was a good day for me to find both the glossy and the white-faced ibis in the same area. (July 17, 2005)

The colors of the plumage of this glossy ibis (*above, right*) are stunning! Iridescent green, bronze, and reddish-brown feathers dominate, making the bird stand out as it feeds in a muddy rice field in a south Louisiana marsh. (July 17, 2005)

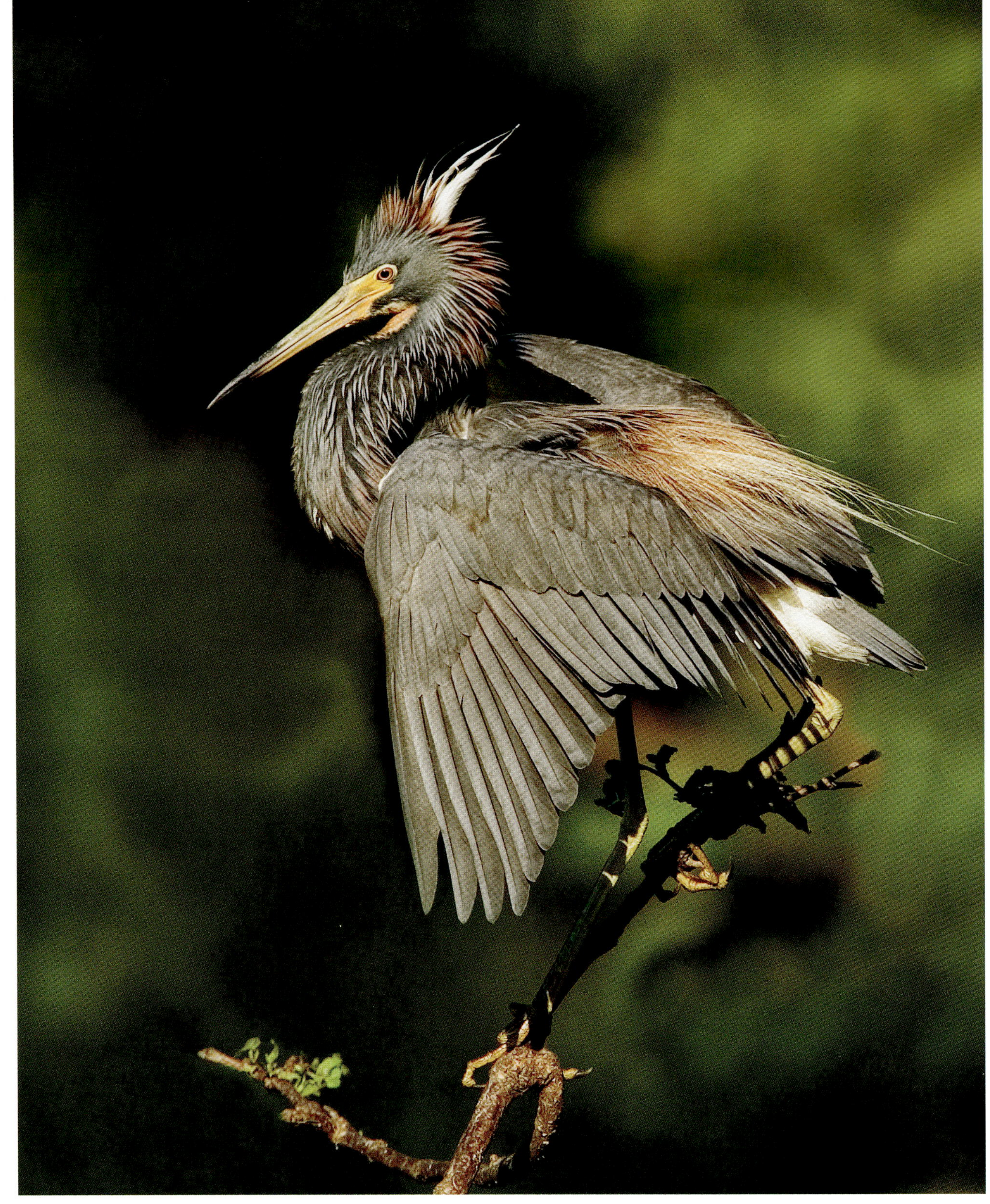

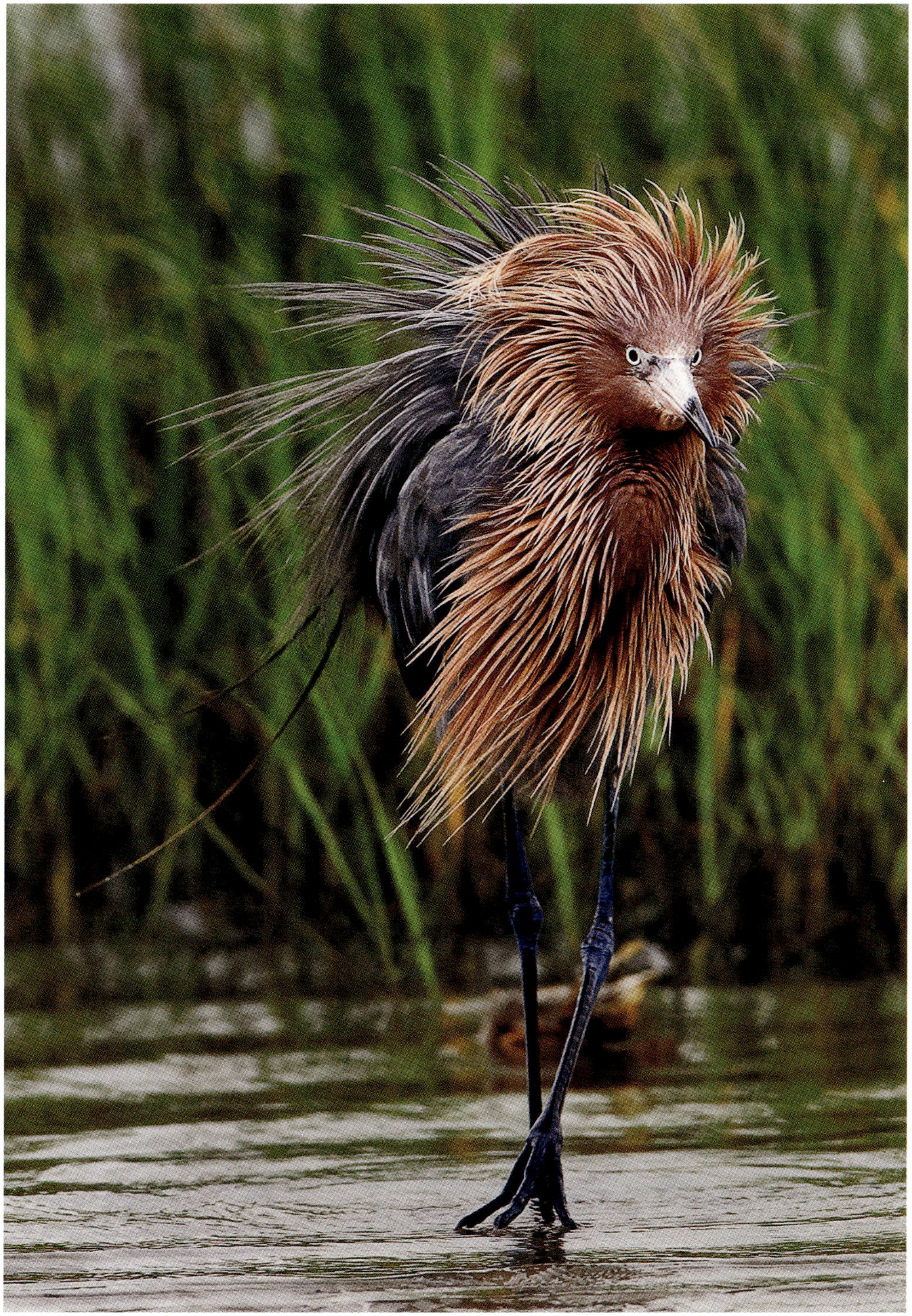

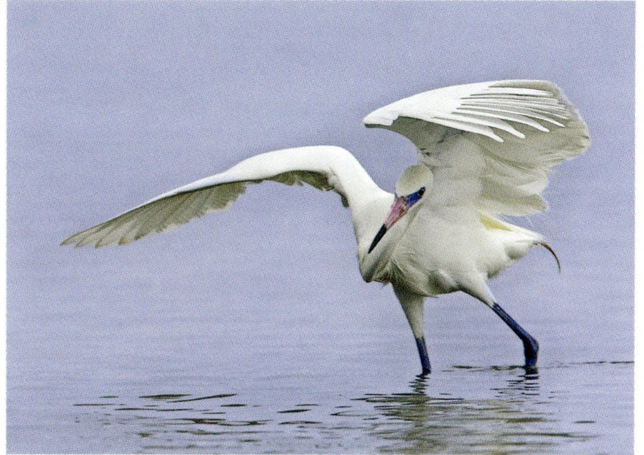

Above: A reddish egret in its white morph stage doing what is called canopy feeding. The bird will spread its wings over its head, like an umbrella, to form a canopy over its potential prey. (June 29, 2007)

Left: I love this shot of this reddish egret with its shaggy plumes lolling about a lagoon. I call him the Lion King. I was lucky to snap him wading ashore near Cameron, Louisiana, since they are pretty rare. This one happens to be a dark morph (there is also a white morph) with its slate-blue body, reddish head, and somewhat shaggy plumes along the neck. When they are foraging, they flap their wings vigorously while running through shallow waters. It makes them look like they're dancing a jig. (April 29, 2007)

Facing page: Biding my time at Lake Martin, I found this tri-colored heron perched on the branch of a button willow. (June 15, 2005)

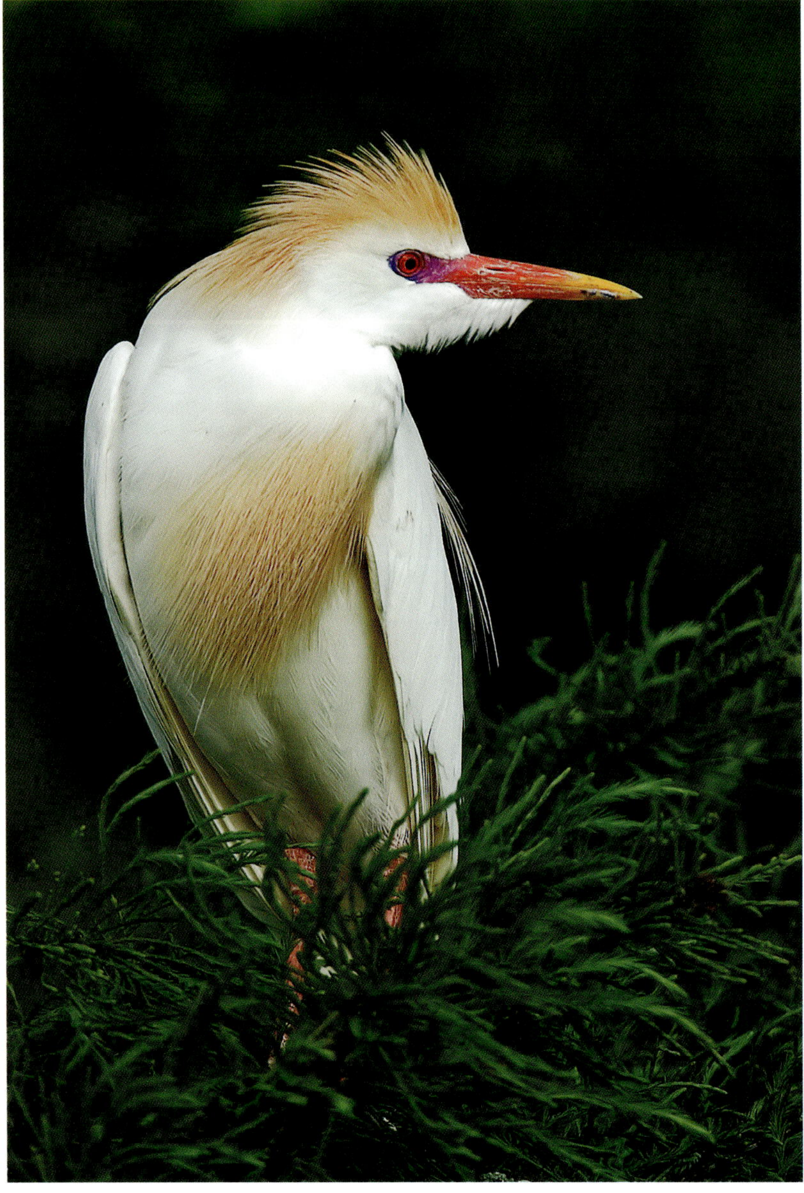

Left: There are those who think these cattle egrets are very ordinary looking, but I beg to differ. They forage just about anywhere—behind tractors and other farm machinery, in marshy areas, around cattle and other grazing animals—for insects that have been disturbed or flushed up. I love watching them ride on the back of cows and horses in a pasture. (May 6, 2005)

Facing page: Preening in a bald cypress tree at Lake Martin, this great egret shows off its delicate, lace-like plumes, which were in high demand in the late 19th century and early 20th century as adornments on ladies' fashionable hats. Called "nuptial plumes" because they appear during the breeding season, they were in such demand that the egret population diminished so significantly, the federal government passed the Lacey Act in 1900 banning the sale of the egret feathers not only in the United States, but also abroad. (March 27, 2005)

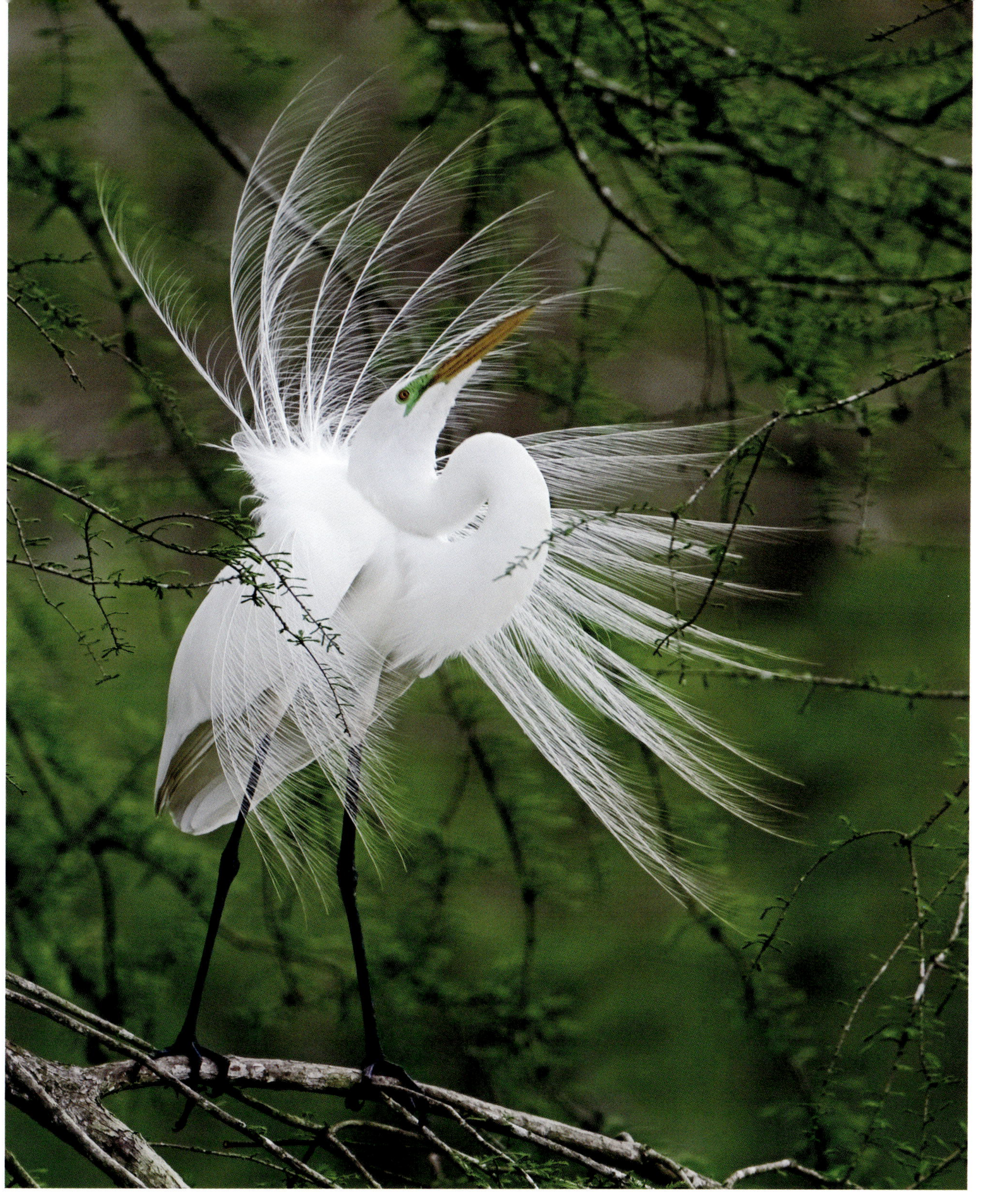

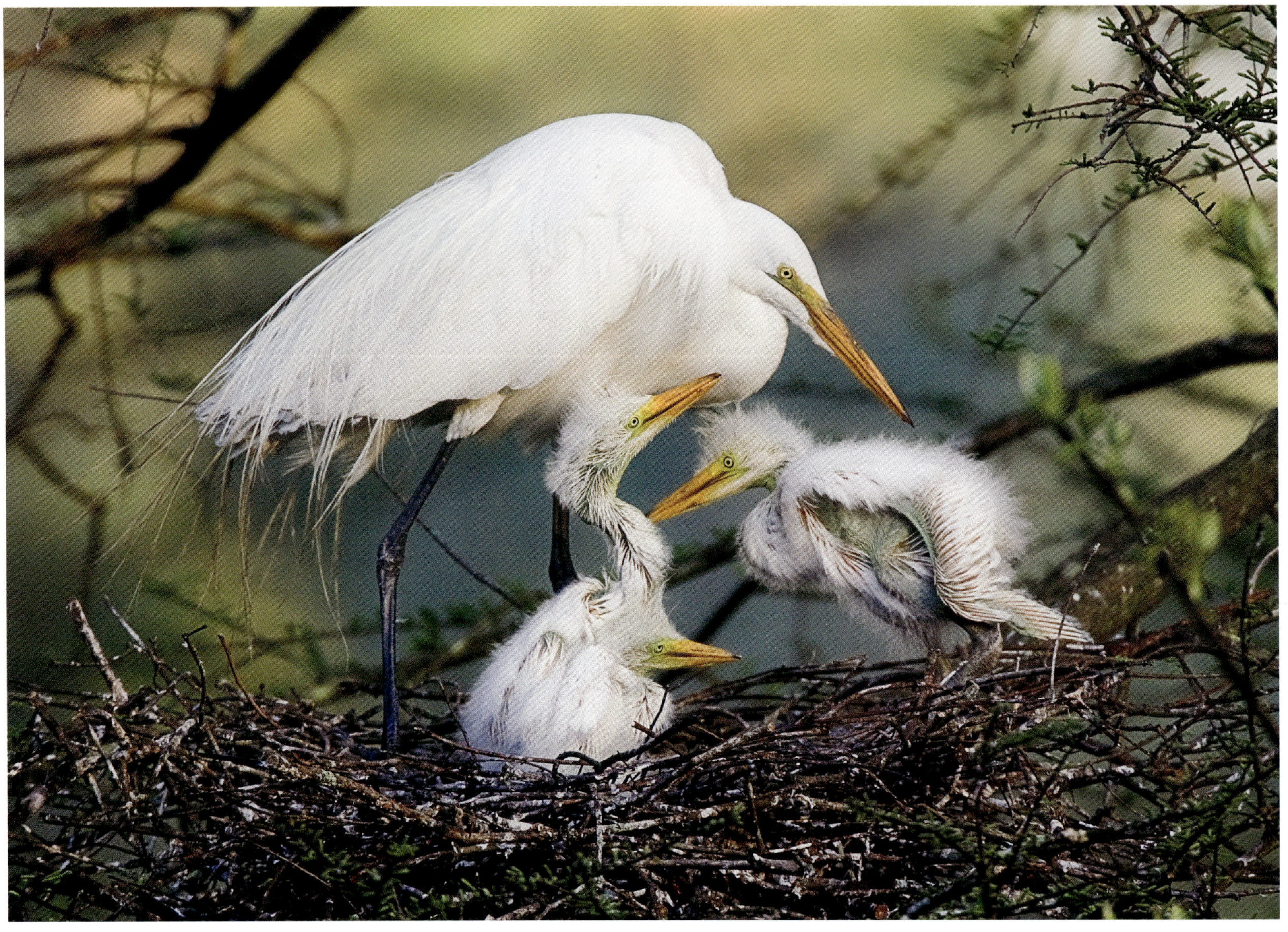

Above: One of my prize photographs—a great egret with baby chicks. The light on this nest was ideal on an April morning, the peak of the nesting season at Lake Martin. The adult egret goes out to find food, partially digests it, and then returns to feed its chicks. Nature at its best. (April 3, 2005)

Facing page: These great egrets, also called white herons, are large birds with a wing span of about fifty inches. The all-white plumage accented by the bright yellow bill and the S-curved neck makes these birds very dramatic to observe. (March 24, 2007)

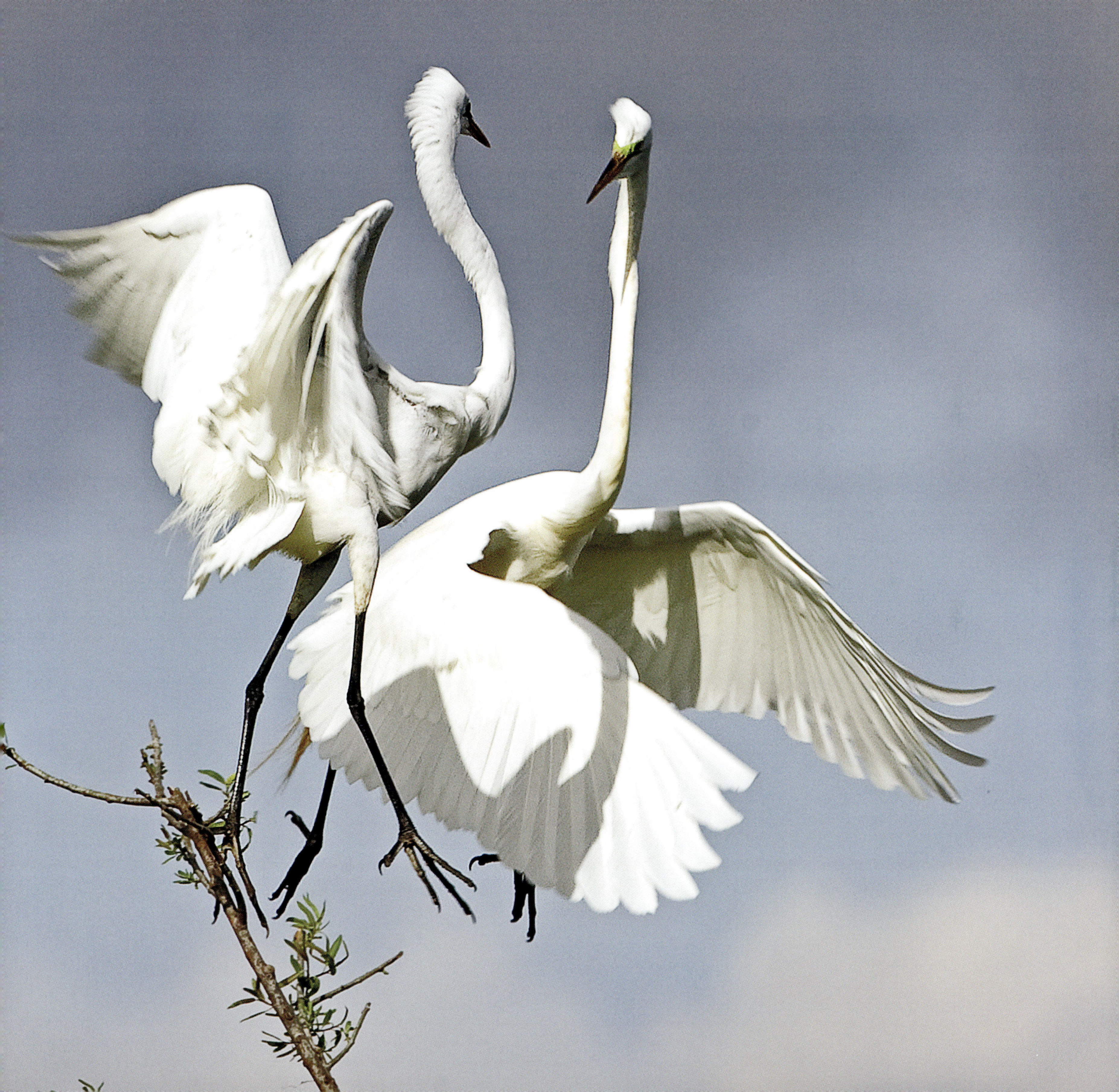

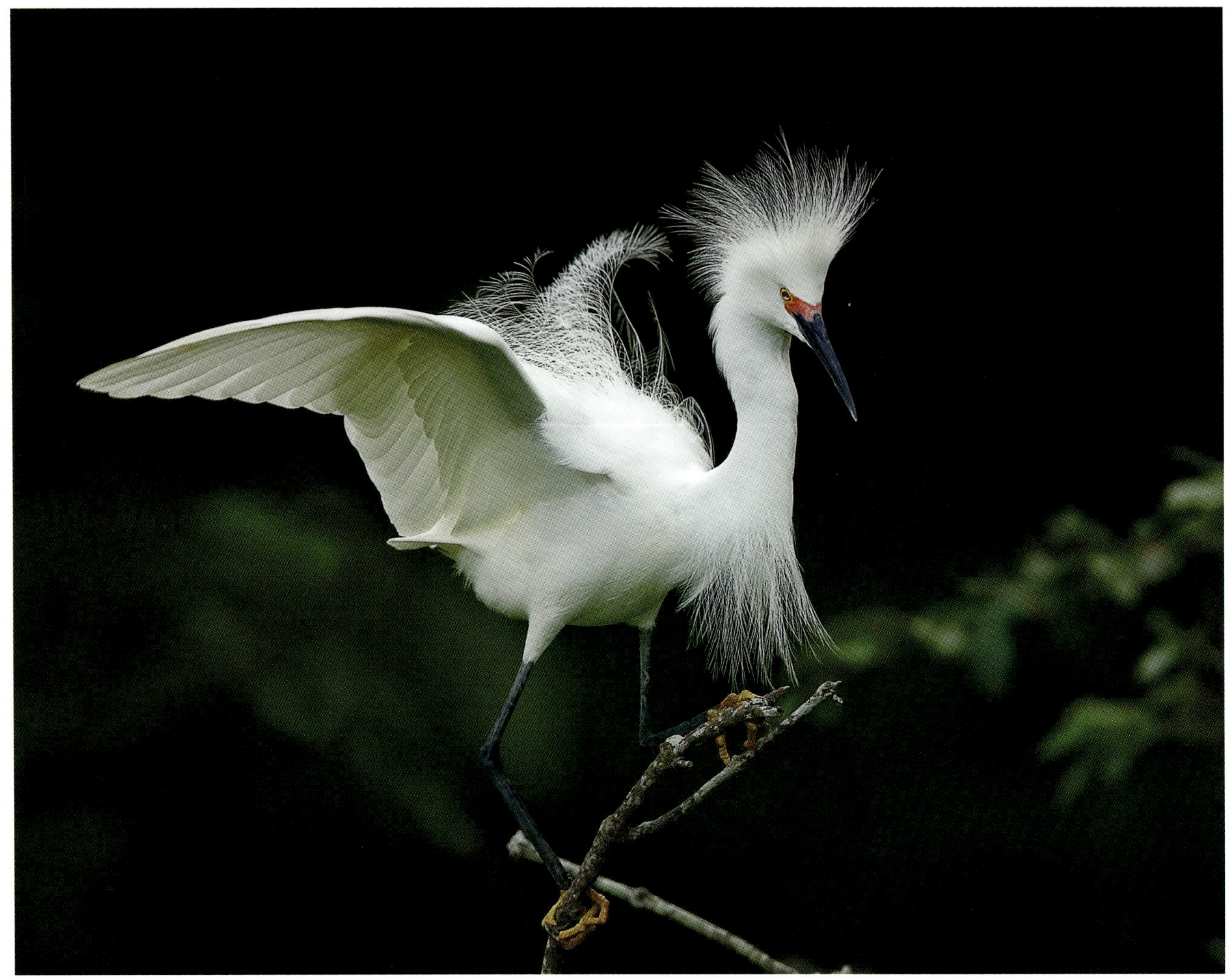

Above: The snowy egret is smaller in size than the great egret and is easily distinguished by its black bill and yellow feet. Here, a stately snowy egret perches atop a tree at Lake Martin. I can easily understand why the delicate plumes were considered *de rigueur* by the millinery trade in the late 1800s. After the snowy egret population plummeted, Edward Avery "Ned" McIlhenny, renowned naturalist and Tabasco sauce heir, took it upon himself to construct what is now known as Bird City in the Jungle Gardens on Avery Island in Iberia Parish. There the egrets could nest on bamboo platforms built by McIlhenny, safe from plume poachers. (May 30, 2005)

Facing page: Great blue herons are indeed huge with a wing span of about eighty inches. I've observed these patient birds stand in shallow water (usually freshwater) to catch fish, frogs, water snakes, and large insects by making stabbing motions with their long, sharp beaks. (April 14, 2007)

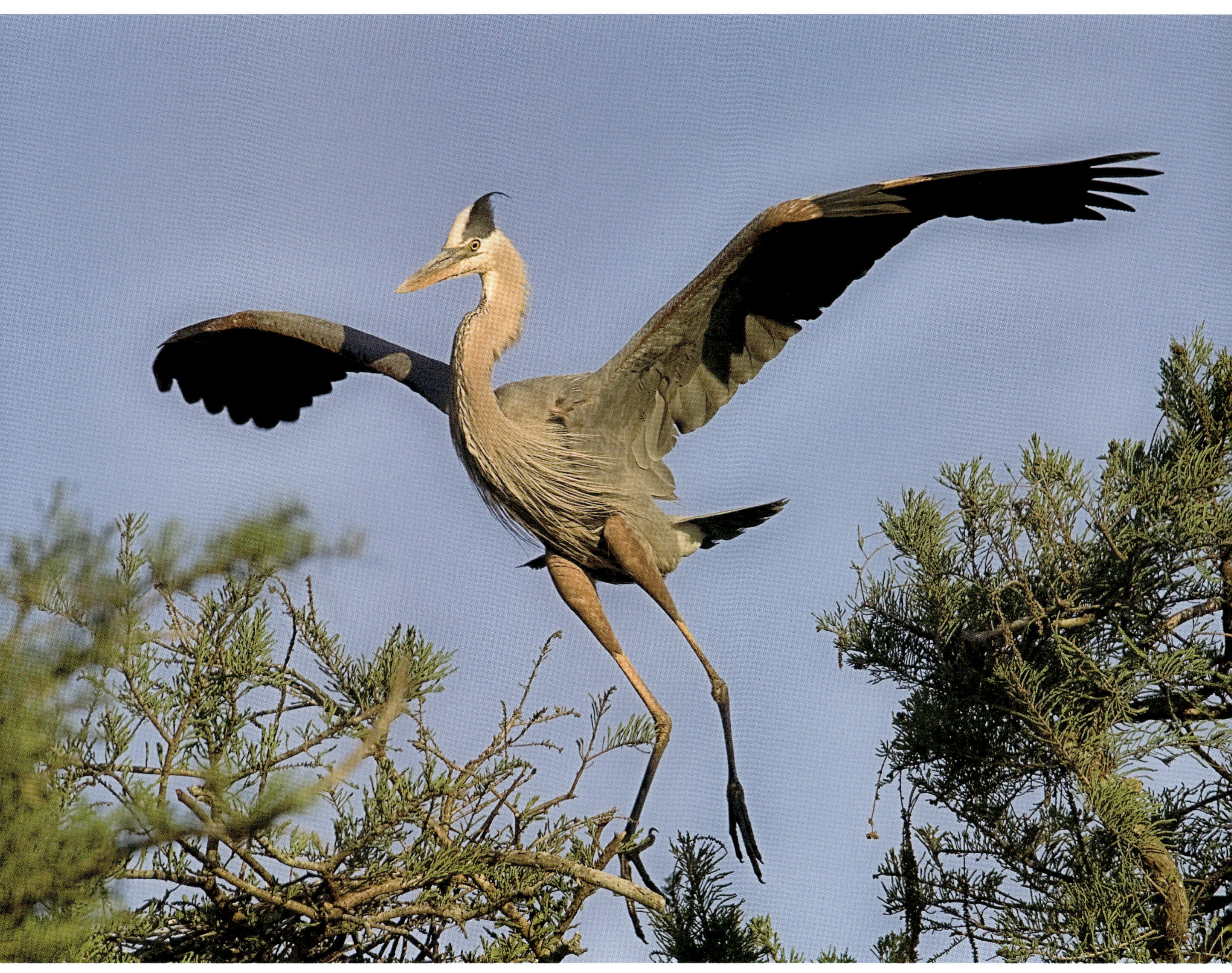

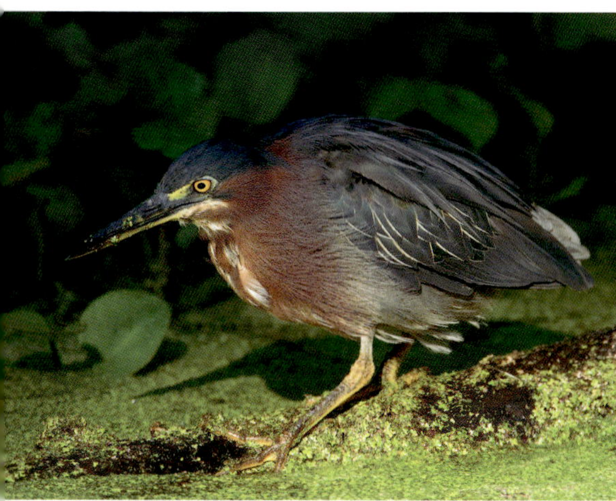

Above: Man, can this bird squawk! The green heron is a small, stocky wading bird that I see mostly in grassy wetlands. It is a good fisherman—using bait such as insects or bread crusts to lure small fish into its grasp. (April 12, 2007)

Right: Little blue herons are easily identified by their bluish-gray feathers. I've observed them along the coast of Louisiana and at Lake Martin. They have a deep, hoarse croak that sounds something like *kraaank*. (October 10, 2004)

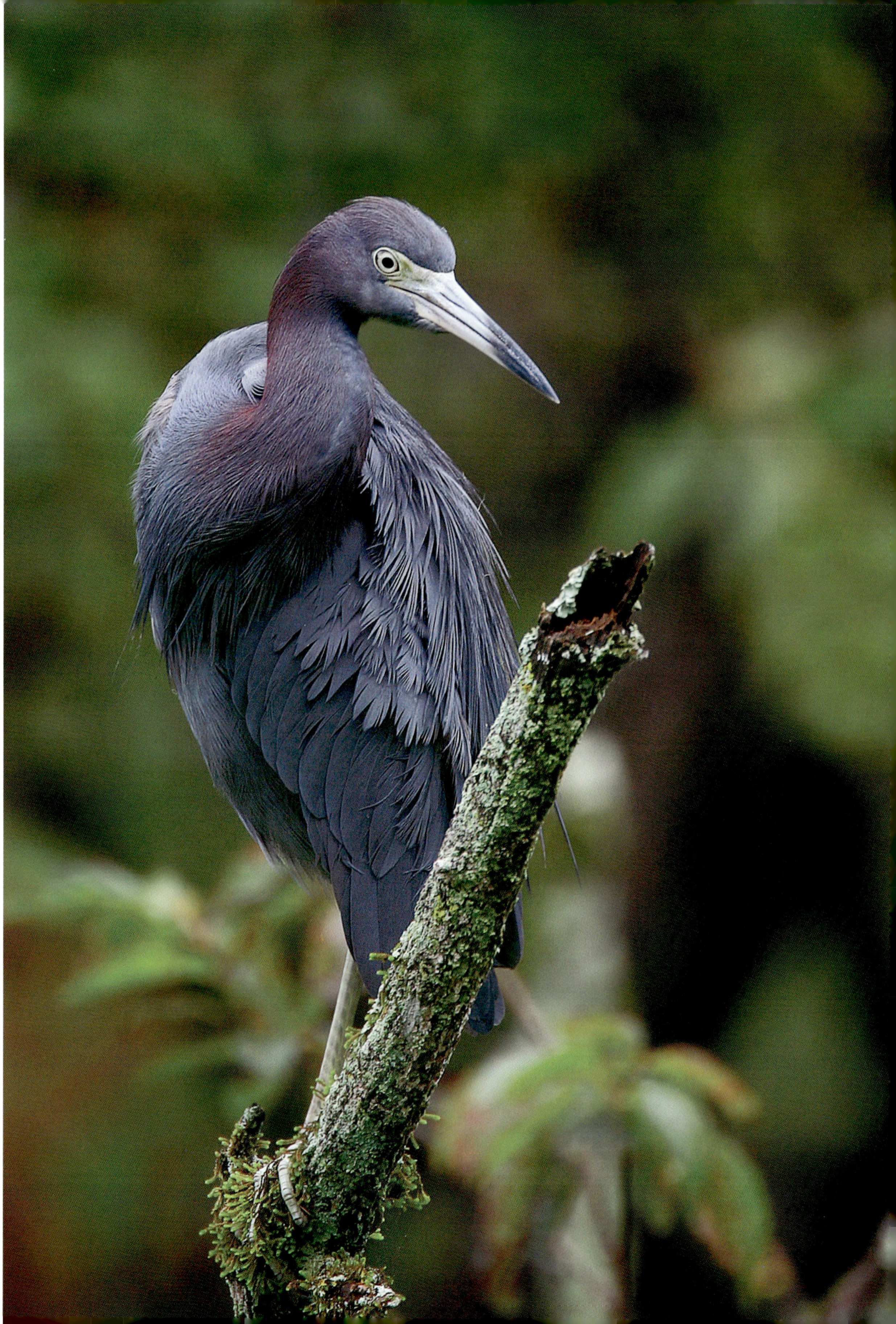

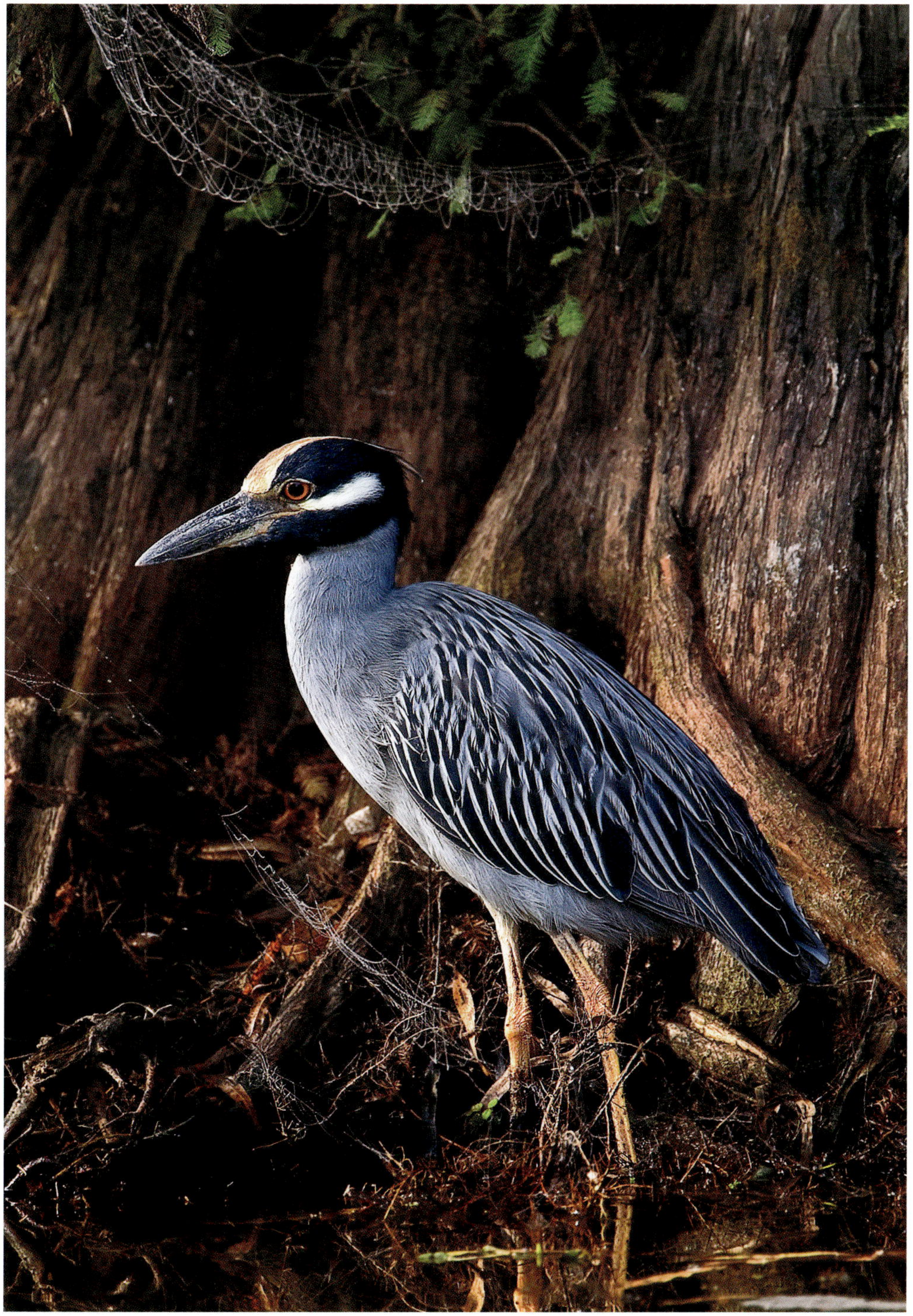

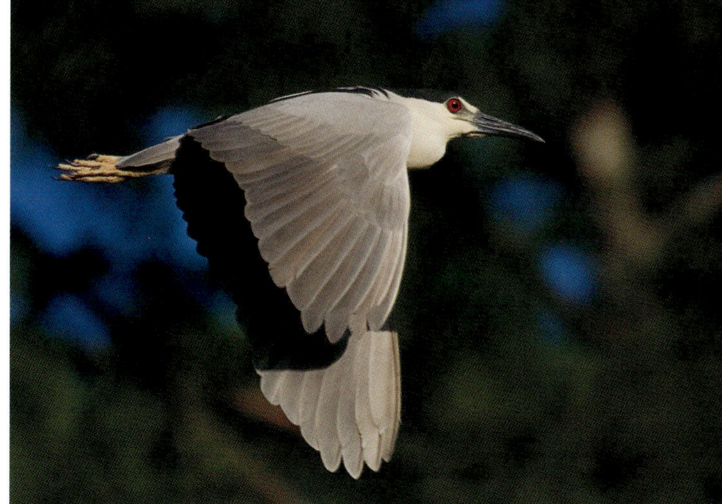

Above: An adult black-crowned night heron is rather stocky with short legs and neck and is similar in size to an American bittern, although the coloring is different. The orange-red eyes stand out like garnets in the crowned head. Apparently they like parenthood as they will brood chicks that are not their own. (April 11, 2006)

Left: A yellow-crowned night heron has attractive and distinct markings, making it easy to identify amidst the trees trunks at Lake Martin. Much like the larger herons, they stalk their prey at the water's edges, mostly at night, looking for insects, small fish, and frogs. (September 30, 2004)

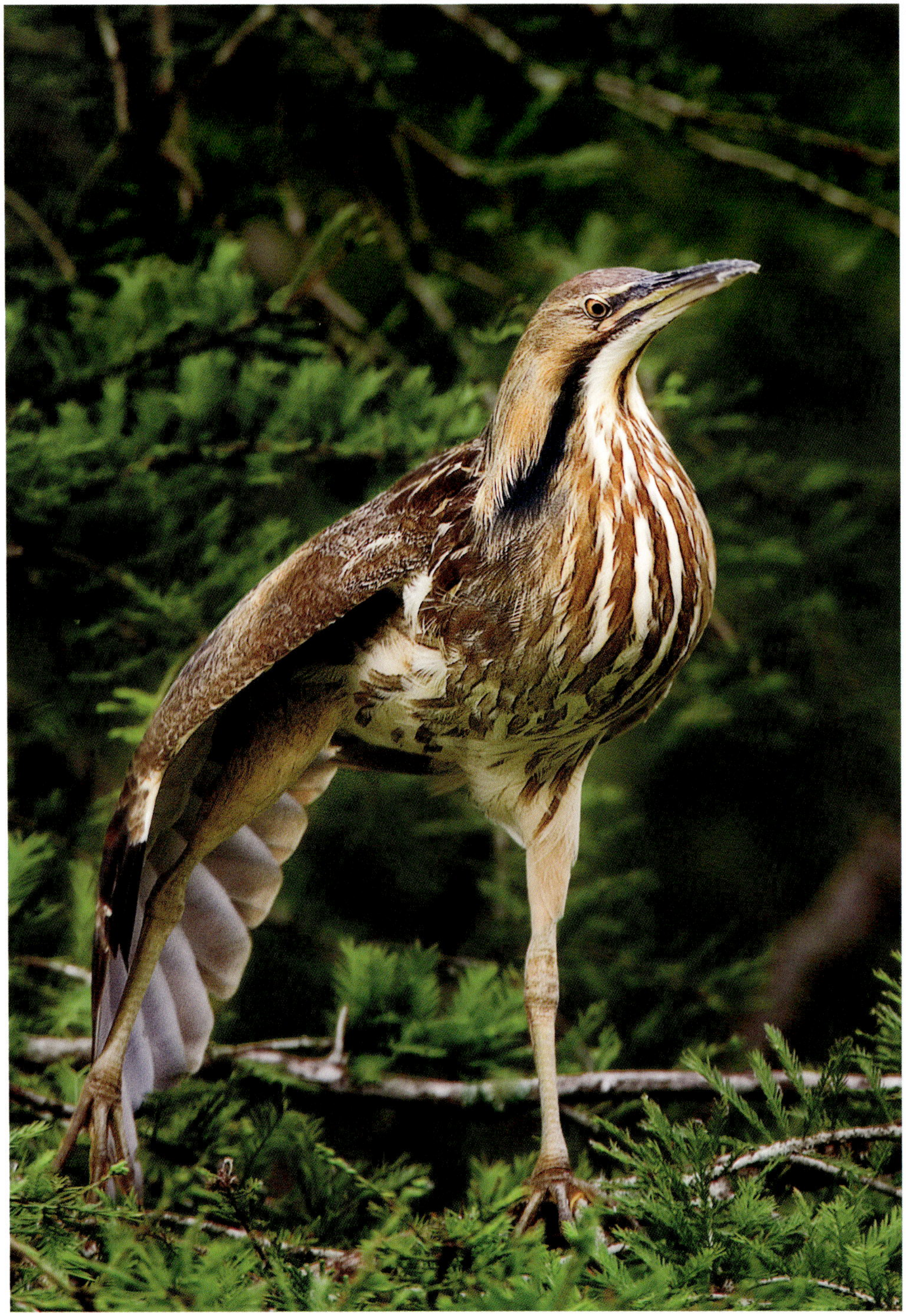

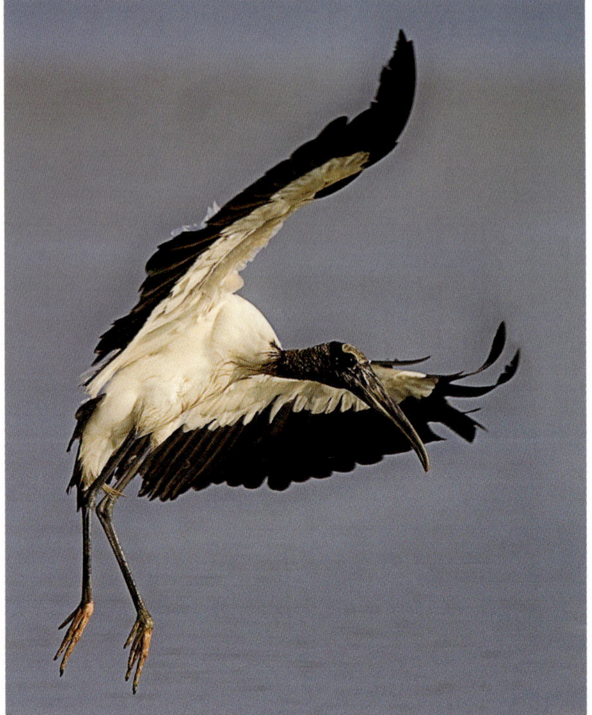

Above: The wood stork, formerly called a wood ibis, is usually found in freshwater wetlands. They are large waders with a wing span as wide as sixty inches, and their bald, featherless faces allow them to forage in deep water. You can hear the flapping wings as a wood stork comes in from a soar, with neck outstretched and legs extended. Like other waders, the wood stork walks slowly and steadily in shallow water seeking its prey—fish, frogs, and large insects. (August 7, 2007)

Left: Because of its brown, white, and buff speckled feathers, the American bittern can usually hide in freshwater marshes and swamps among cattails and other similar vegetation. When it senses it has been seen, this heron points its bill upward, making it appear like the reeds in which it forages. It mostly travels alone and has an annoying pumping sound—*oong-ka-choonk*—that you can easily recognize. (April 4, 2007)

WETLAND FLYERS

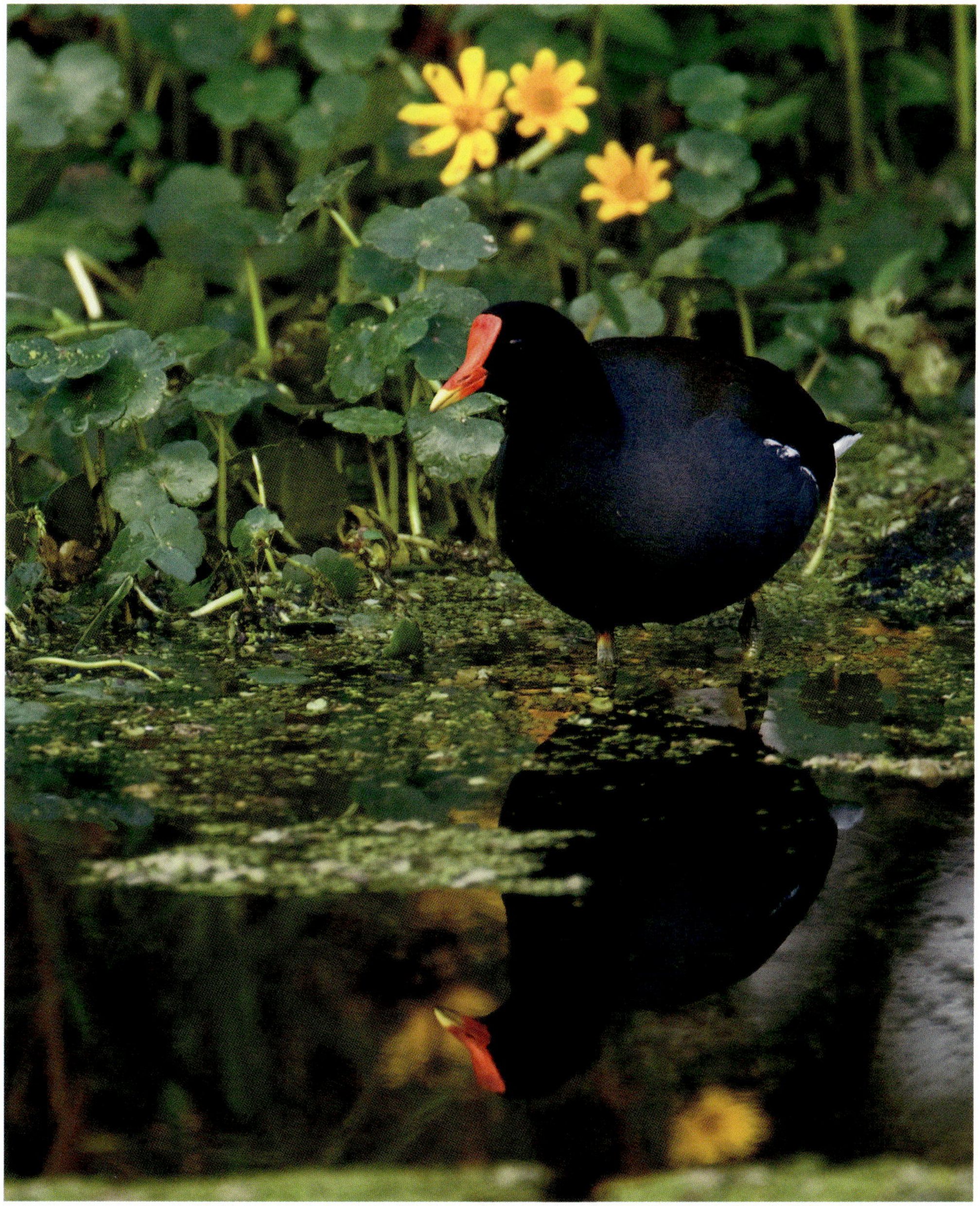

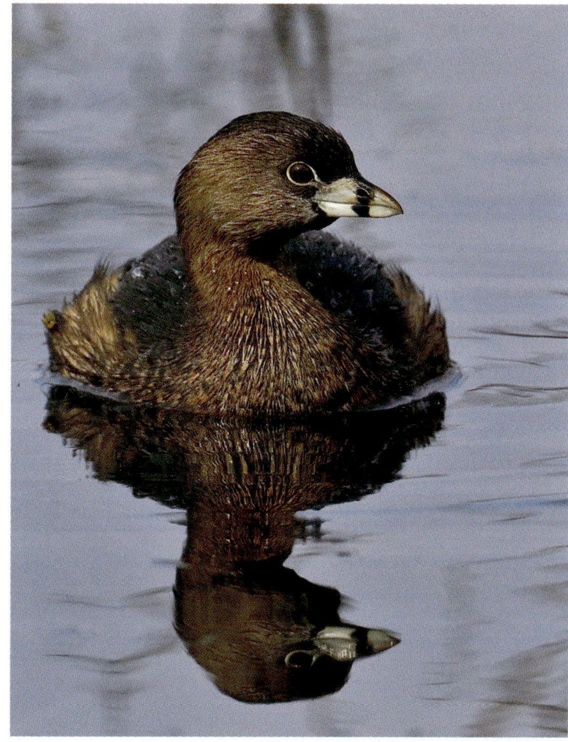

Above: I spotted this pied-billed grebe one morning while trying to photograph waterfowl in flight at the Florence Club in southwest Louisiana and was lucky to get a mirror image on the first snap. (February 10, 2007)

Left: A common moorhen reflected in the water at Lake Martin, the focal point of the Cypress Island Preserve, which is home to myriad birds. Moorhens are busy birds, always twitching their heads and necks as they feed on plant material, small animals, and insects. (November 14, 2005)

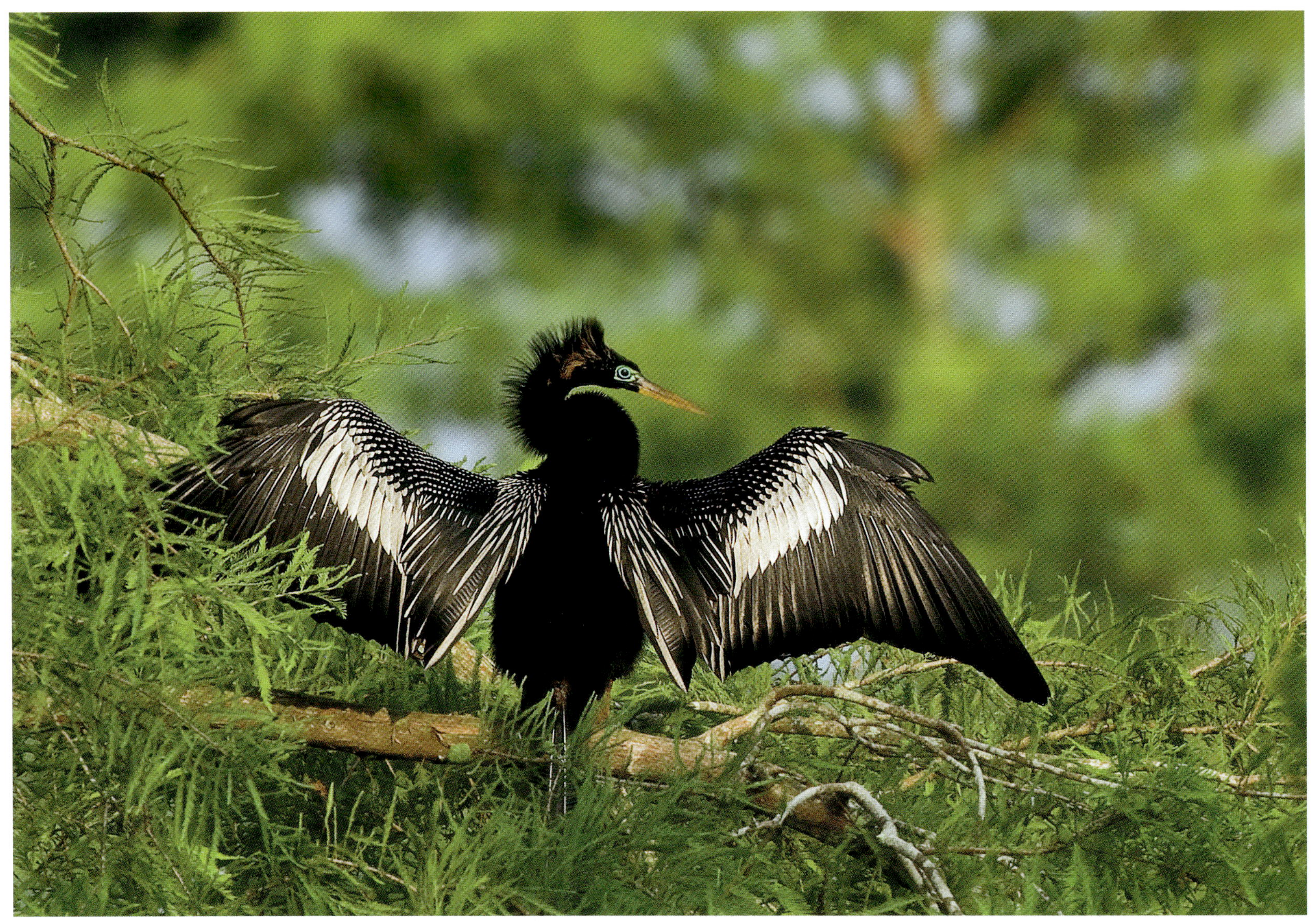

One of my earlier photographs taken with a Canon EO2 20D. I was impressed by this exquisite bird perched in the branches of a bald cypress tree at Lake Martin. Similar to cormorants, anhingas are aquatic and swim almost fully submerged. Like cormorants, they require long periods of drying with wings spread due to their wettable plumage. Their blue-ringed eyes are absolutely piercing. (January 1, 2000)

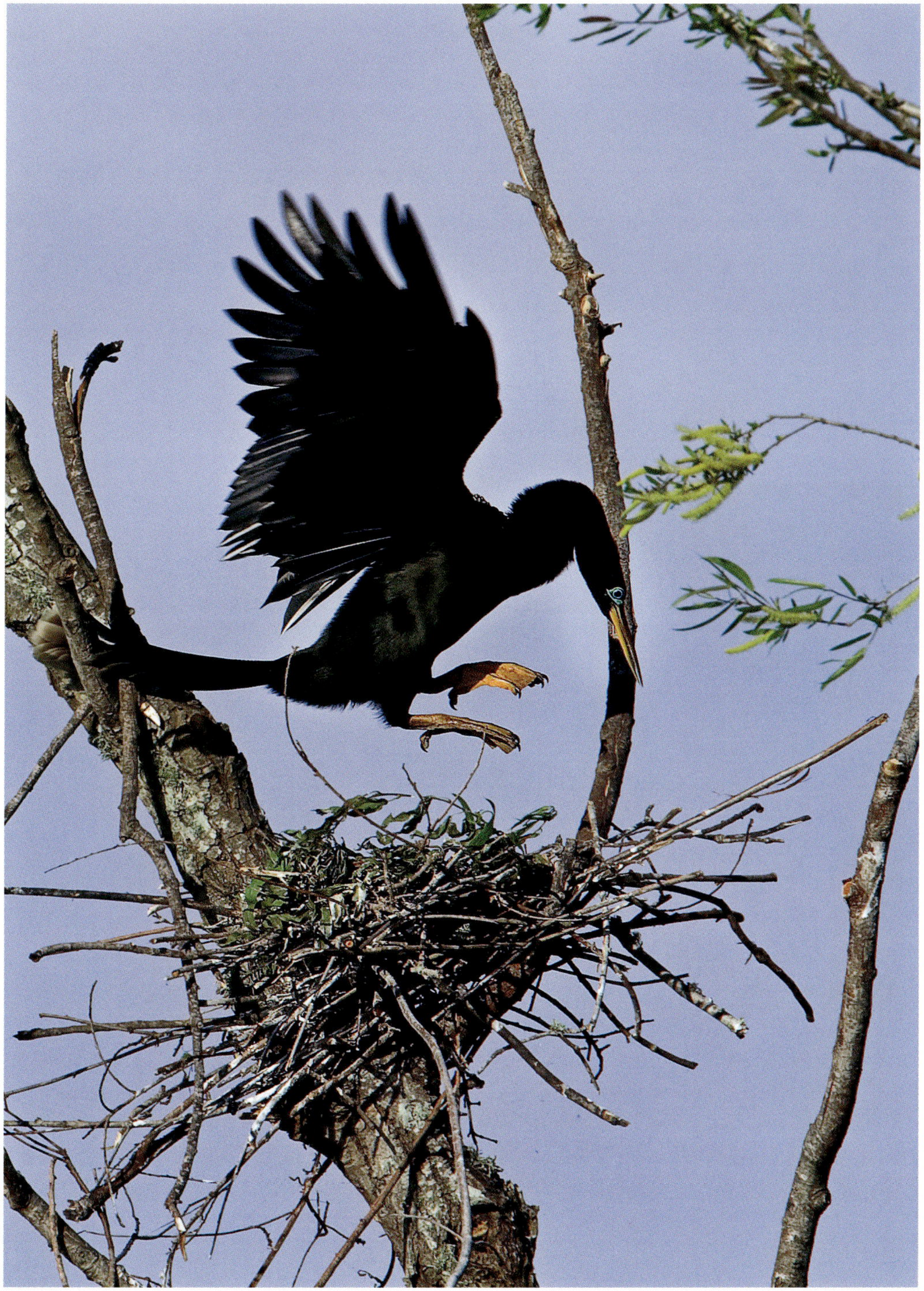

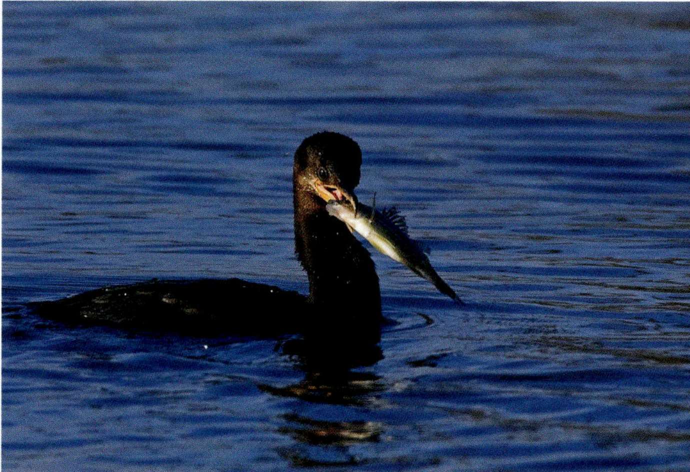

Above: A cormorant is a diving bird that feeds underwater on fish and sometimes snakes. After their fishing trips, it is typical to see them on the shore holding their wings out in the sun to dry. The feathers of a cormorant are not waterproof, which may enable them to dive more quickly since their feathers do not retain air bubbles. (December 5, 2006)

Left: Note this anhinga's snake-like neck and shiny black plumage. (March 24, 2007)

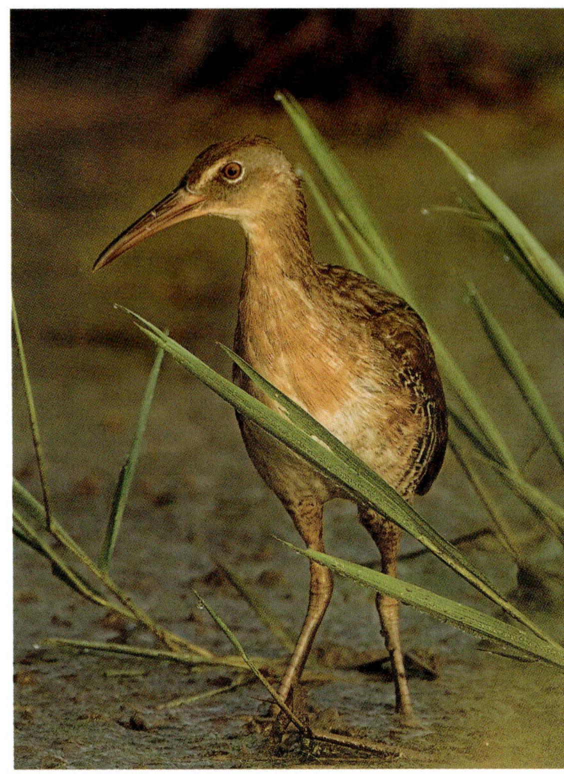

Above: Rails are shy and secretive birds and are difficult to observe. When I do spy them, they are usually in Louisiana wetland habitat. This particular clapper rail was spotted wandering out of a flooded crawfish pond. (July 23, 2005)

Right: These purple gallinules never fail to catch my attention with their colorful plumage of blue and green feathers, spindly long, yellow legs and toes, and bright red bills with a yellow tip. While not great fliers, they are excellent waders and can tiptoe over lily pads and other water vegetation scavenging for frogs, insects, and plants. I captured this image in Lacassine National Wildlife Refuge near Lake Arthur in the southwest part of Louisiana. (May 29, 2006)

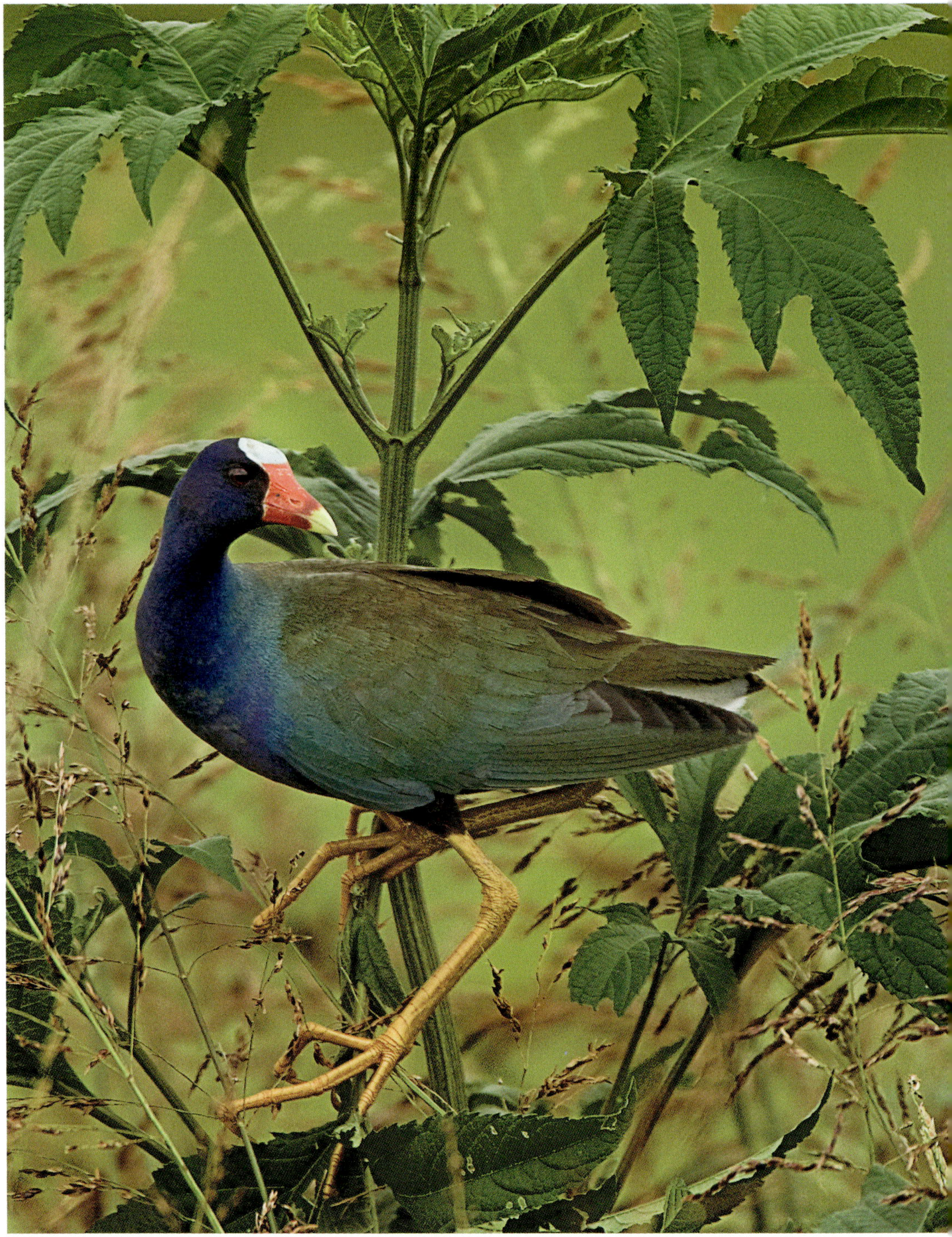

BIRDS OF PREY

Owls, kites, falcons, harriers, and hawks, as well as large ospreys and giant bald eagles, are all birds of prey, also known as raptors. They hunt primarily on the wing, using their highly-acute senses, especially their vision and hearing, and their large, powerful talons and beaks to snare and eat their prey.

Although I don't usually go out looking for these birds, I can almost always count on seeing them in rice fields, marshes, swamps, and woodlands. I'll also see them as I drive along country roads. The largest concentration of hawks can be observed during the winter months.

I am always fascinated watching them soar, sprint, swoop, and dive while they hunt for prey. Small animals like rodents, young opossums, and field mice are easy prey for owls, hawks, and kites, while ospreys and eagles feed primarily on fish and reptiles.

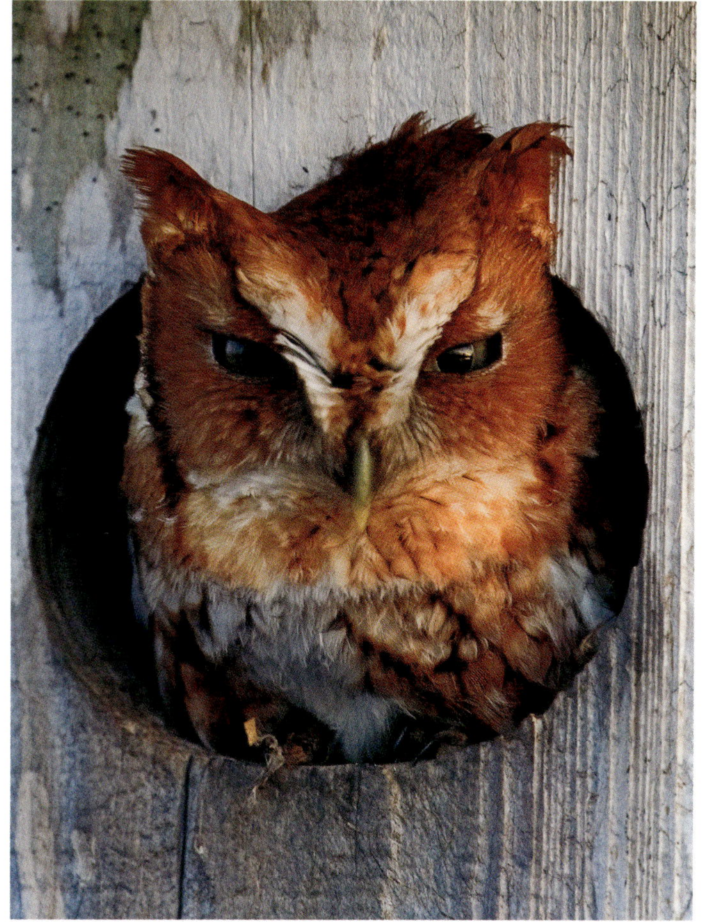

Whoa! When this screech owl poked his head out of the opening in a wood duck box at the Florence Club where I was planning to photograph ducks, he surprised me. What didn't surprise me, though, is that these owls seek cavities in hollow trees and deserted buildings to raise a family, so the duck box was an ideal spot for this bird to nest. His unruly expression leads me to believe I disturbed him. Sorry, Mr. Owl! (March 3, 2007)

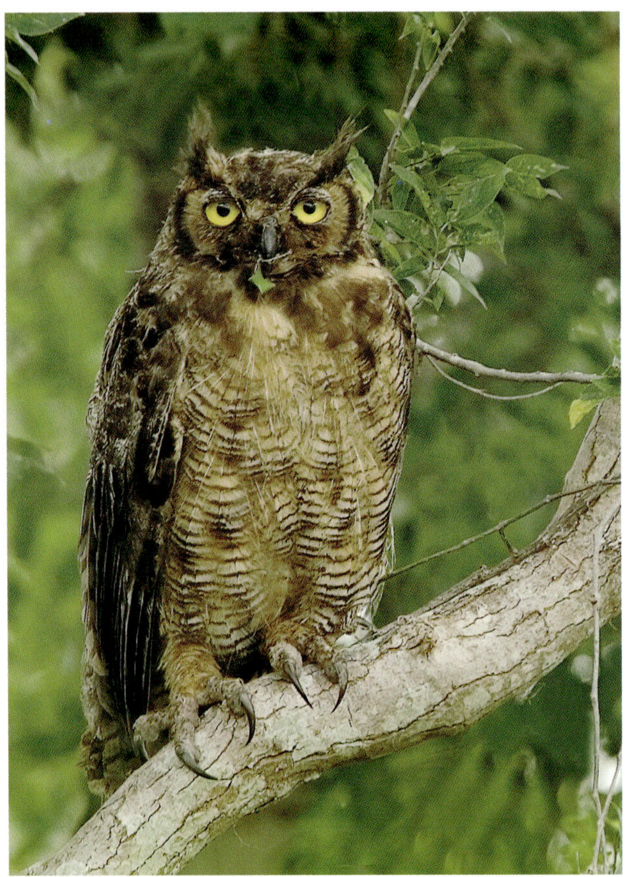

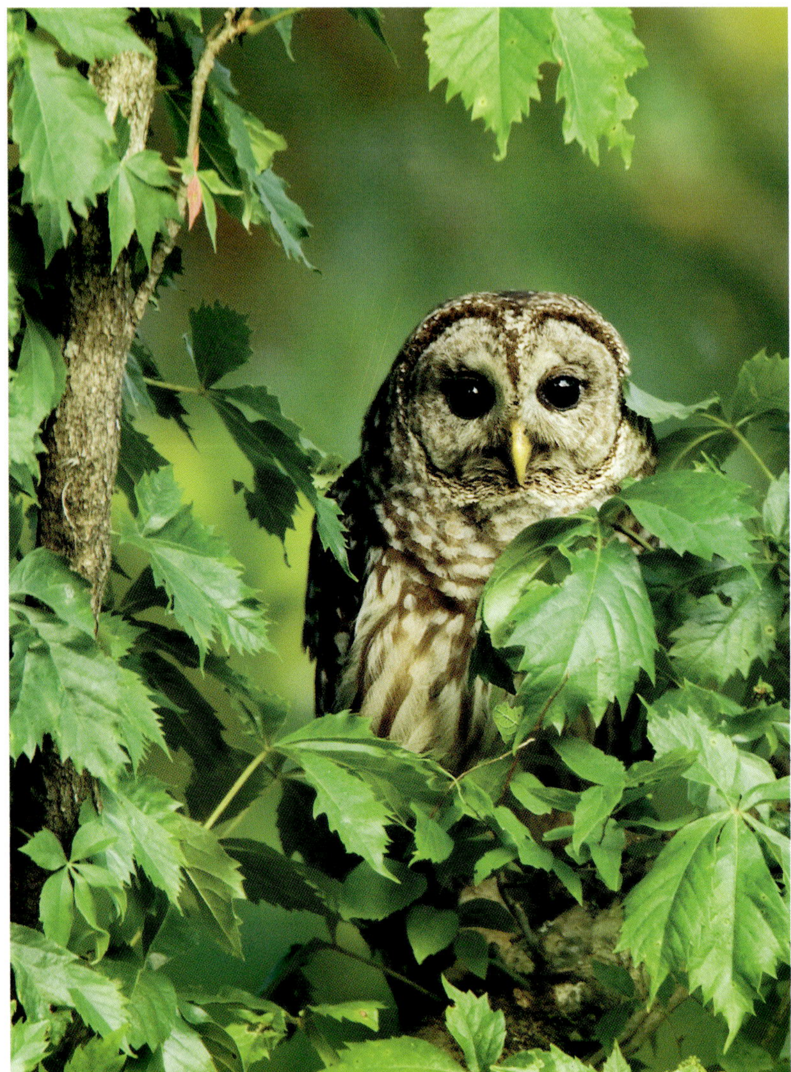

Left: A great horned owl is a formidable bird and a fierce predator. Check out the feathered talons, which enable this rather large owl to prey on mammals the size of a large rabbit. I've seen one of these owls scoop up a young opossum in an easy swoop. They can see in the dark and have stereo hearing, so finding their prey is easy! What appear to be horns are merely feather tufts. The piercing yellow eyes remind me of cat eyes. I found this one at my duck lease near Pecan Island in south Louisiana. (September 23, 2006)

Right: This barred owl appeared while I was trying to capture a photograph of a summer tanager at Sherburne Wildlife Management Area in the Atchafalaya Basin. I looked to my left as he swooped in, and I swung around and got him! Serendipity at its best! (June 4, 2006)

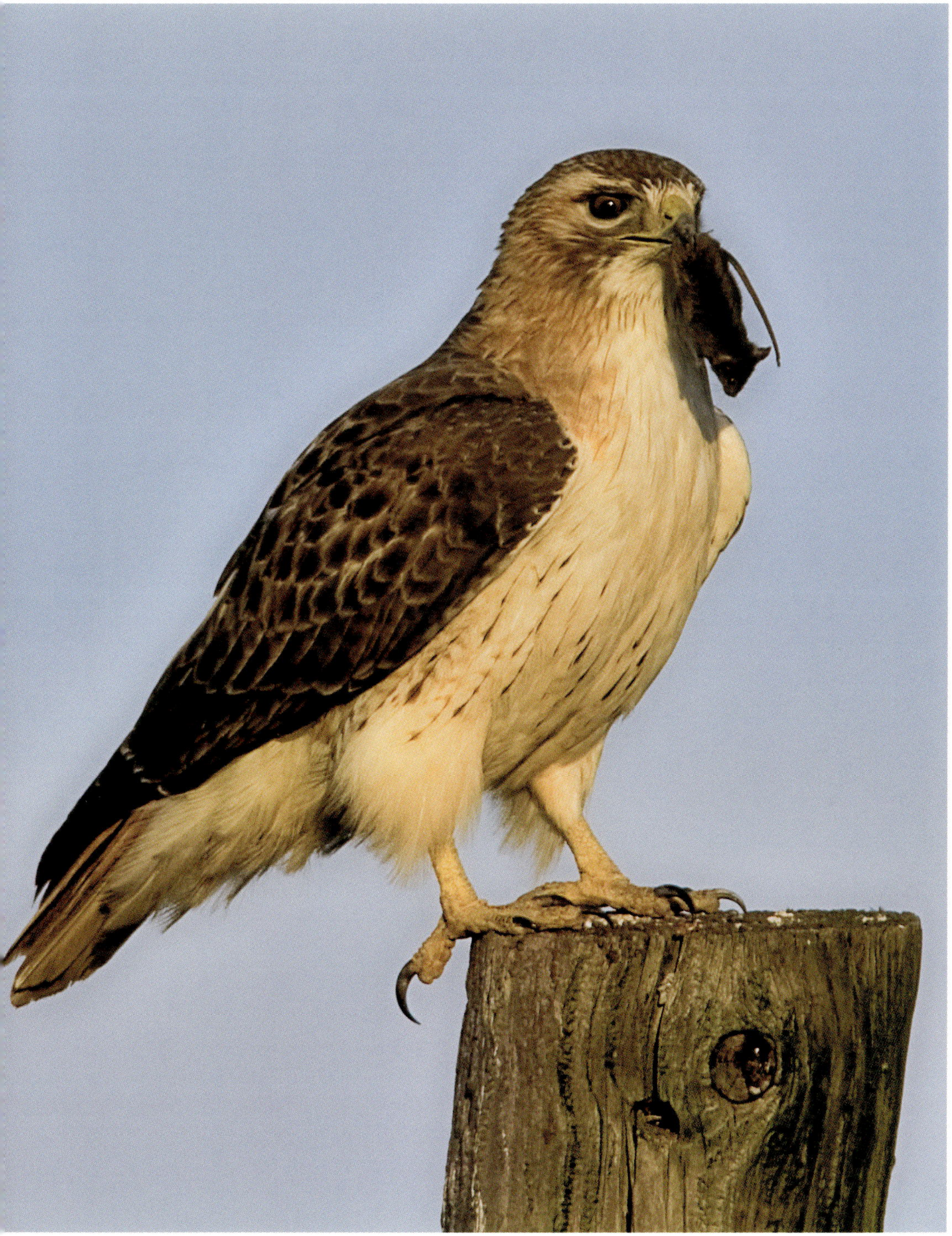

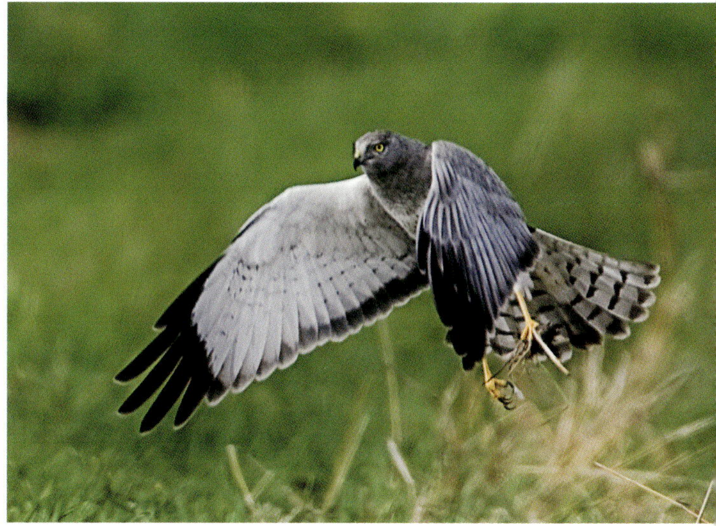

Above: Also known as a marsh hawk, this male northern harrier has pale grey plumage with black-tipped wings, which look like they were dipped in ink. Note the rodent in his talons. (January 10, 2007)

Left: Looks like this red-tailed hawk got his supper—a field mouse. I was photographing ducks and geese at the Florence Club when I happened to spot this guy on a fence post. (March 3, 2007)

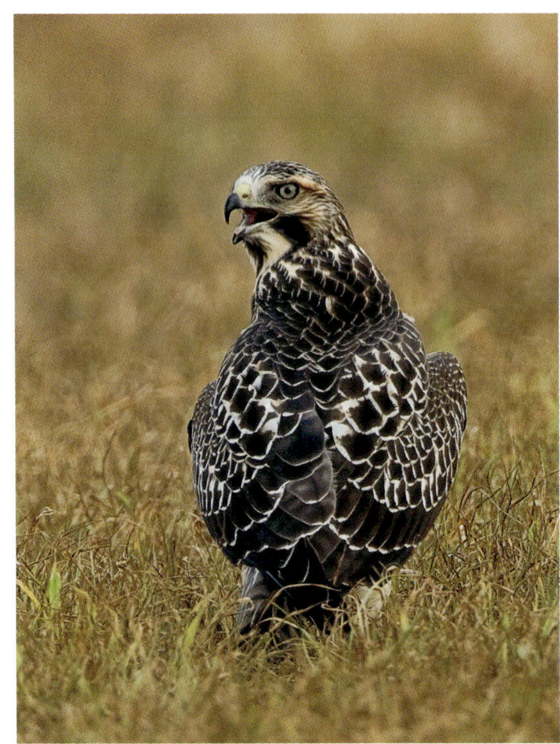

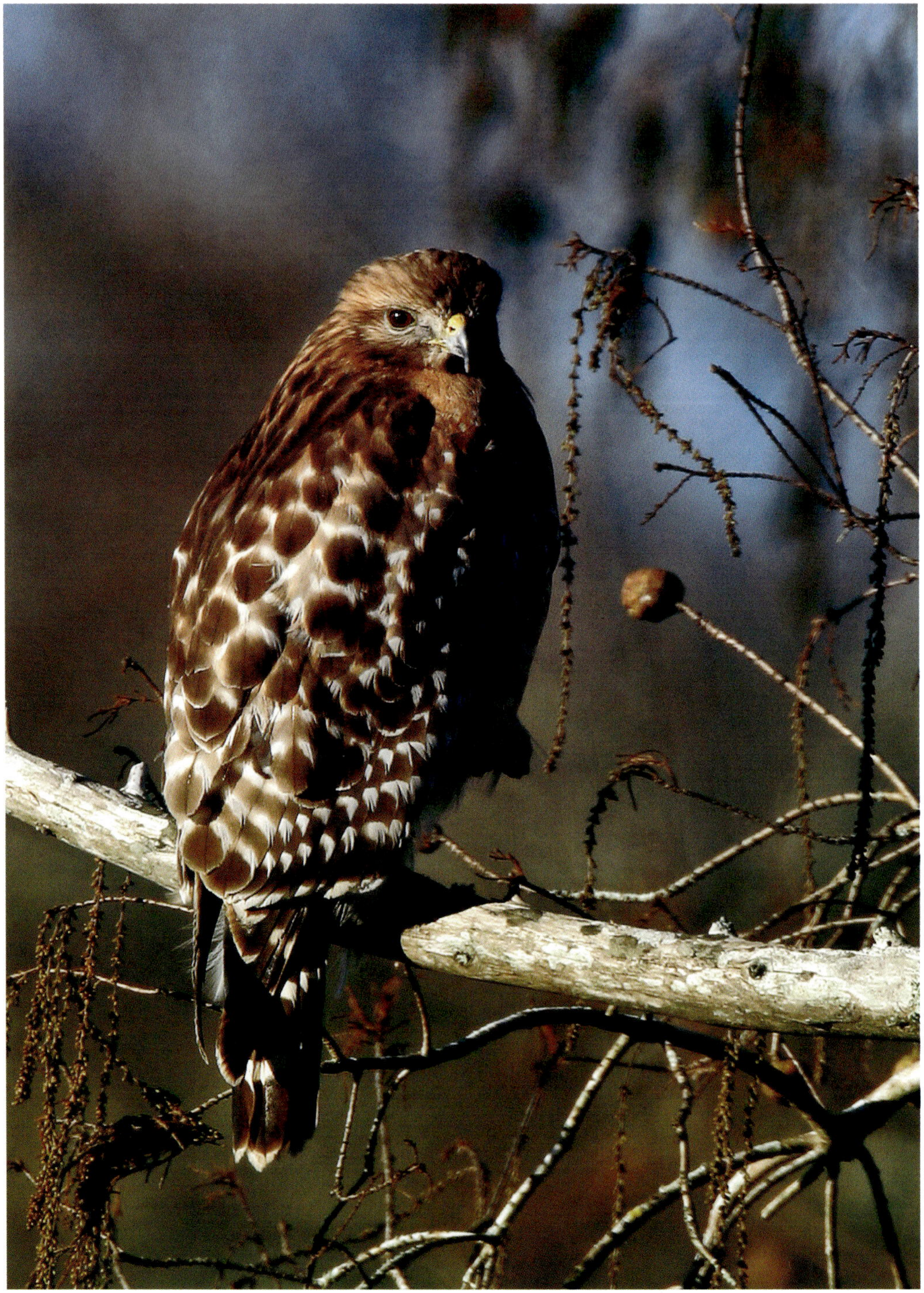

Above: Swainson's hawk, a fierce-looking bird, is rarely seen in south Louisiana. Generally they are found west of the Texas-Louisiana border, but, lucky me, I snapped this photograph near Kaplan, Louisiana. They will travel as far south as Argentina to winter. (August 20, 2005)

Right: A red-shouldered hawk at Lake Martin in December. They are called default raptors because they can be found all over North America in urban settings. They are prone to albinism and can be totally white. I happened to see one such white hawk in Yellowstone National Park, and at the time I couldn't identify it. (December 16, 2004)

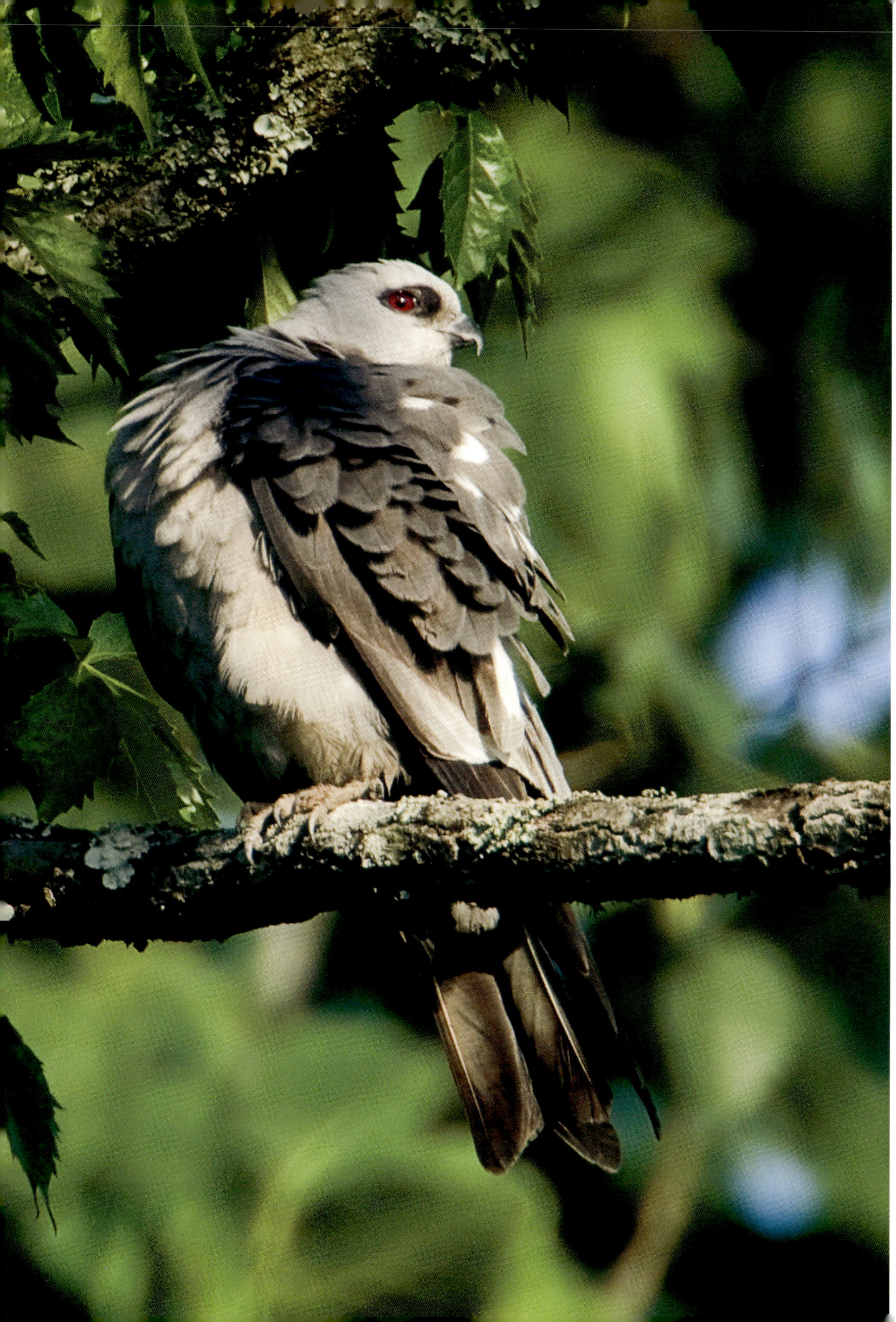

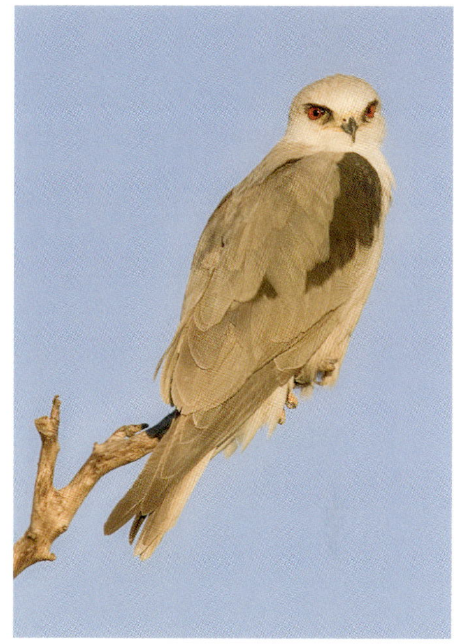

Above: Distinguished by dark shoulder feathers, the white-tailed kite seldom ventures away from its migration route, but I was able to see and photograph this bird in the setting sun at Lacassine National Wildlife Refuge in southwestern Louisiana. The gray two-toned plumage is set off by piercing red eyes amid a white-feathered head. These kites primarily feed on rodents. (January 14, 2006)

Left: This Mississippi kite looks more like a falcon than any other kite. It is buoyant and soars on flat wings high up in the thermals, catching and eating insects on the wing. I spied this kite in Sherburne Wildlife Management Area in the Atchafalaya Basin. Those red eyes gleam like garnets. (May 15, 2005)

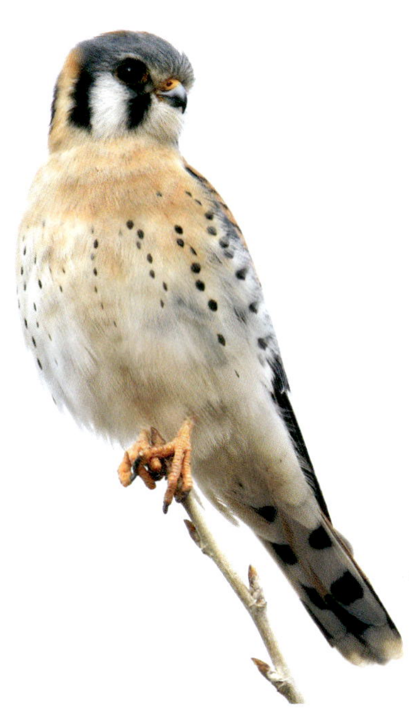

Above: The American kestrel is the smallest and most common falcon. I noticed this one perched on a small limb as he searched for prey—usually insects, small mammals, and reptiles. This adult male shows the typical dark marks around his white cheeks, which frame the dark eyes. American kestrels can usually be spotted on utility lines in rural areas. They are small but I think very pretty to observe. (January 11, 2005)

Right: I spied this peregrine falcon at Henderson Lake on the way back from photographing nesting eagles. Also known as a duck hawk, I've seen photographs of them with mallards in their claws, but they more often prey on doves, pigeons, and songbirds There has been some debate about their speed in the air, but some report clocking them at 200 miles, and more, per hour—like a bullet. The force of this high-speed dive can kill its prey on impact! (May 10, 2005)

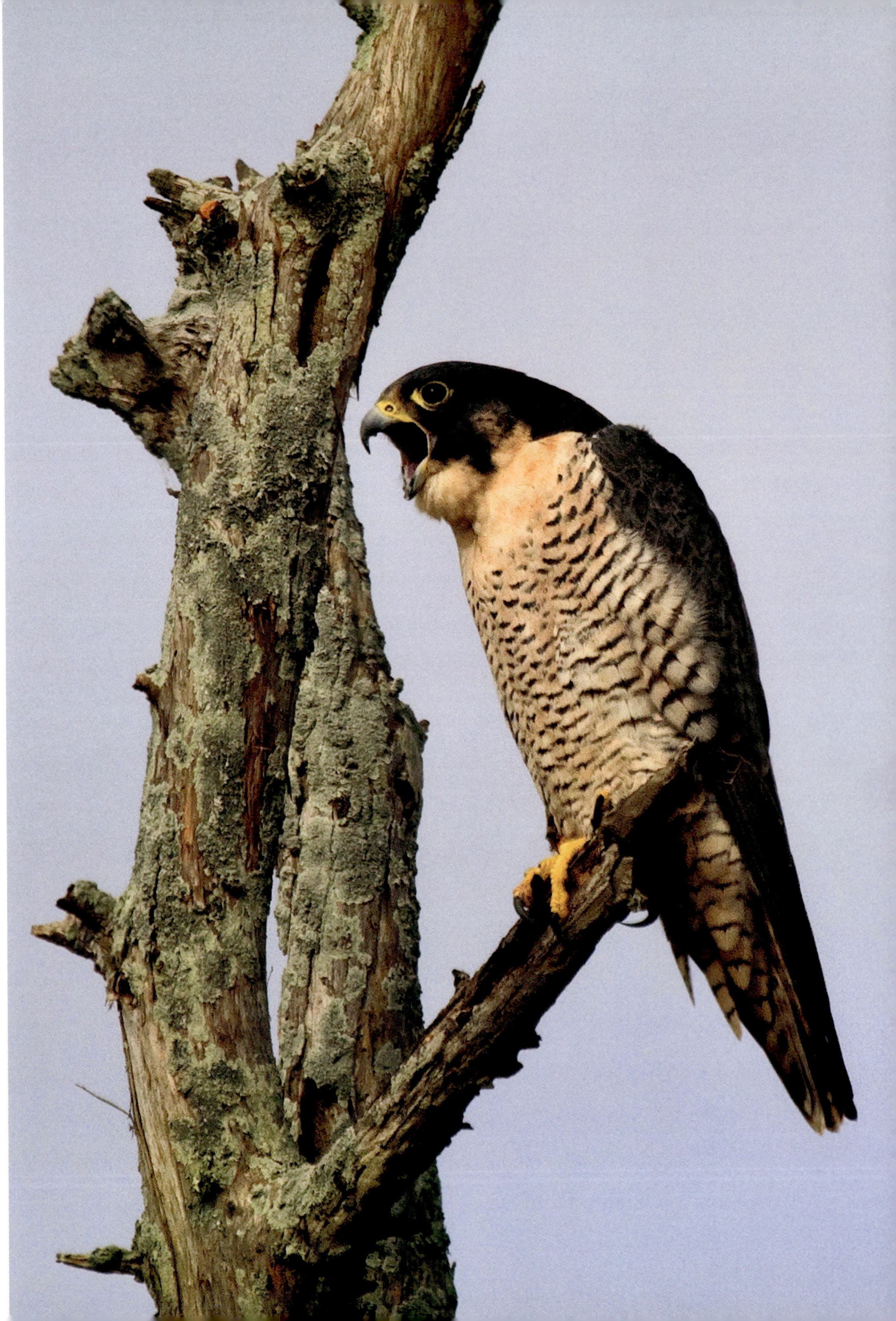

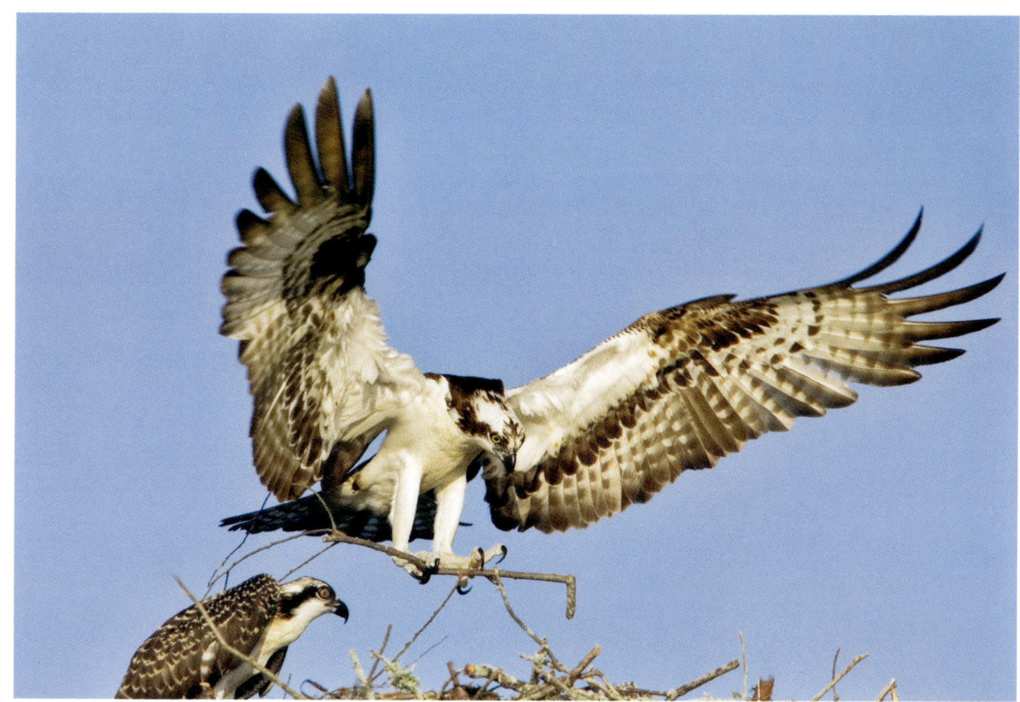

Above, left: An osprey building a nest in the Atchafalaya Basin. (June 11, 2005)

Below: Ospreys, also called fish hawks, are huge birds and, as their name implies, feed primarily on fish. The bull bream in this bird's talon is large enough to feed a family of four. Their wing span averages about 5 feet, and I've seen these birds plunge from high altitudes into the water to capture fish. You might find them nesting on telephone poles, channel markers, and even in duck blinds. These photos were taken in the Atchafalaya Basin while I was photographing bald eagles. (June 15, 2004)

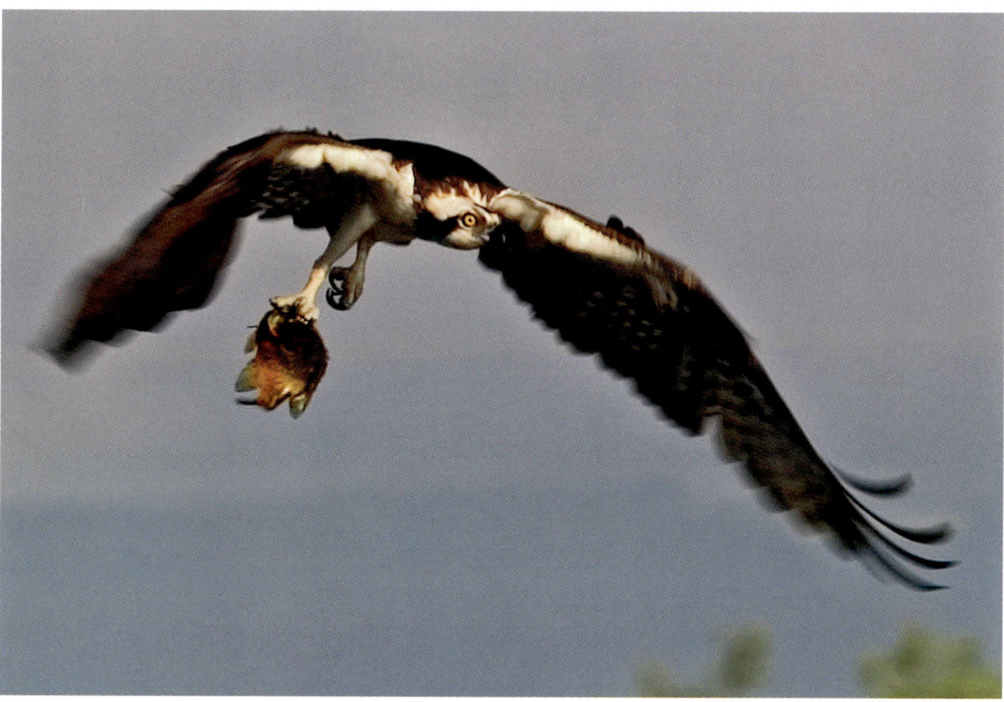

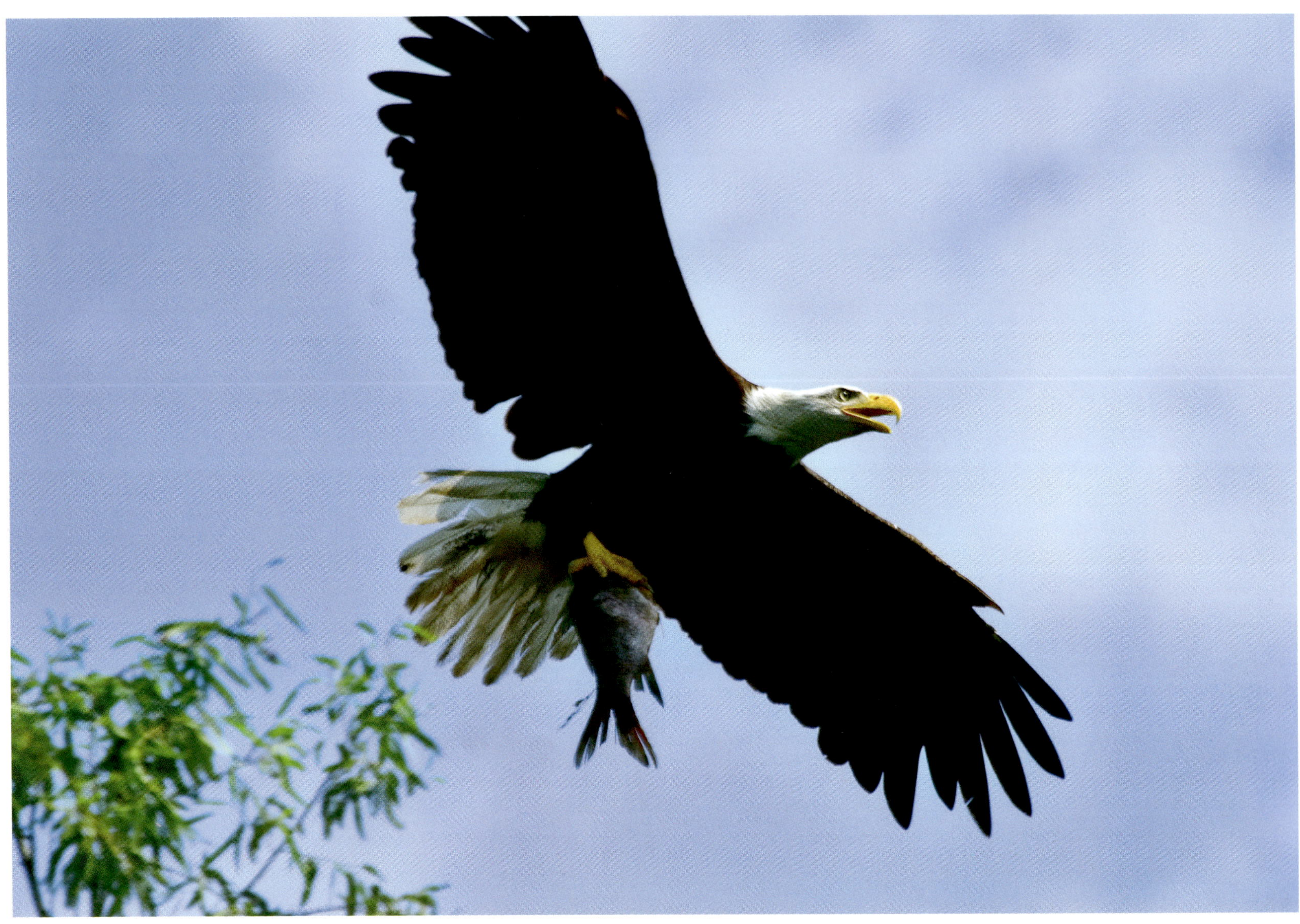

Ah, the granddaddy of birds—the bald eagle—is indeed a sight to behold. Even larger than ospreys, bald eagles feed on fish but also prey on waterfowl, and often they "steal" the kill from other raptors. The American bald eagle is the symbol and national bird of the United States, and in the late 20th century was on the endangered species list. Now, the population has stabilized, and they are no longer on the list. (There are over 400 in Louisiana.) Watching them soar and hearing their piercing screams is thrilling indeed. Photographed near Henderson Lake in the Atchafalaya Basin. (May 8, 2004)

WOODLAND RESIDENTS

The birds in this chapter are what I call "tweety" birds simply because most of them are small and have enjoyable songs and sounds. Commonly known as passerines, or small woodland songbirds, they comprise half of all bird species. Fortunately, many kinds of these birds can be observed practically year-round in Louisiana.

Resident birds, those that are here year-round, increase during the winter when their relatives join them from "up north." These are the most familiar birds since they can be spotted at the feeders in your backyard or perhaps in a park—think mockingbirds, cardinals, Carolina wrens, chickadees, several species of woodpeckers, and blue jays.

Then there are the colorful neotropicals that migrate, spending the winters in South and Central America but returning to the United States to breed. They begin arriving from late January to early May, peaking in April. These are far less common to observe, but they are quite common in our woodlands, swamps, and marshes. These include the prothonotary, northern parula, summer tanager, some vireos, blue grosbeak, wood thrush, and the indigo and painted bunting.

Other migrants that nest in North America and winter in the tropics only pause in south Louisiana long enough to refuel on their north and south migrations during the spring and fall. In fact, this is the group most watched by birders in April, when they stop in the woodlands along the Louisiana coast. Most are only around for a few hours or several days, depending on the weather. This group includes over two dozen species of warblers, the rose-breasted grosbeak, some vireos, and the scarlet tanager.

The wintering birds, which arrive in October and November and depart in March and April, may be familiar to the average person since many spend time around town. Common winter birds include cedar waxwings, blue-headed vireos, house and winter wrens, and yellow-rumped warblers.

I had very little interest in these small songbirds, but in the spring of 2006, for some reason yet to be determined, many birds that I usually photograph—egrets, herons, and roseate spoonbills—didn't show up, and what few did nested far from the road at Lake Martin. Naturally I, along with many other photographers and birders, was very disappointed. It was at that time that my friend and fantastic birder Danny Dobbs suggested that I give some thought to photographing the smaller species—the passerines.

I got myself an MP3 player, loaded it up with birdsongs and sounds, and set up at Lake Martin and later at several other wildlife areas. Within a few minutes after turning on the MP3 player and selecting the song of a particular bird, that bird would come to investigate. Bingo! I was entranced.

One day, I was sitting in my car with the windows rolled down and the MP3 playing, and a prothonotary warbler flew and perched on my rearview mirror. I think we were both surprised when we were suddenly eye to eye. Another time, a bird flew into my car and headed to the speaker to listen to the birdsongs!

Since then, I've devoted quite a bit of time photographing my new-found friends. These birds are small, but they make up for it with their beauty and music.

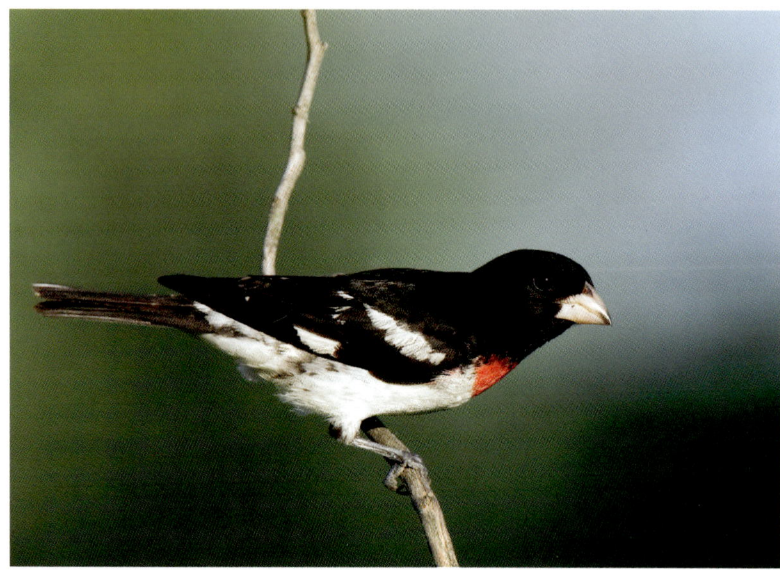

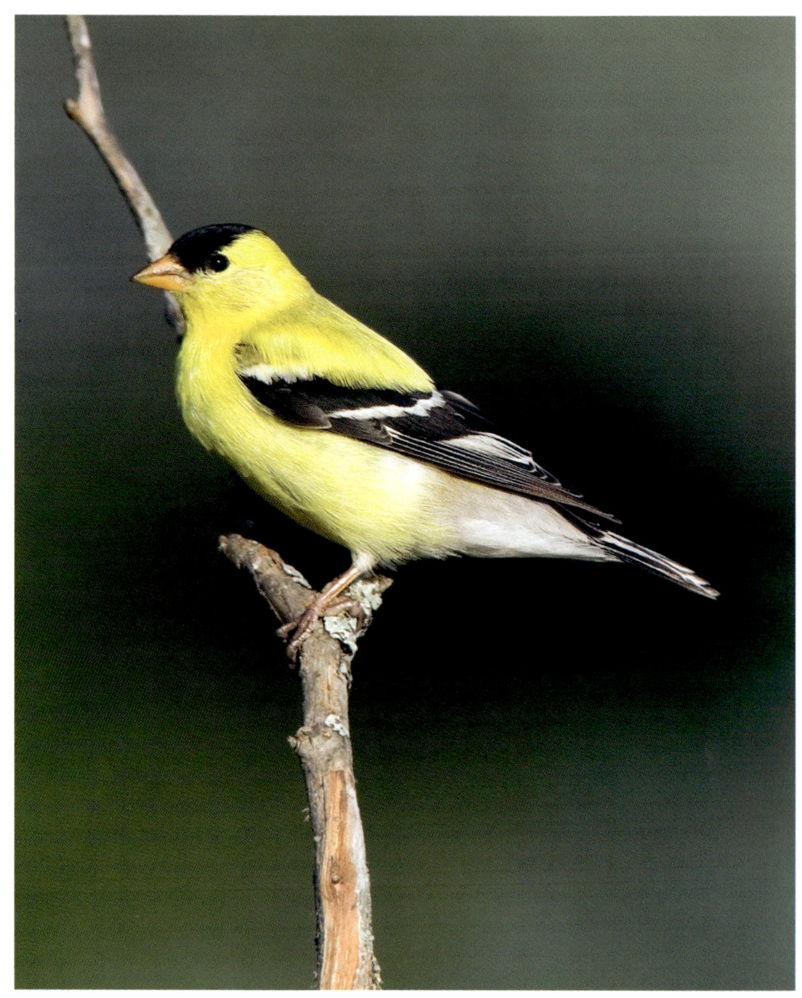

Above: This adult male rose-breasted grosbeak sings much like a robin, but its song is more varied and richer. Grosbeak comes from the French *gros bec,* or fat bill. The fat bill allows the bird to expertly shell sunflower seeds. (June 13, 2007)

Right: With its bright yellow plumage, the American goldfinch is sometimes referred to as a wild canary. Its orange, conical beak is ideal for consuming seed heads. During the summer, the male is a vibrant yellow but turns an olive color during the colder months. Its bright plumage attracts females during the breeding season. A social bird during the nonbreeding season, it is often found among large flocks. If you listen closely to their tweets, it sounds like they are chirping *po-ta-to-chip.* (June 13, 2007)

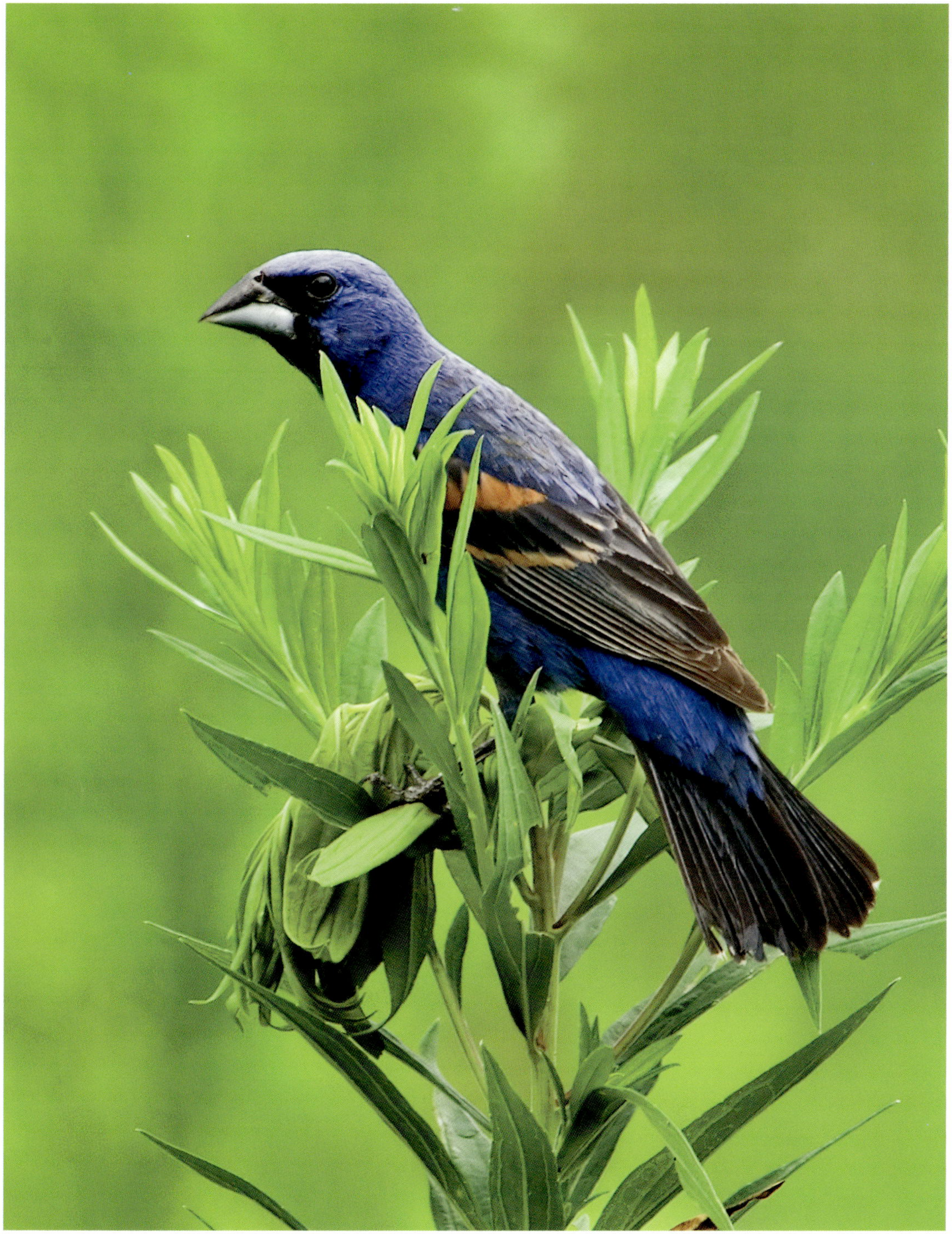

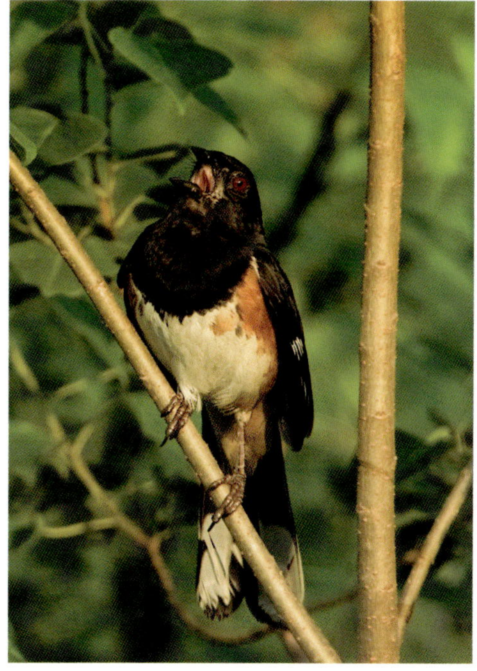

Above: While I was trying to photograph a painted bunting on the fringes of heavy brush at Sherburne Wildlife Management Area in the heat of summer, this brightly-colored eastern towhee popped out of the foliage and seemed to pose for the camera! (July 2, 2006)

Left: When I spotted this bird at Sherburne Wildlife Management Area in the Atchafalaya Basin I first thought it was an indigo bunting because of its bright blue feathers, but then I noticed its fat bill and larger size. This male blue grosbeak seems to be on the watch, perched on this bright green bush. (July 17, 2006)

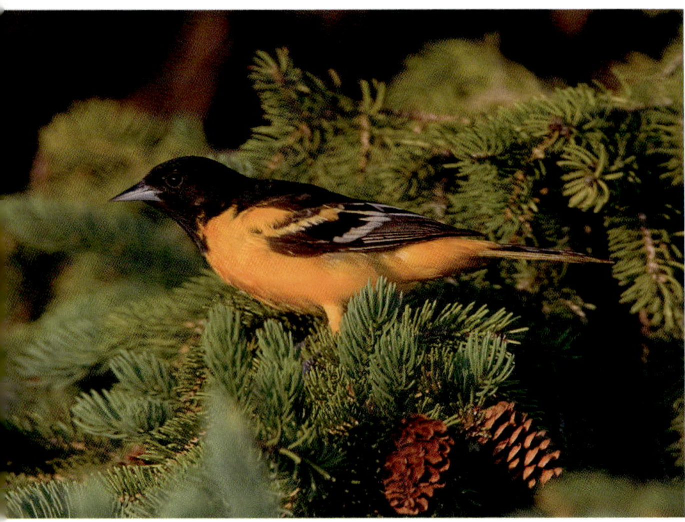

Above: A bit of trivia—this bird got its name because the male's bright colors resembled the coat of arms of Sir George Calvert, Lord Baltimore, who colonized and named the region that is now the state of Maryland. If you ever watch a Baltimore Oriole baseball game, you'll understand why their uniforms are bright orange and black. The bird's colorful plumage stands out in the foliage of the woods, and their loud, fluty whistle is easily recognizable. This photo was shot in Michigan, but orioles can be spotted in Louisiana as they come through during the spring and fall migrations. (June 10, 2007)

Right: An orchard oriole is the smallest of the orioles but makes up for its size with bright brick red-and-black feathers and a rich, whistled warbling. (July 2, 2006)

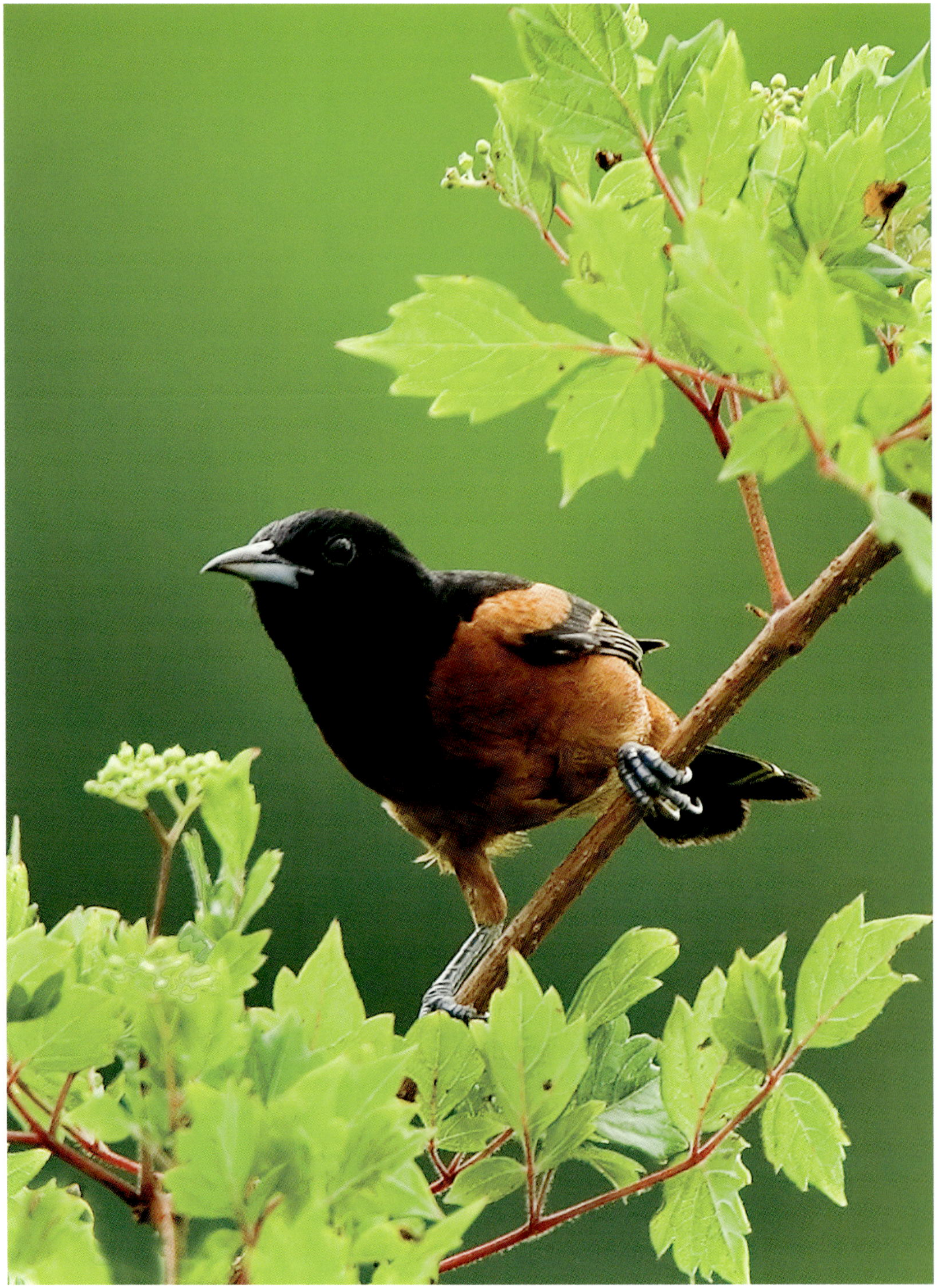

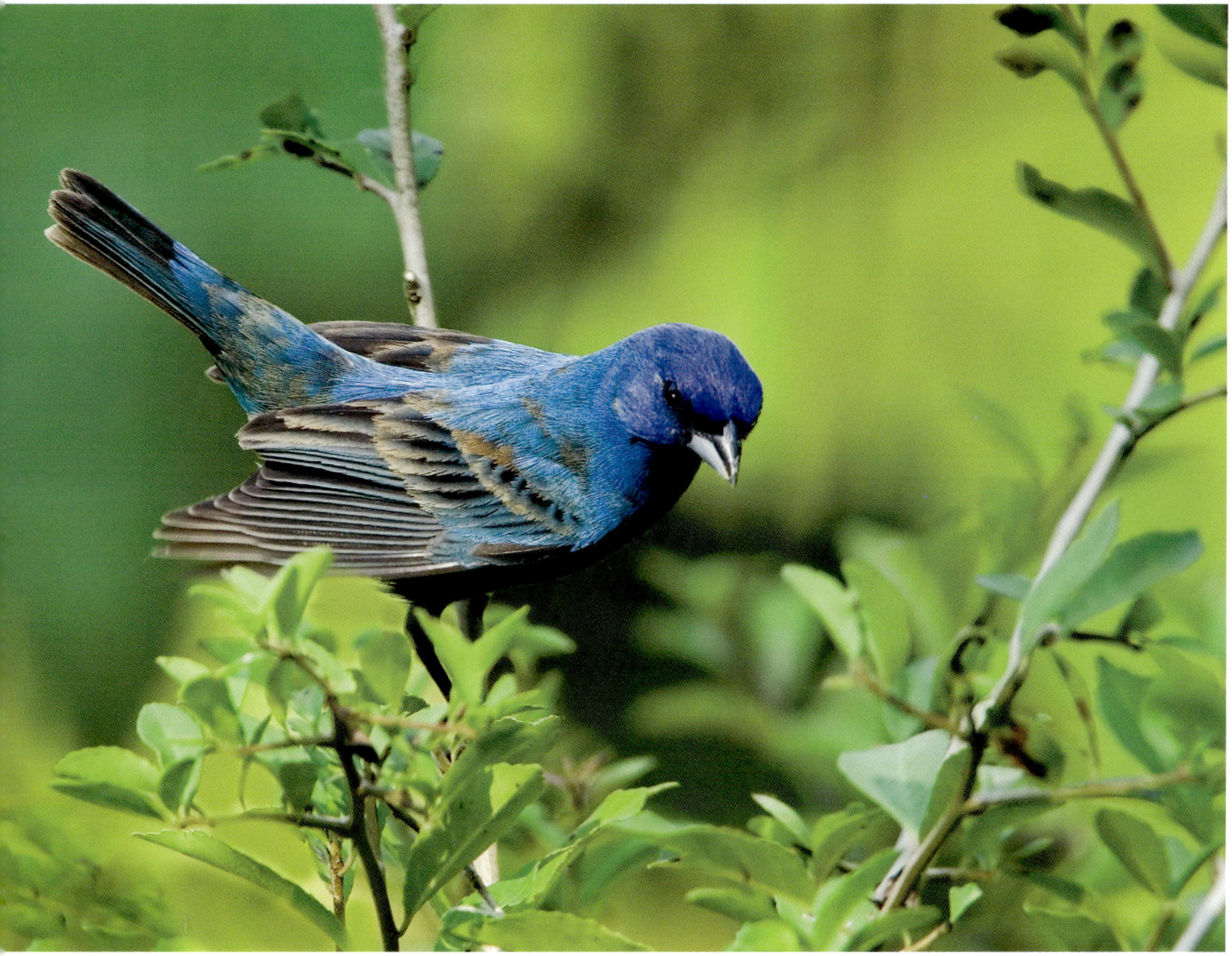

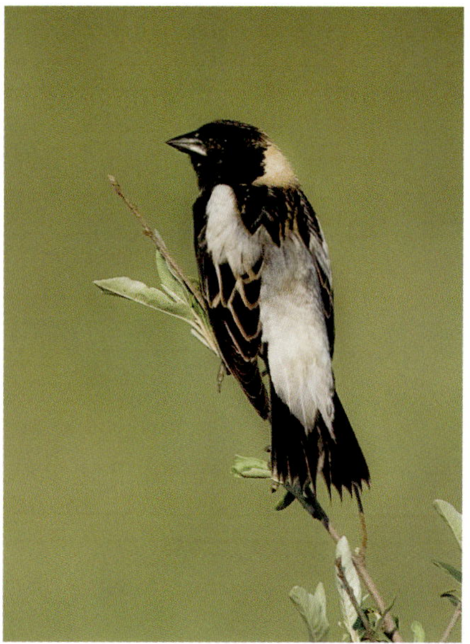

My first thought when I spied this small, black bird, a bobolink, was that it looked like he had on a tuxedo in reverse—the black feathers were predominant on the underside with the white ones appearing on the lower back. It was a sight to behold, and his song was this bubbling, jangling series of notes that indeed sounds like *bob-o-link bob-o-link, blink blank blink*. (June 10, 2007)

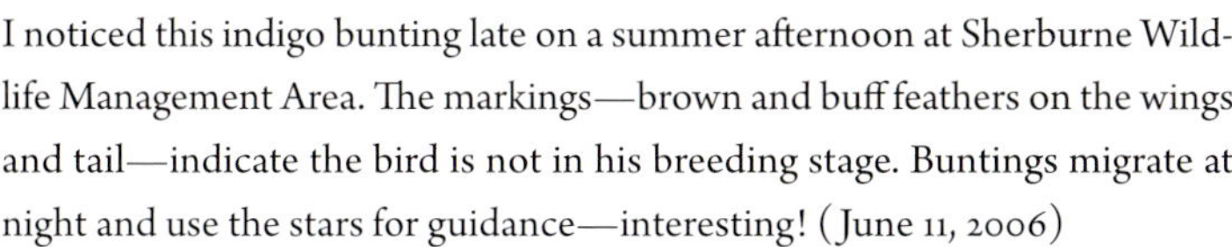

I noticed this indigo bunting late on a summer afternoon at Sherburne Wildlife Management Area. The markings—brown and buff feathers on the wings and tail—indicate the bird is not in his breeding stage. Buntings migrate at night and use the stars for guidance—interesting! (June 11, 2006)

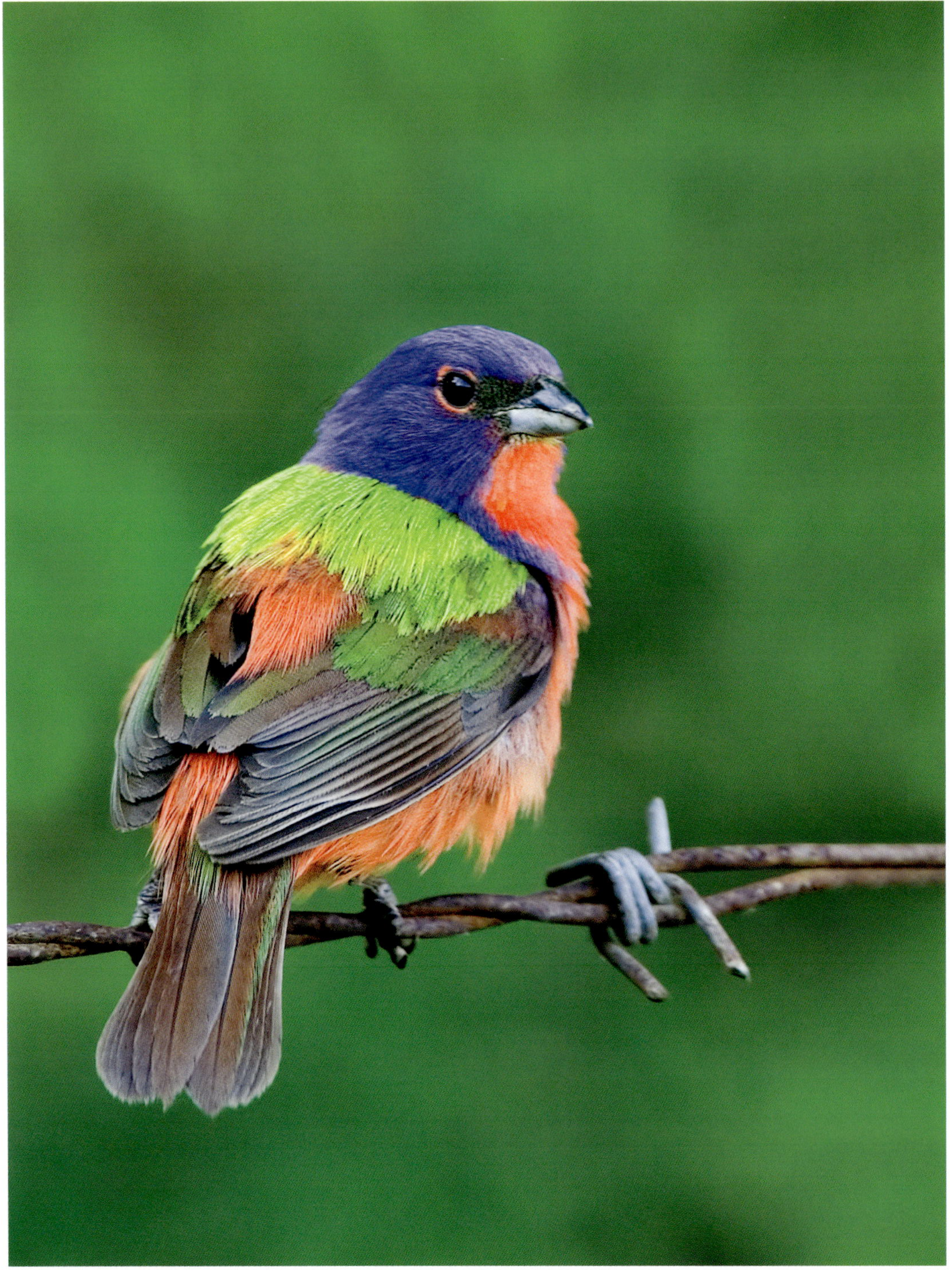

When I have the privilege to come upon these exotic colorful birds I am in total awe. Their tropical vibrant colors almost defy description. It's as if an artist went wild with his palette of colors! Note the vivid red around the black pearl-like eyes. I was fortunate enough to spot this beauty in a wooded area in south Louisiana. (May 24, 2006)

TANAGERS AND CARDINALS

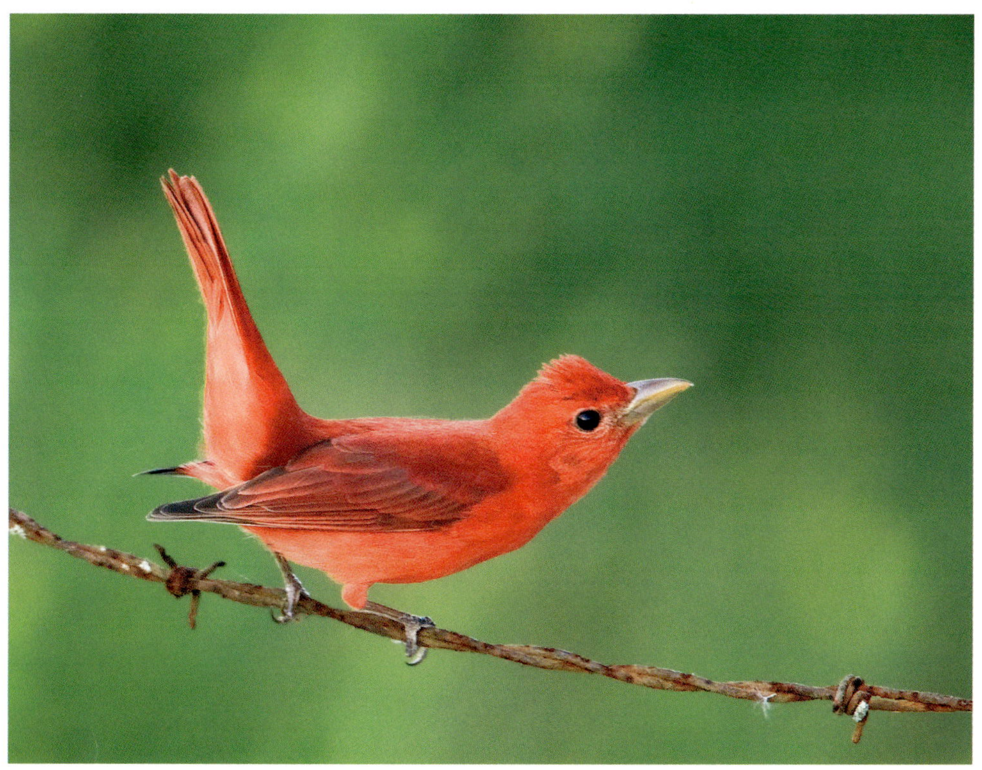

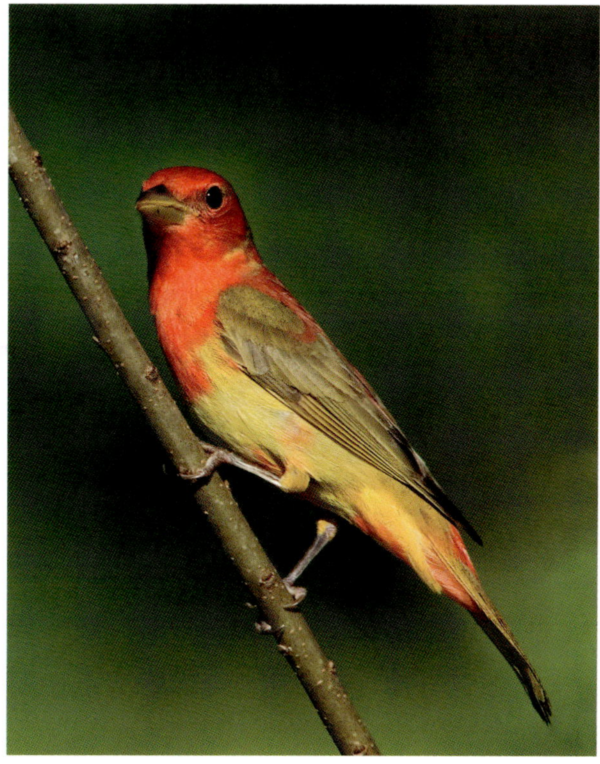

Left: This bright red, male summer tanager just popped out of the foliage in the forests of the Atchafalaya Basin where I spied it one spring when the bald cypress and willows were leafing out. They feed on insects and are considered to be bee and wasp specialists. They can catch a bee in flight, kill it by beating it against a branch, and then remove the stinger by rubbing it off on a branch before popping the bee or wasp into their mouths. (April 20, 2007)

Right: This first-year adult tanager shows the typical markings—a mixture of red and yellowish green and a bright red head. (April 21, 2007)

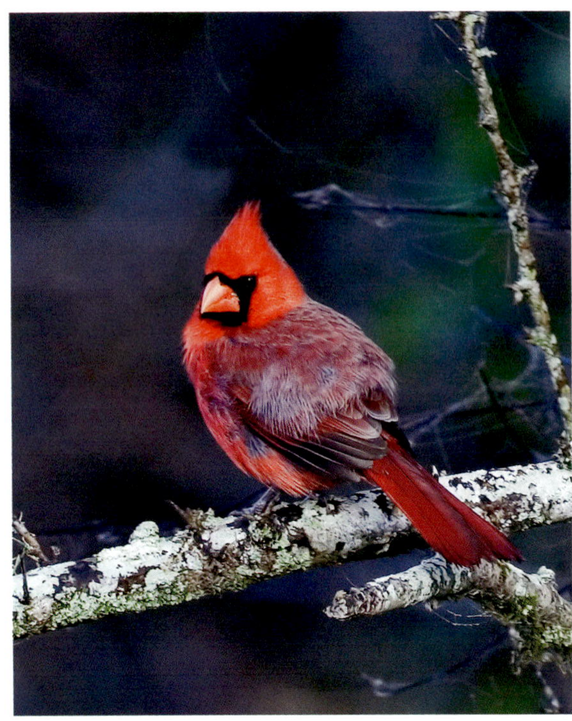

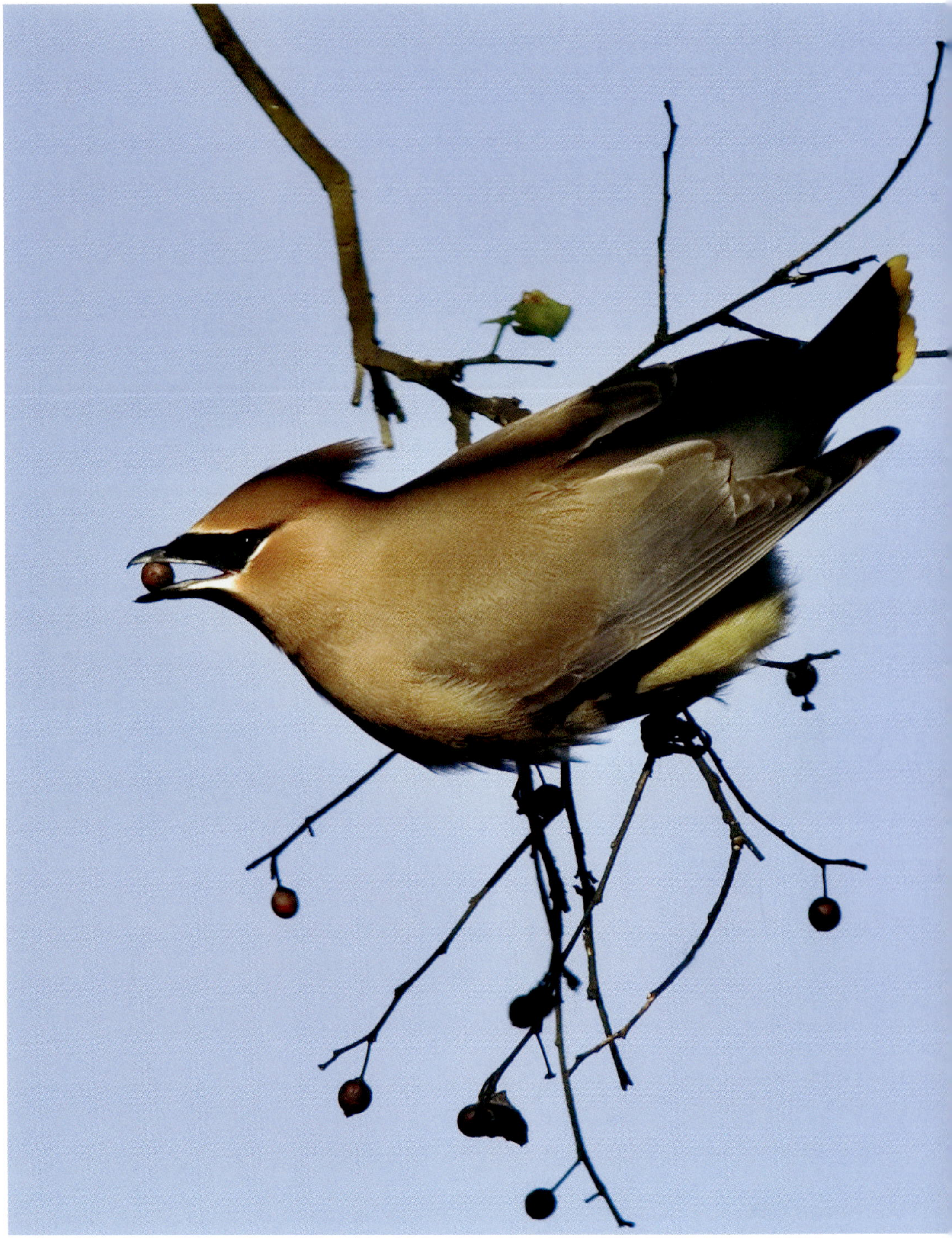

Above: A male cardinal is easy to recognize with his bright red beak and coal black eyes. (January 11, 2006)

Right: Cedar waxwings feed on berries and sugary fruit. Here one looks like he's found a branch with one of his favorite foods. These birds favor open forest habitats, where there are berry sources as well as running water. I found this one at Lake Martin, where both are plentiful, but they also like fountains and birdbaths, so you might see one in your backyard. (January 25, 2007)

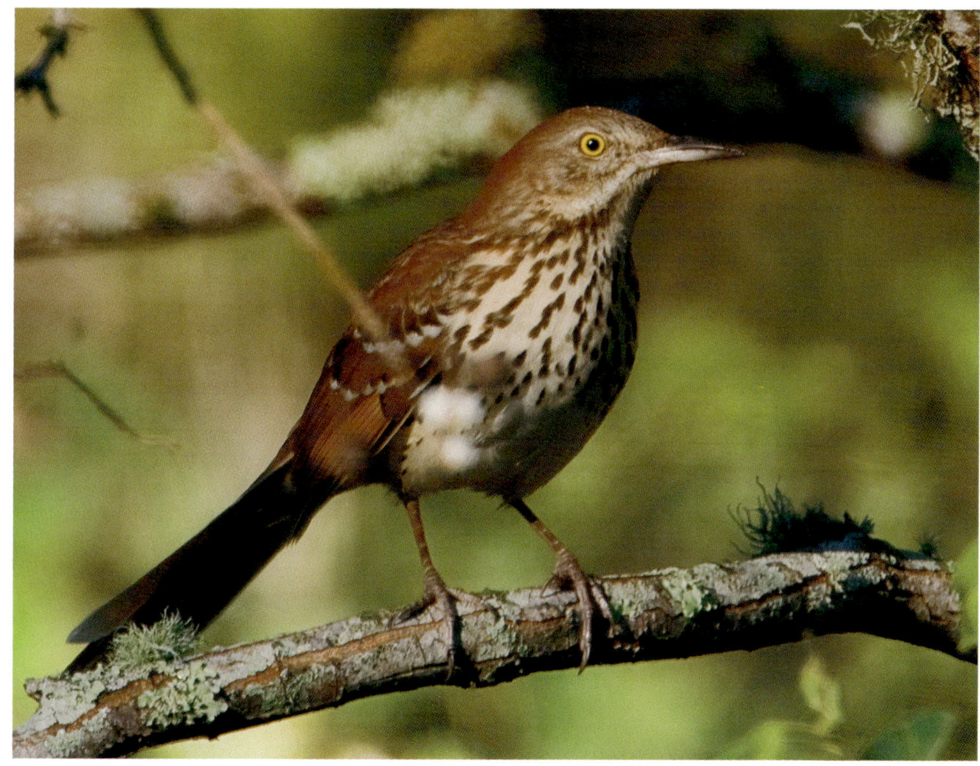

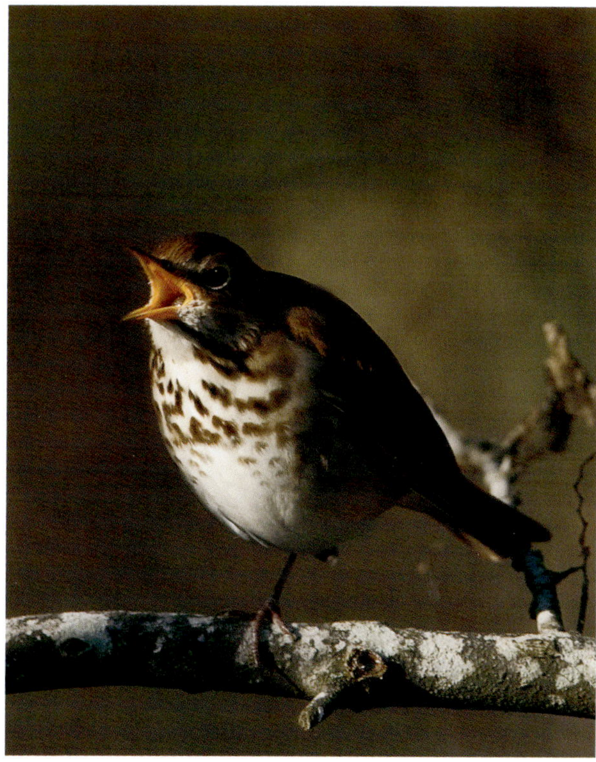

Left: A rather drab brown thrasher, this bird can belt out some fine songs, which is how I usually find these birds in the woods. (November 2, 2005)

Right: I was at the mud-boat house at my duck lease near Pecan Island when I heard this Swainson's thrush chirping his heart out. He's not very striking in appearance, but he was so happy, I snapped him. (December 31, 2006)

WARBLERS, VERIOS

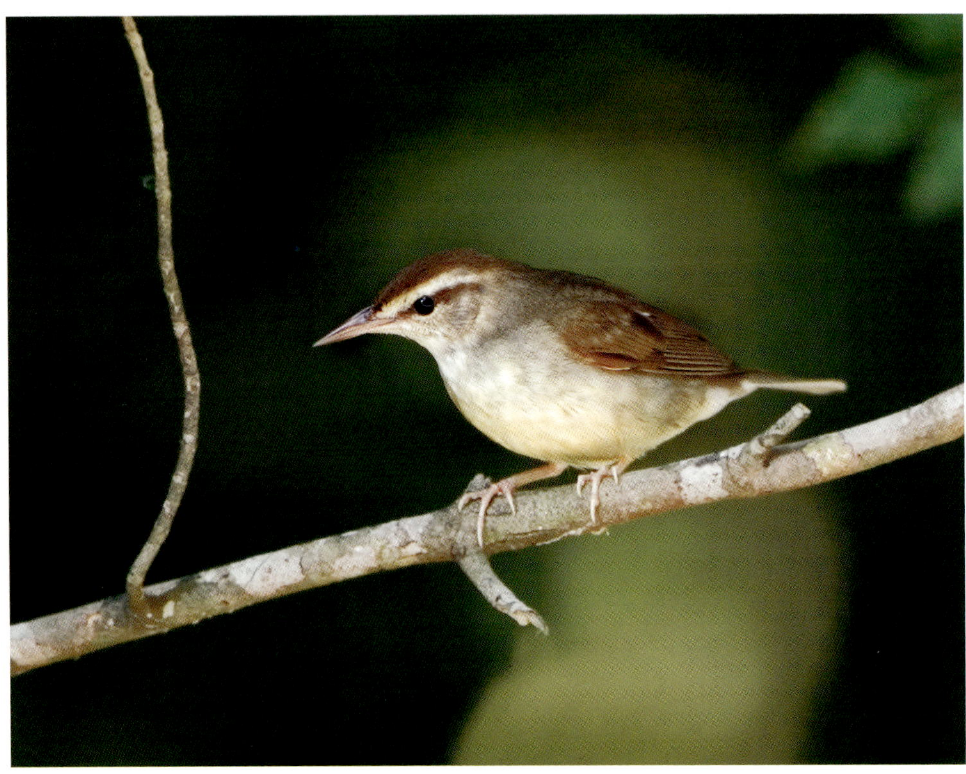

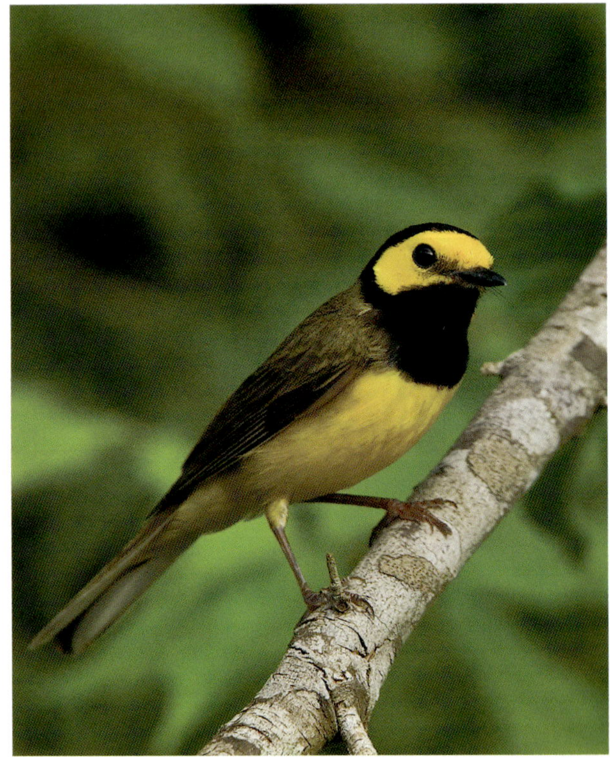

Left: Photographed in the Sherburne Wildlife Management Area in the Atchafalaya Basin, the Swainson's warbler is rather uncommon, but I've observed them occasionally in the swamplands of south Louisiana. Their song is a series of long, ringing whistles ending in *so, so, so, so, sweet-to-hear.* (June 2, 2007)

Right: I love the markings on this hooded warbler—like it is wearing a mask. I spied it singing loudly in the Sherburne Wildlife Management Area where it darted around eating insects and spiders. Its nest is usually made of dried leaves and strips of bark. (June 28, 2006)

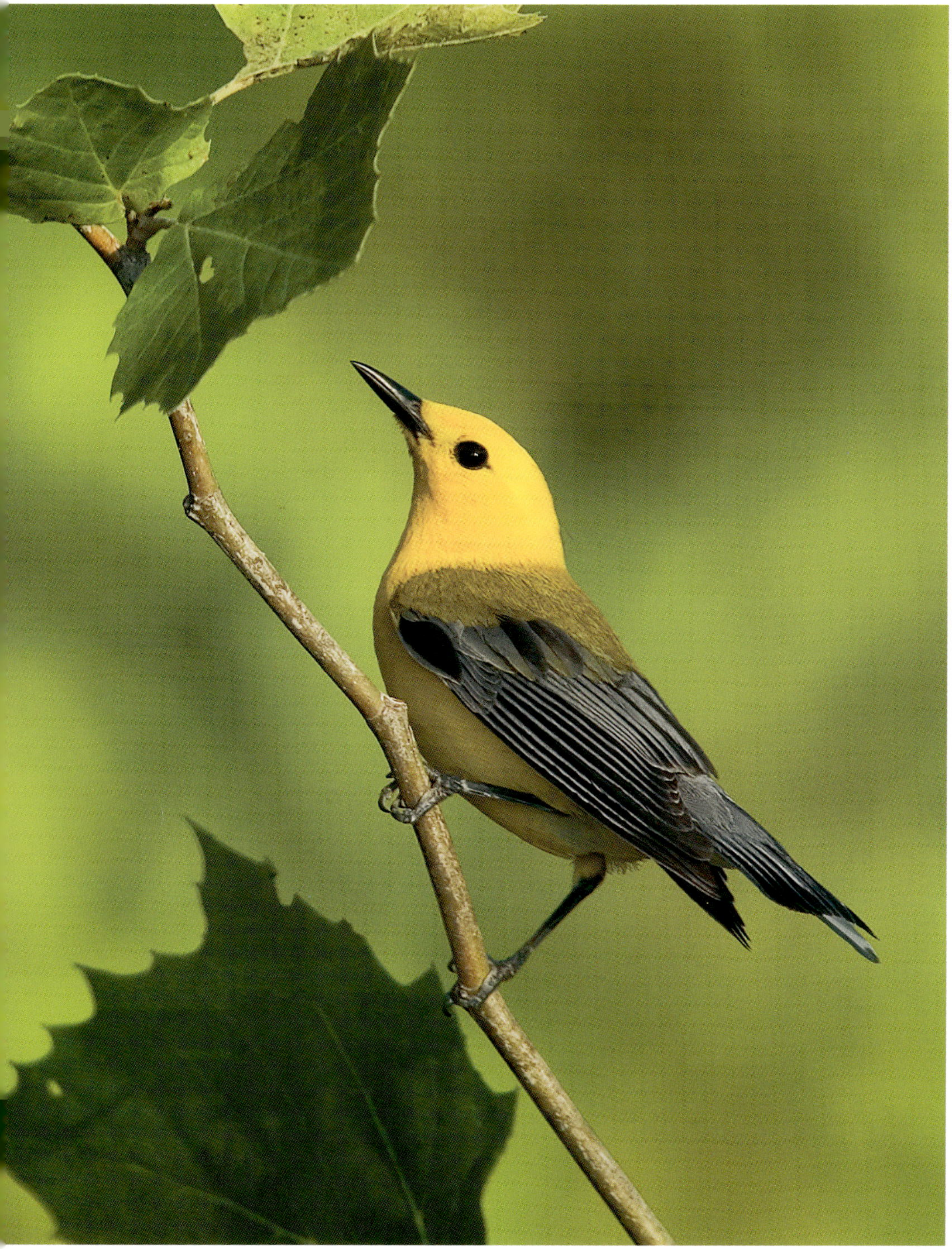

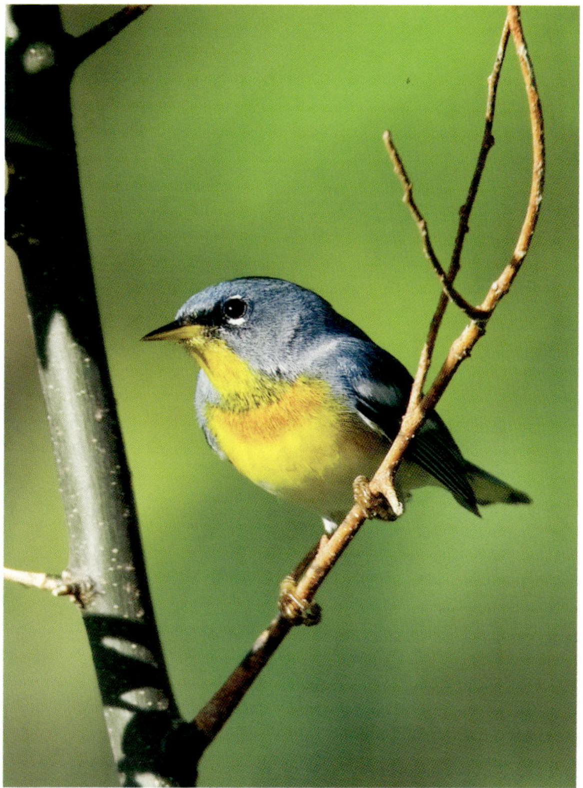

Above: A bird with an attitude, huh? It looks like this northern parula was rather annoyed when I snapped his photograph, but this is his normal expression due to his facial markings. Because they like to hang out among Spanish moss, they are fairly common in south Louisiana woods. (April 18, 2007)

Left: I was in the Atchafalaya Basin at Butte LaRose photographing bald eagles when this bright yellow bird, a prothonotary warbler, caught my attention with its soft, ringing *tweet, tweet, tweet, tweet,* all on one pitch. I understand that the name prothonotary refers to clerks in the Catholic Church, who at one time wore bright yellow robes. (May 16, 2006)

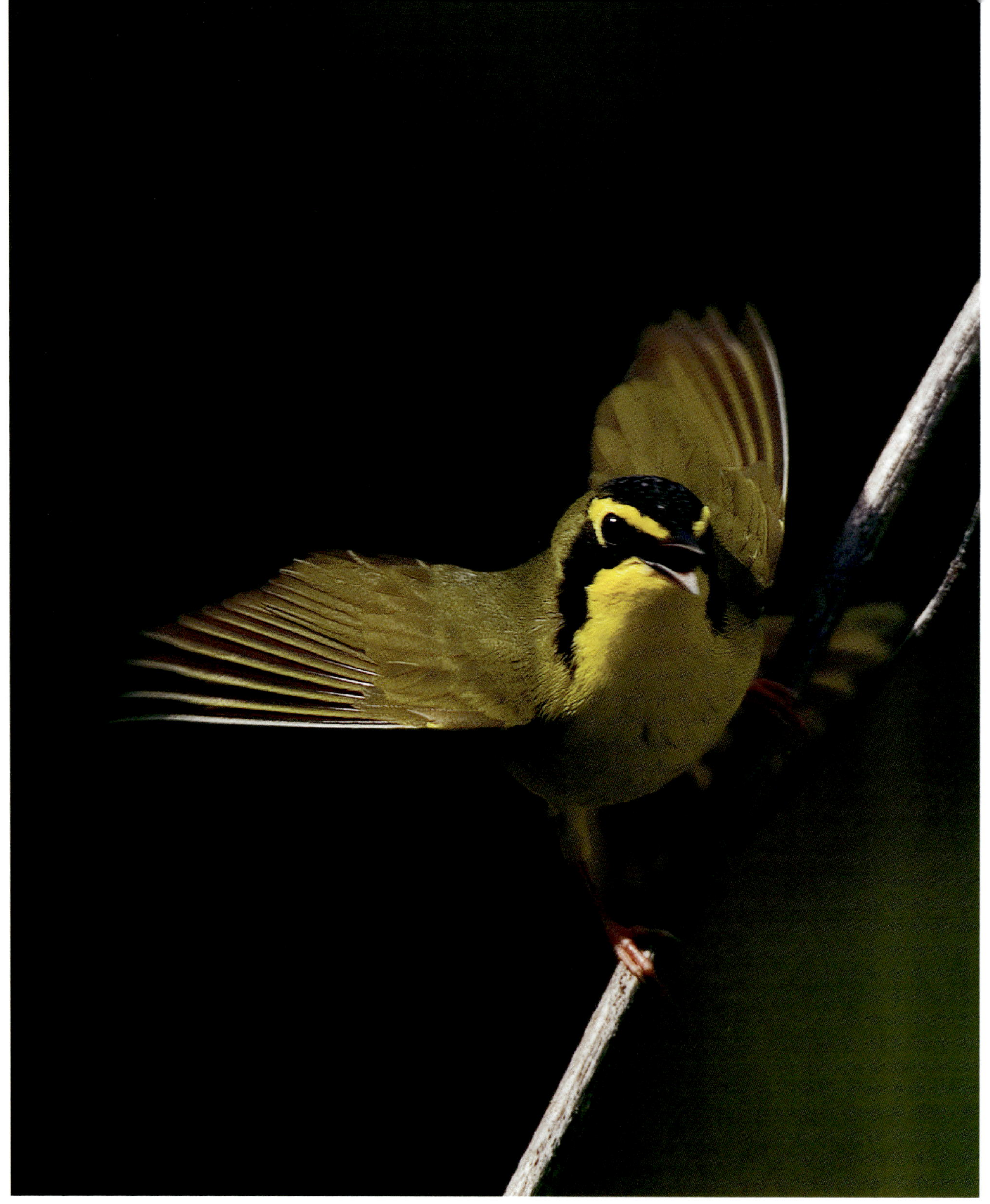

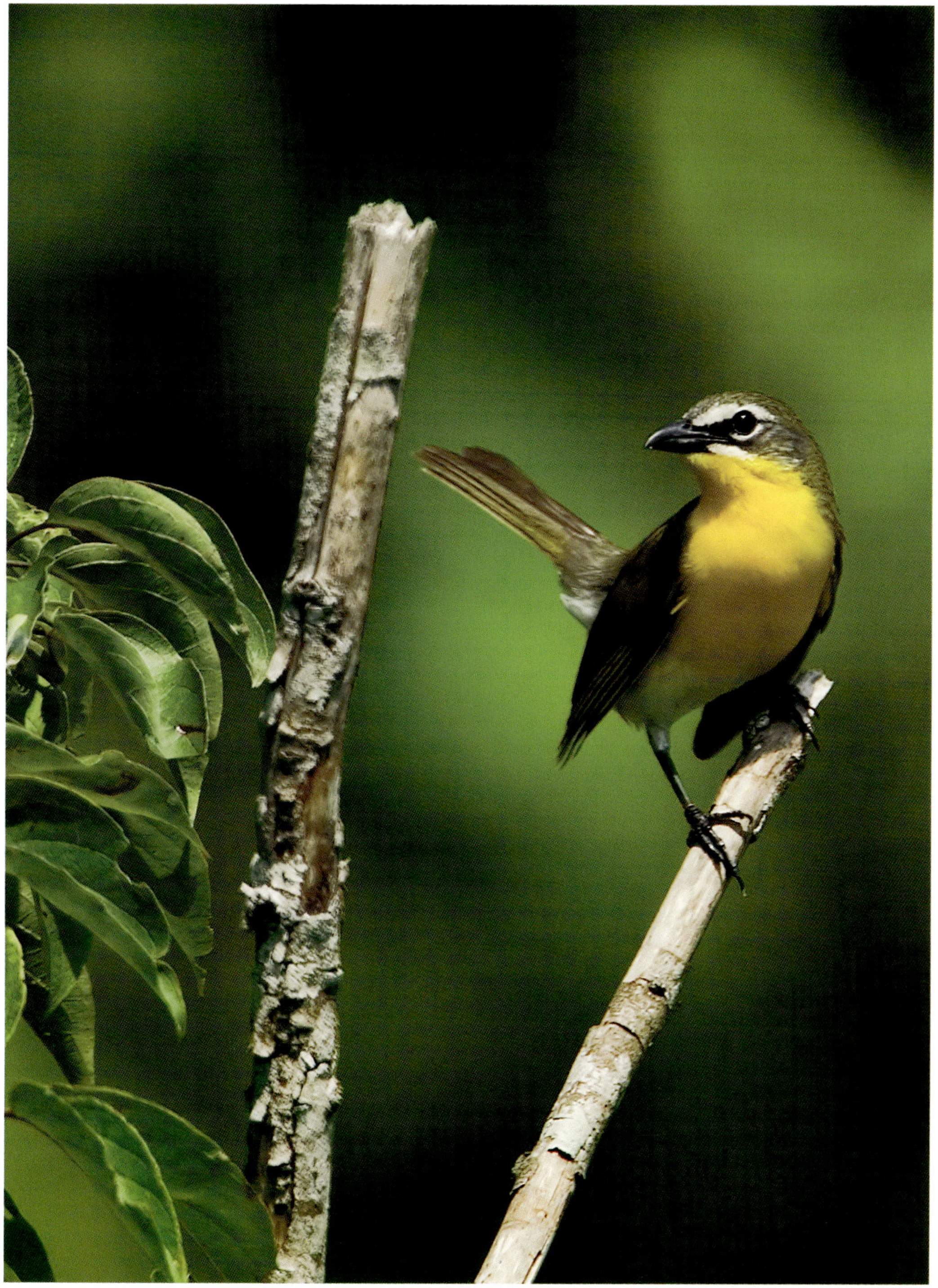

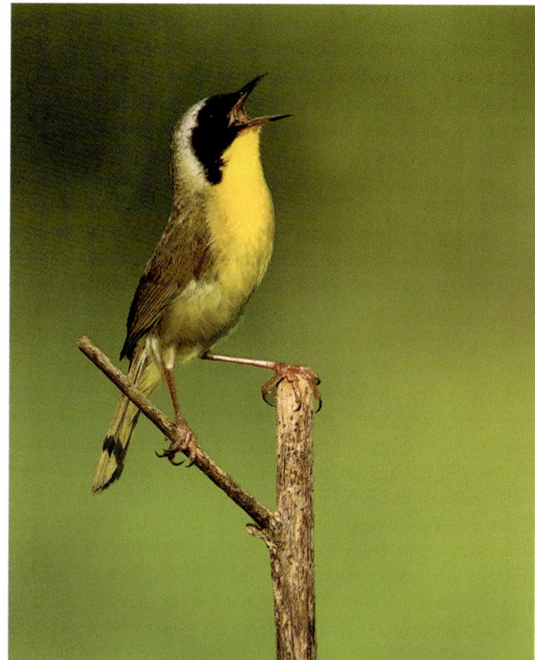

Above: I think these little common yellow-throated warblers are rather stunning with their bright yellow throats and chest and black faces. As they like habitats with pine and cypress, both swampy and dry woods, I see them from time to time in the Atchafalaya Basin. (June 25, 2006)

Left: The yellow-breasted chat is one of the larger warblers at six to seven inches long. He has a very distinctive song—a combination of clucking, mewing, gurgling, and whistles—and will sing sometimes late into the evening. (June 24, 2006)

Facing page: I usually hear the Kentucky warbler with its loud, distinctive *churree, churree, churree* song before I spot it. The olive green of its back and neck contrasts beautifully with the bright yellow throat and belly. Note the bright pink legs. They like to nest close to the ground and feed mostly on insects, caterpillars, and spiders they find in the underbrush of moist deciduous forests. (April 13, 2007)

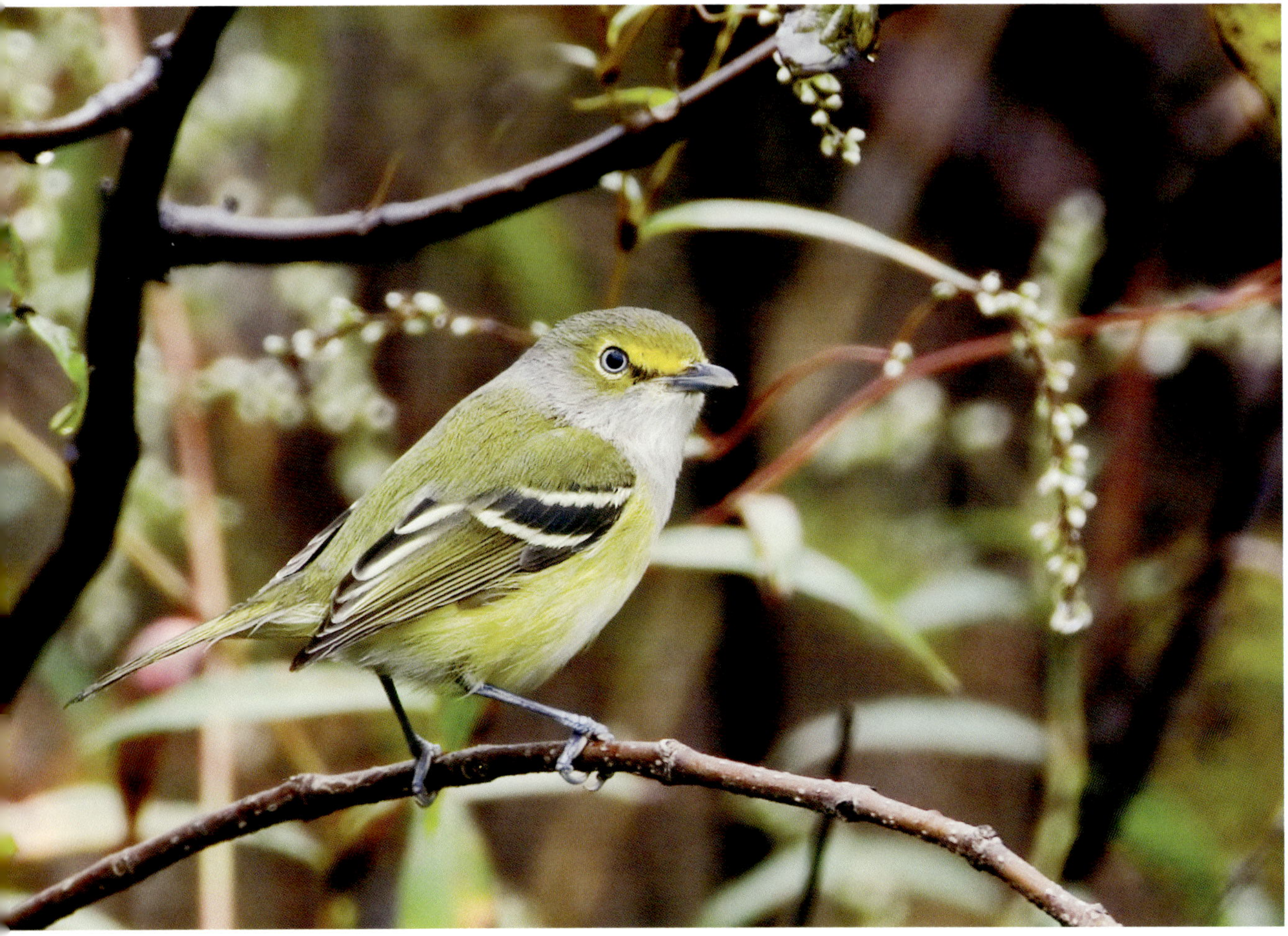

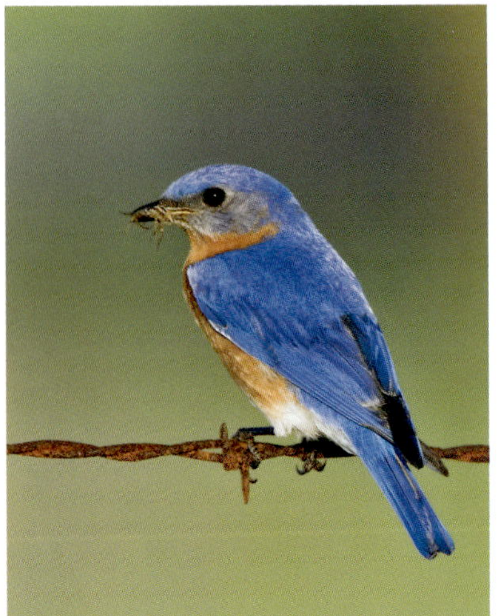

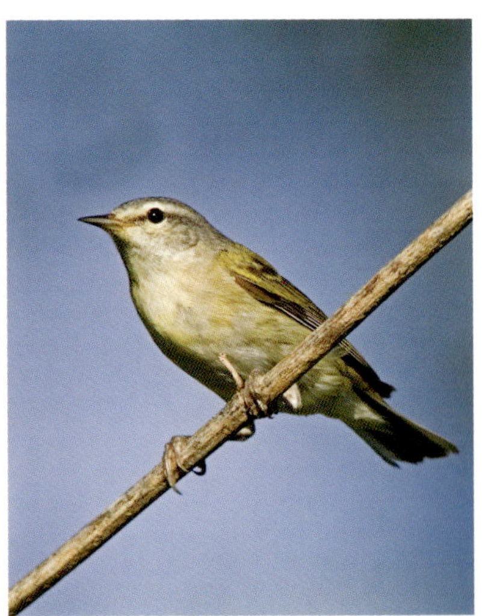

Left: White-eyed vireos frequent the Sherburne Wildlife Management Area in the Atchafalaya Basin, where they flit around in the dense thickets and undergrowth. (November 10, 2005)

Above, right: Ah, the Bluebird of Happiness—the plumage is outstanding with bright blue feathers and brick-red throat and breast. To attract him to your yard, put out peanut butter mixed with raisins. (April 4, 2007)

Although this female Tennessee warbler (*below, right*) is rather plain and dull, she has a song of musical notes and trills, so she deserves a picture, right? (April 19, 2007)

WOODPECKERS

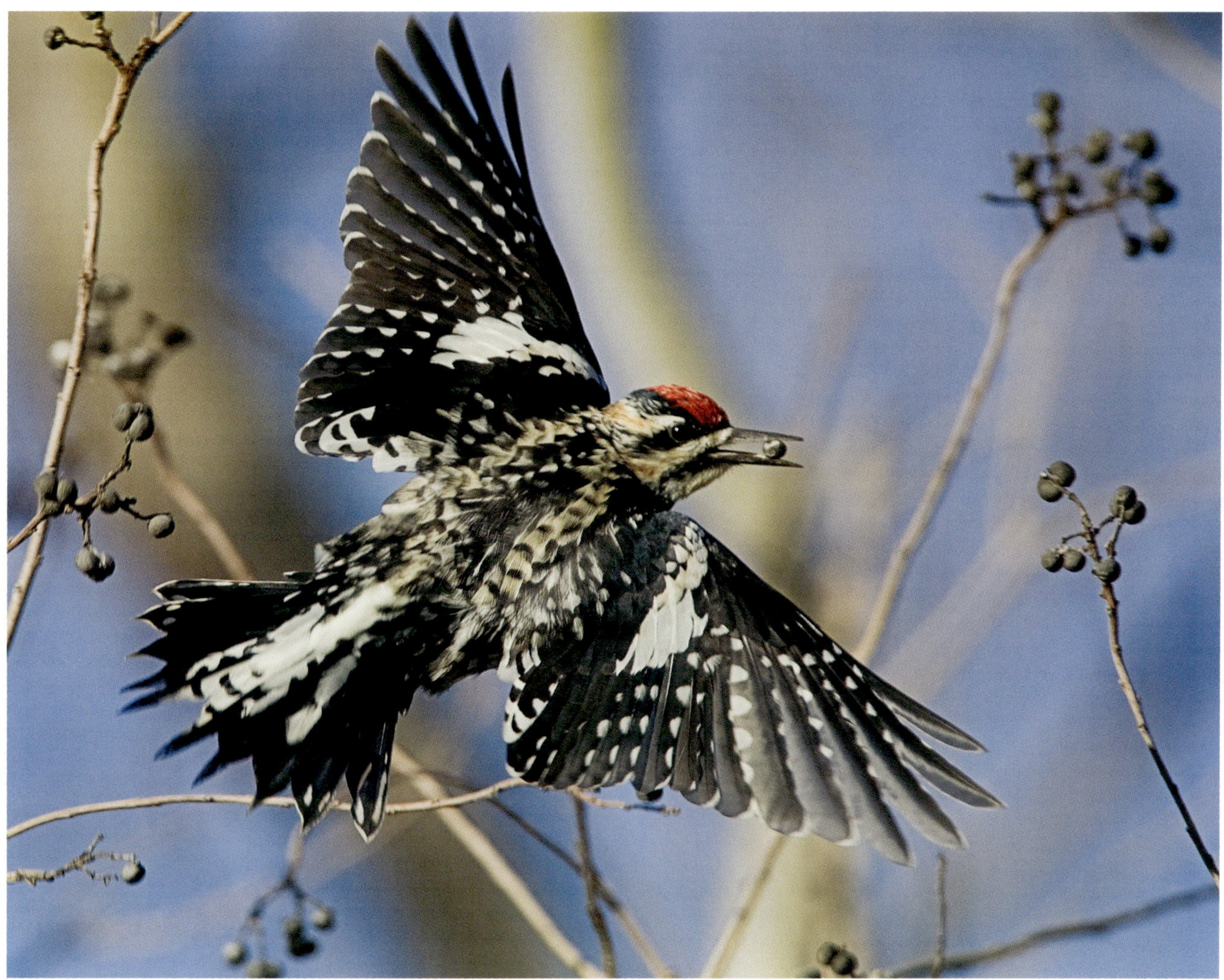

A yellow-bellied sapsucker inserts its bill into tree trunks to, you guessed it, suck out the sap. The black-and-white dotted feathers are quite intricate and attractive. (January 18, 2006)

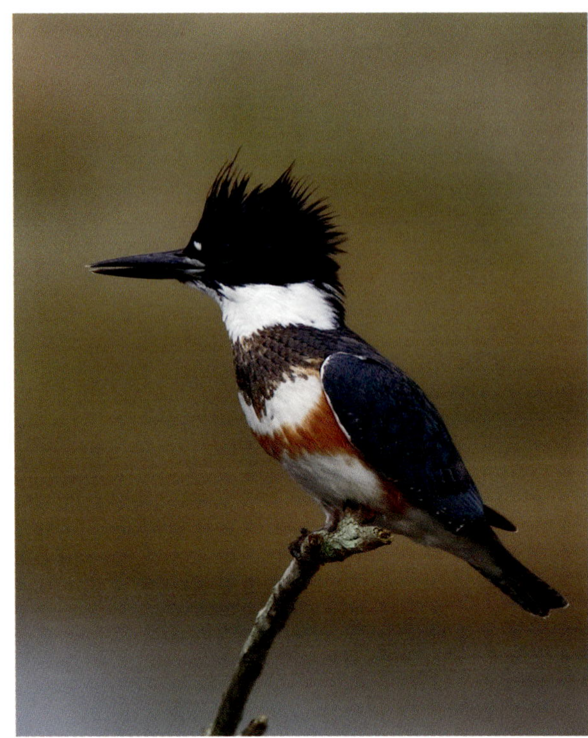

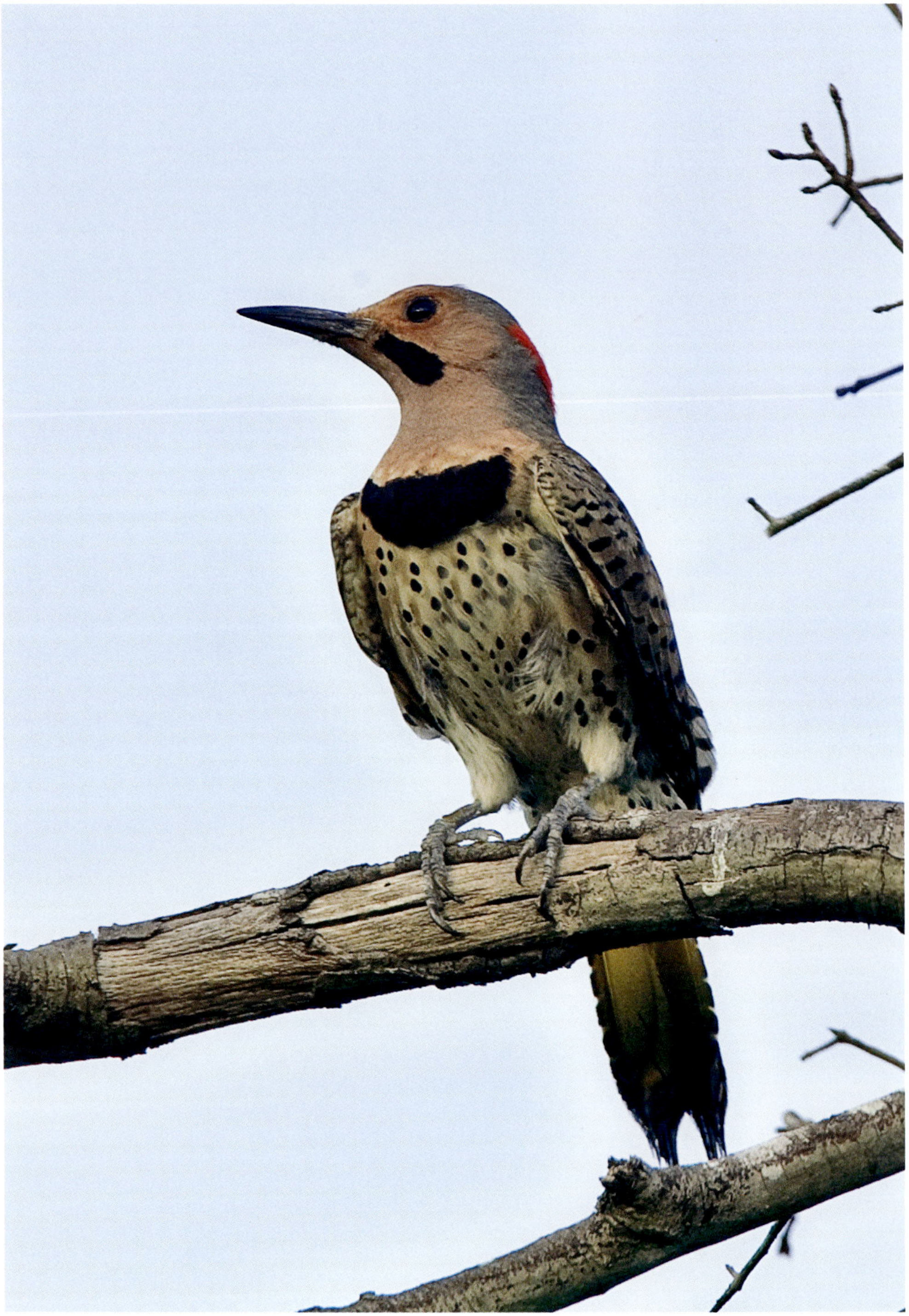

Above: I was putting out decoys on the pond of my duck lease near Pecan Island on a beautiful clear day when I spied this belted kingfisher with its bushy crest. It hung around for a few days plunging head-first in the water for small perch and snakes. (December 22, 2007)

Right: Northern flickers, using their long barbed tongues, love to peck for ants on rotten wood on the ground or in soft soil, but they can also climb on tree trunks to hammer away. The black markings on this adult male, photographed at Sherburne Wildlife Management Area, give him the appearance of a gentleman with a moustache and a black bib. Note the red "cap" on the back of his head and the black-dotted plumage. (June 22, 2006)

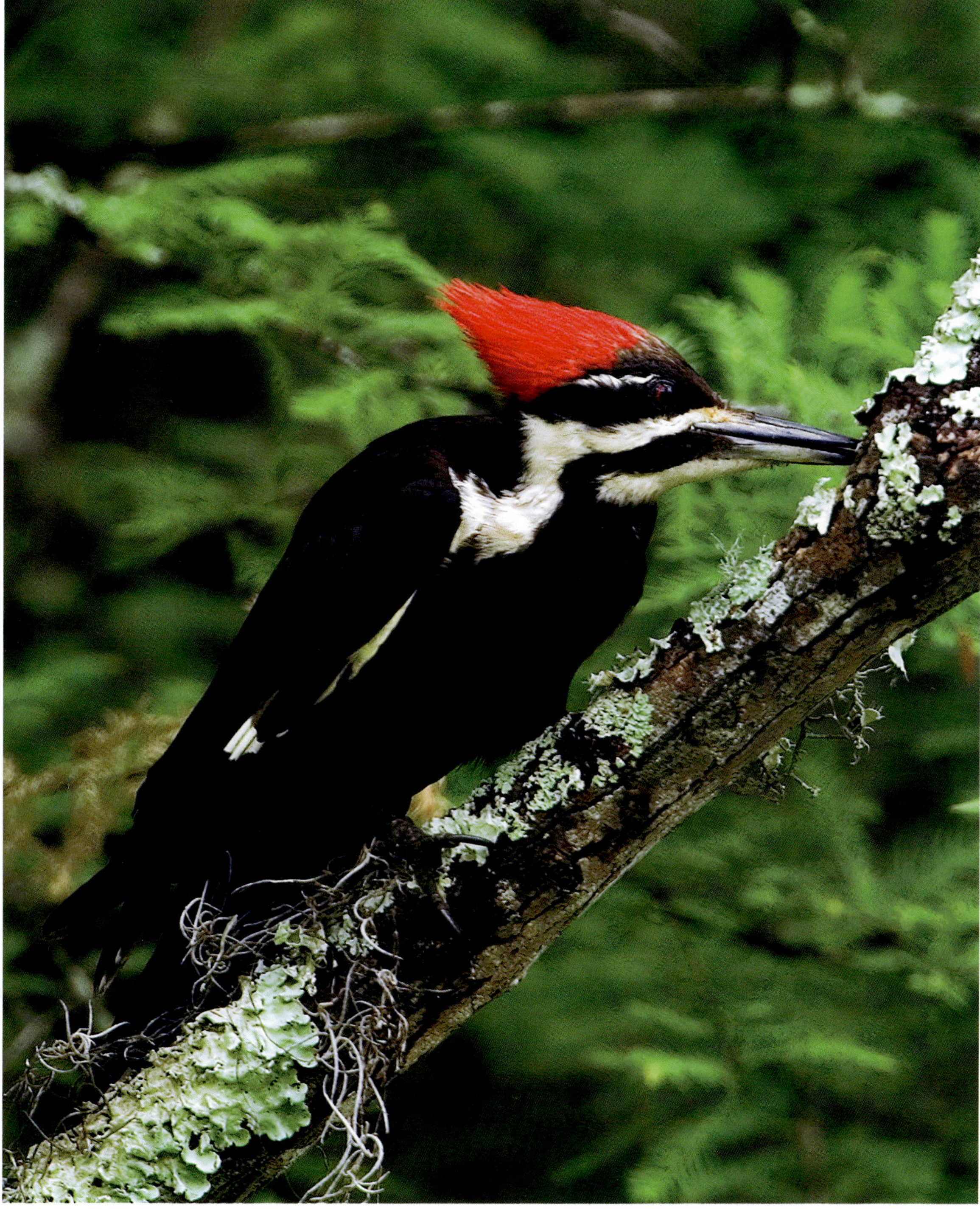

With its red-capped head, a pileated woodpecker is usually easy to spot, especially in forests that offer deadwood in which it can nest. Large as a crow, this woodpecker is voracious when looking for carpenter ants and wood-boring beetles in dead trees. If you want to attract them to your backyard feeders, put out suet—they love it. (April 30, 2005)

WRENS AND CHICKADEES

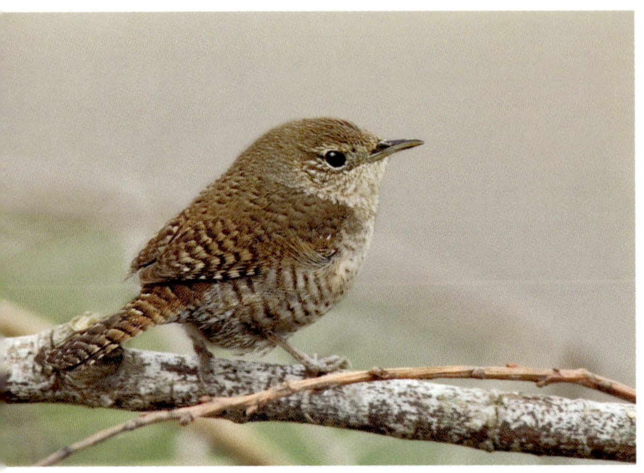

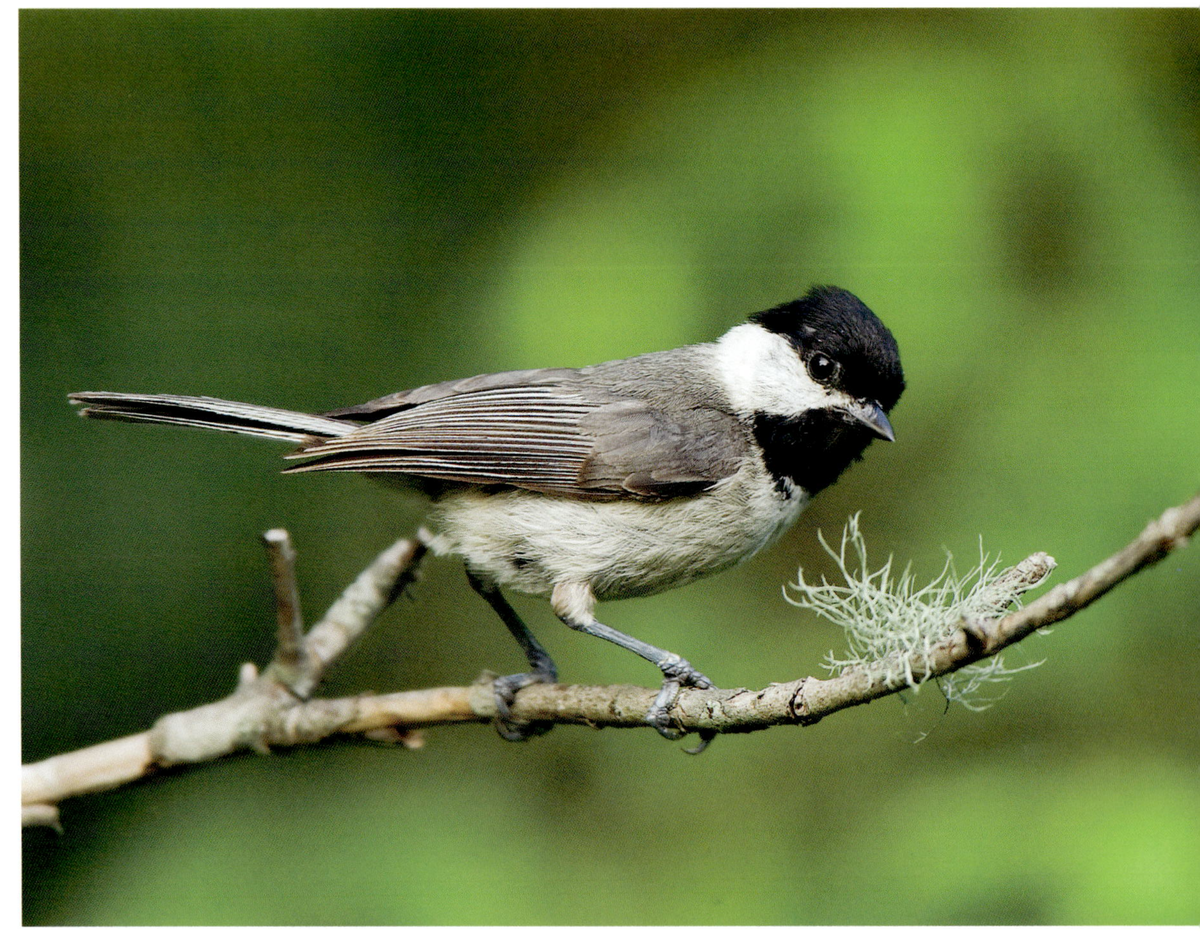

Above: I often see these tiny winter wrens in the shady woods at Lake Martin, where they like to feed on spiders and insects near rotting logs and leaves. Their complex melodies are striking and loud considering the small size of these birds. (February 20, 2007)

Right: I love these small Carolina chickadees—what wonderful innocent faces! They like nesting in birdhouses, but I like to watch them in the woods near Butte LaRose in the Atchafalaya Basin, where they feed on seeds and berries. (May 25, 2006)

MIGRATION IN THE MARSHES

During the fall and winter in Louisiana, several millions ducks and geese follow a great migratory route (called the Mississippi Flyway) that is shaped like an enormous funnel with its tip at the Louisiana coast. The neck of the funnel leads up the Mississippi River Valley, widens out at the Missouri and Ohio valleys, and continues to widen west and east until, at the funnel's mouth, the flyway almost spans the continent, from the northwestern tip of Alaska to the eastern shores of the Hudson Bay.

In the southernmost part of Louisiana is the vast and virtually treeless area of wetlands known as marshes. The seemingly monotonous region is broken only by patches of dry land where trees are able to gain a foothold. The fishermen and trappers who once inhabited this area called it *la prairie tremblante,* the trembling prairie. It is here that hunters and wildlife enthusiasts can witness the incredible influx of waterfowl as the seasons change from summer to fall to winter.

Prior to the opening of the regular duck hunting season, I'm out in the wetlands photographing teal, the first ducks to arrive on the scene in September. Seeing strings of rolling teal (from 50 to 200 in a string) across the marsh and rice fields gives rise to my anticipation of the Louisiana duck season. By October, the specklebellies are filtering down. Following them are the gadwalls (Louisiana's mallard) and the pintails. The excitement heightens.

At about the time that I'm assessing the approaching hunting season, sportsmen are performing the arduous preparation of readying decoys, cleaning and preparing hunting camps, servicing mud boats, and checking shotguns. By the time the two-week teal season arrives in mid-September, hunters are anxious to give their equipment and camp sites a trial run before we get into the "serious" hunting season, which begins in November.

By opening weekend of duck season, I am chomping at the bit to get out both to hunt and to photograph the huge concentration of waterfowl. I get goose bumps watching blue-wing and green-wing teal, the smallest of all duck species, as they feed in ponds and lakes. I get a thrill seeing a flock of pintails on the wing over the marshlands. Green-headed mallards are as graceful as ballerinas, and the colorful markings and plumage of wood ducks never fail to amaze me. The loud honking of geese as they fly in their V formation over the waterways is exhilarating. Specklebelly geese, with their large wings flapping, are always entertaining. Large snow geese, brightly white, appear like giant archangels as they descend on the water.

I could go on and on, but I think you get the idea.

After the duck season is officially over, I really get serious about photographing ducks because that is when they are in their full and brilliant plumage—varying shades of lavender appear on the blue-winged teal and pintail sprig, the glowing iridescent colors of the green-headed mallard seem magnified, and the markings on the wood ducks look more pronounced.

DUCKS

TEALS

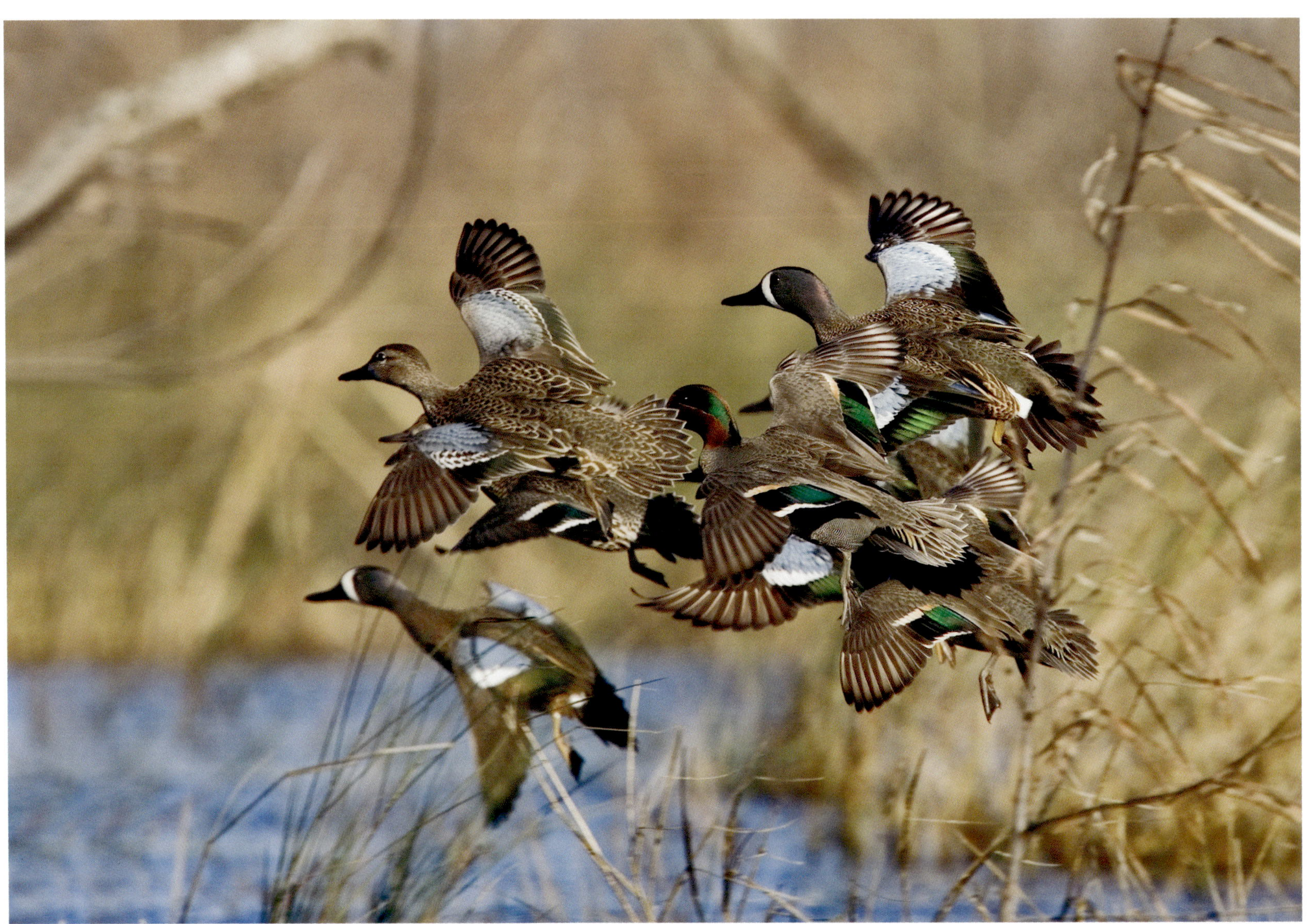

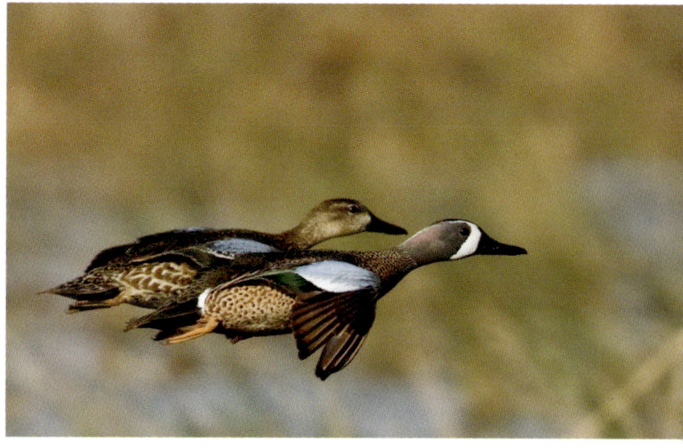

Above: A perfect pair of blue-winged teal flying low over the marsh near Gueydan. I love when I can capture them in this flight mode. Although teal are the smallest of all duck species, about fourteen inches long, they are indeed striking with their blue and green wing feathers that catch the sunlight when they fly. (January 28, 2007)

Left: The blue-winged and green-winged teal are among the last ducks to migrate north in spring and some of the first to migrate south in fall, which gives me plenty of time to photograph these beautiful birds. Here, a pair (male and female) of blue-winged teal are just taking off from a shallow pond in south Louisiana soon after hunting season ended. (February 2, 2008)

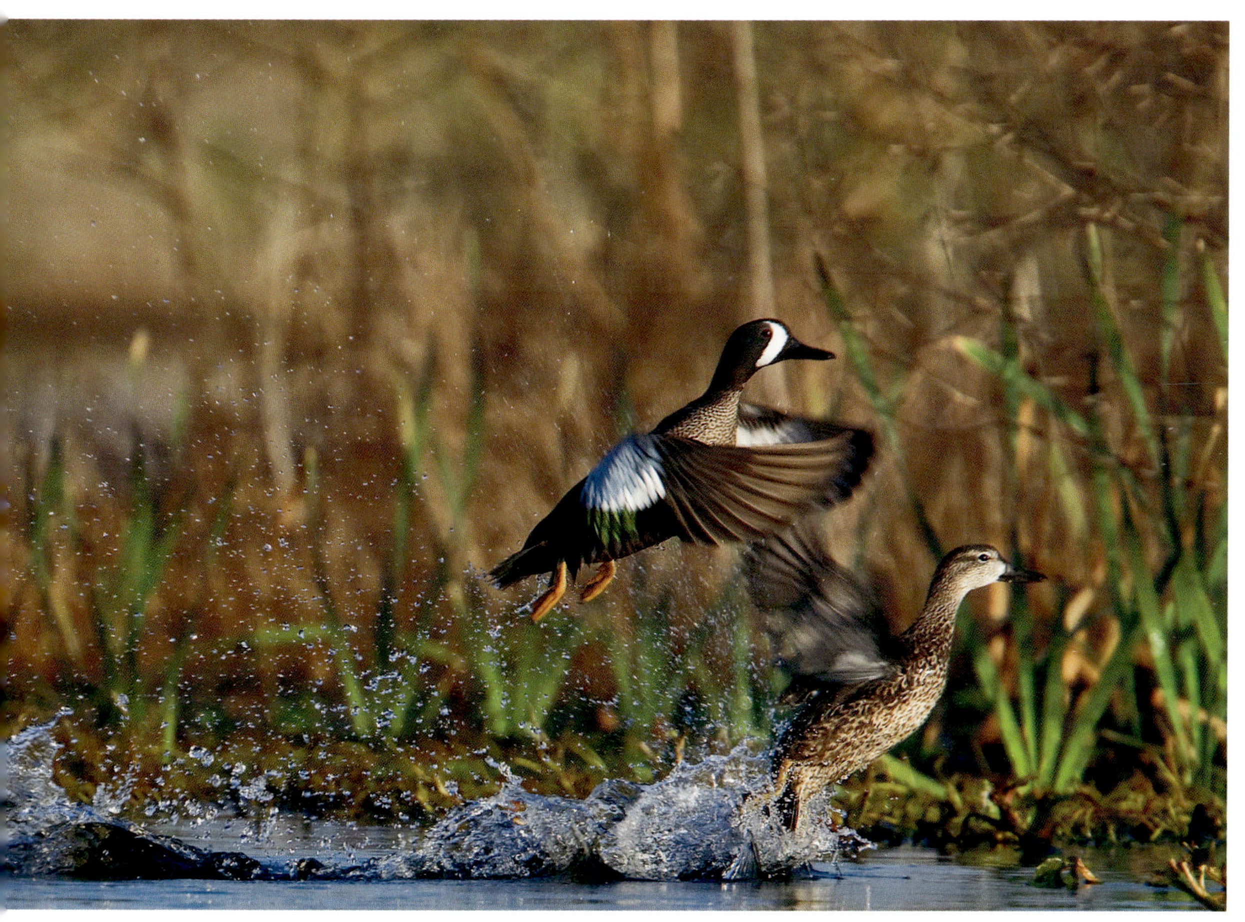

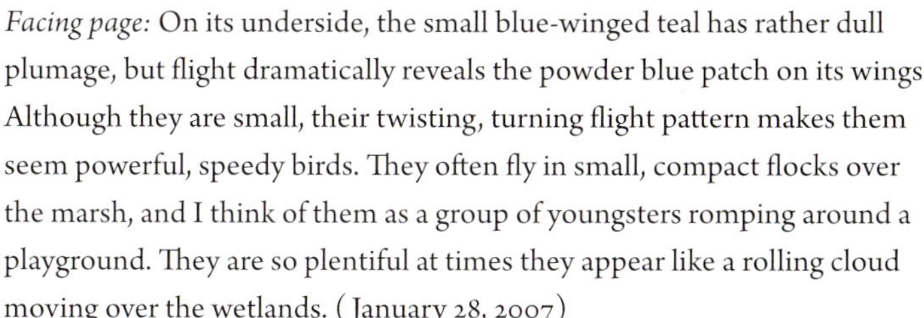

Facing page: On its underside, the small blue-winged teal has rather dull plumage, but flight dramatically reveals the powder blue patch on its wings. Although they are small, their twisting, turning flight pattern makes them seem powerful, speedy birds. They often fly in small, compact flocks over the marsh, and I think of them as a group of youngsters romping around a playground. They are so plentiful at times they appear like a rolling cloud moving over the wetlands. (January 28, 2007)

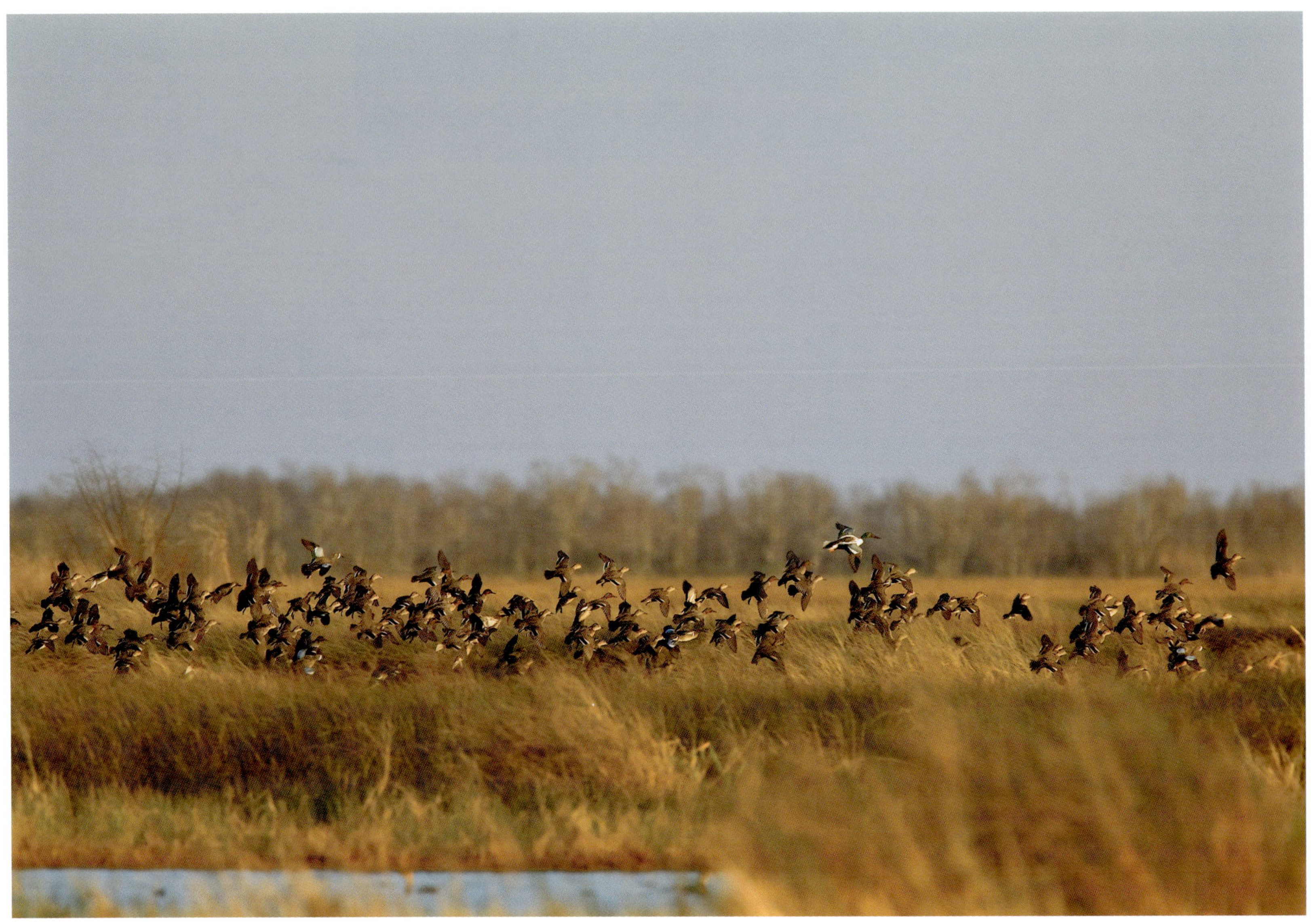

Once the hunting season is over, I spend quite a bit of time photographing thousands of ducks in the marsh. Here a flock of green- and blue-winged teal roll across the marsh in the golden light of the setting sun. A lone shoveler, with its white shoulders and green head, flies above the flock. (February 7, 2008)

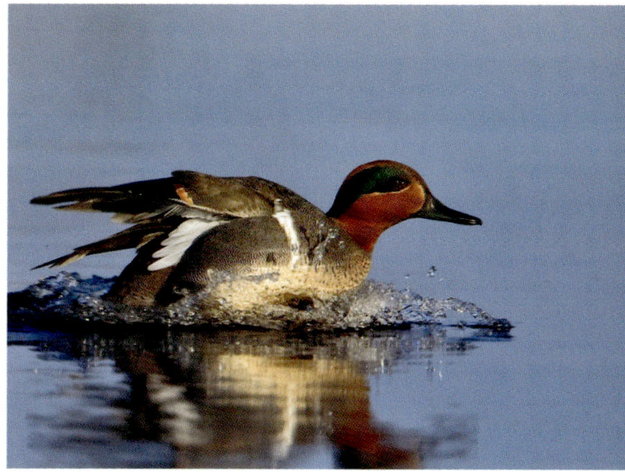

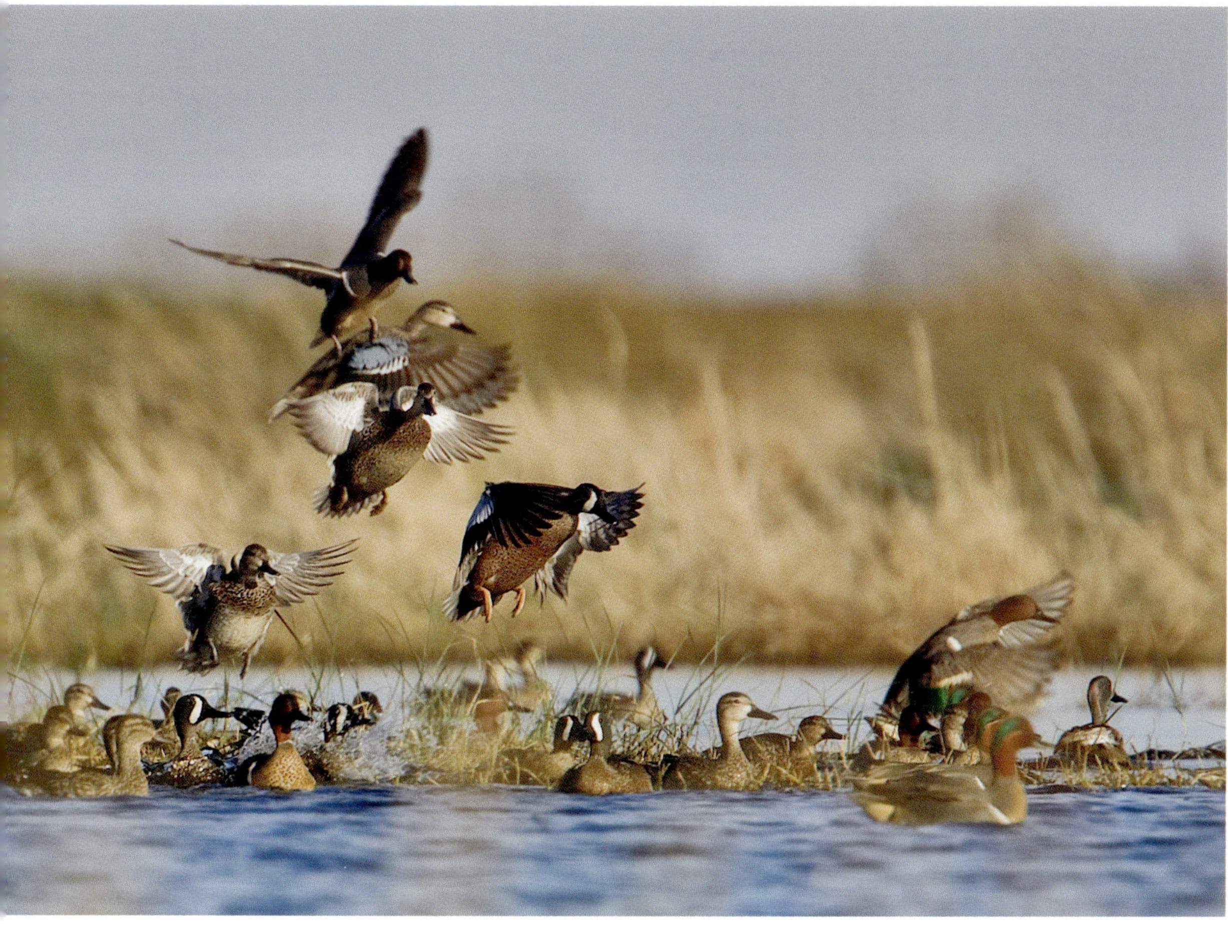

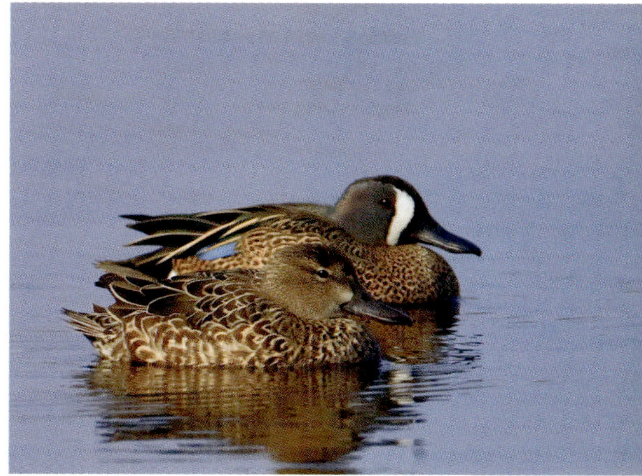

Left: Blue- and green-winged teal have a field day in the marsh. This is the kind of photograph that I like to get after the hunting season is over since the markings on the ducks are so magnificent at that time of the year. (February 7, 2008)

Above, right: This lone green-winged teal landing in the marsh illustrates the exquisite coloring and markings that appear late in the season. (February 2, 2008)

A pair of blue-winged teal (*below, right*) float in the marsh near the Florence Club. The markings on the heads of these ducks are magnificently detailed and stunning. (February 10, 2007)

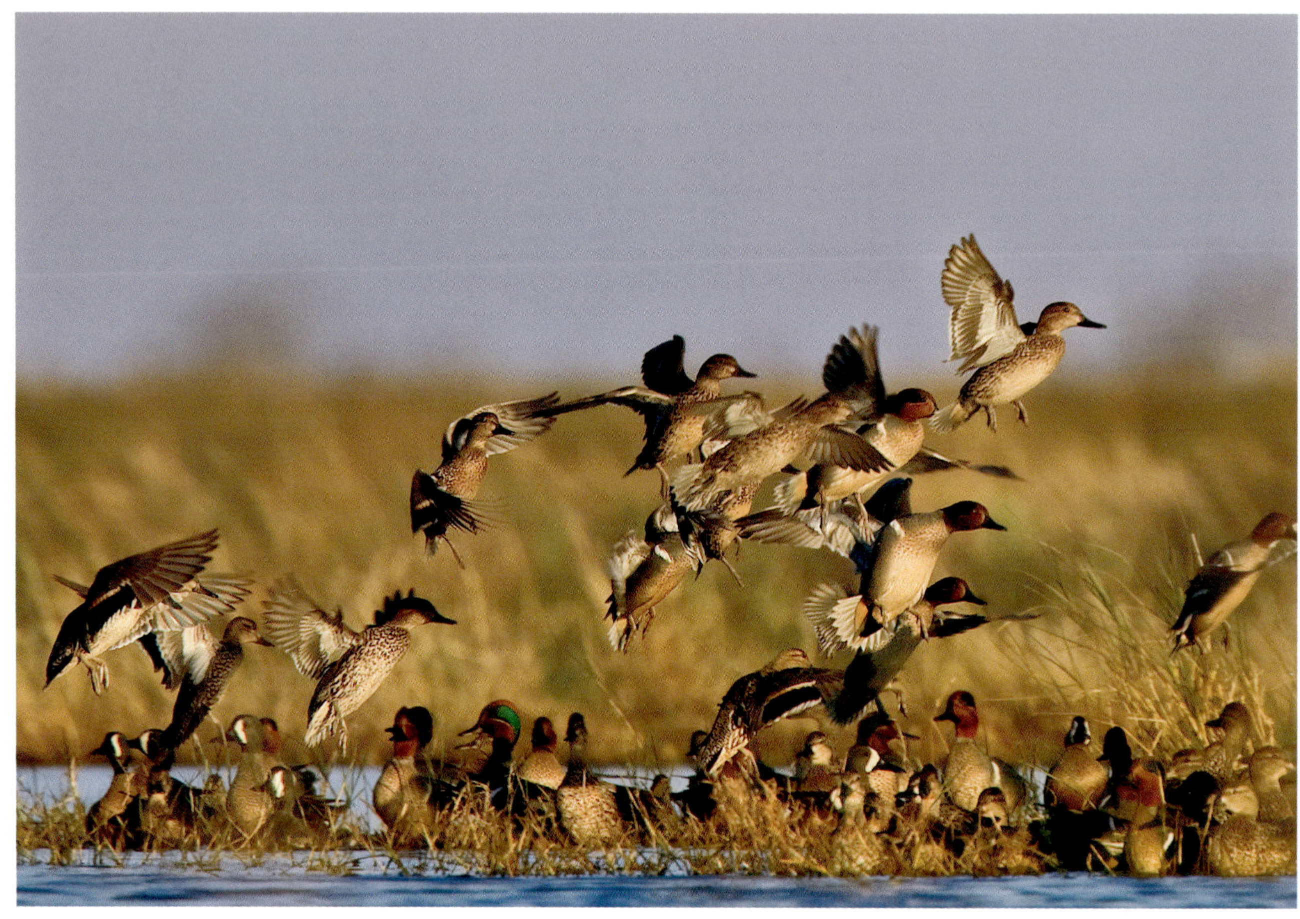

Both green-winged and blue-winged teal are forming a small point in the marsh after the close of hunting season. (February 7, 2008)

PINTAILS

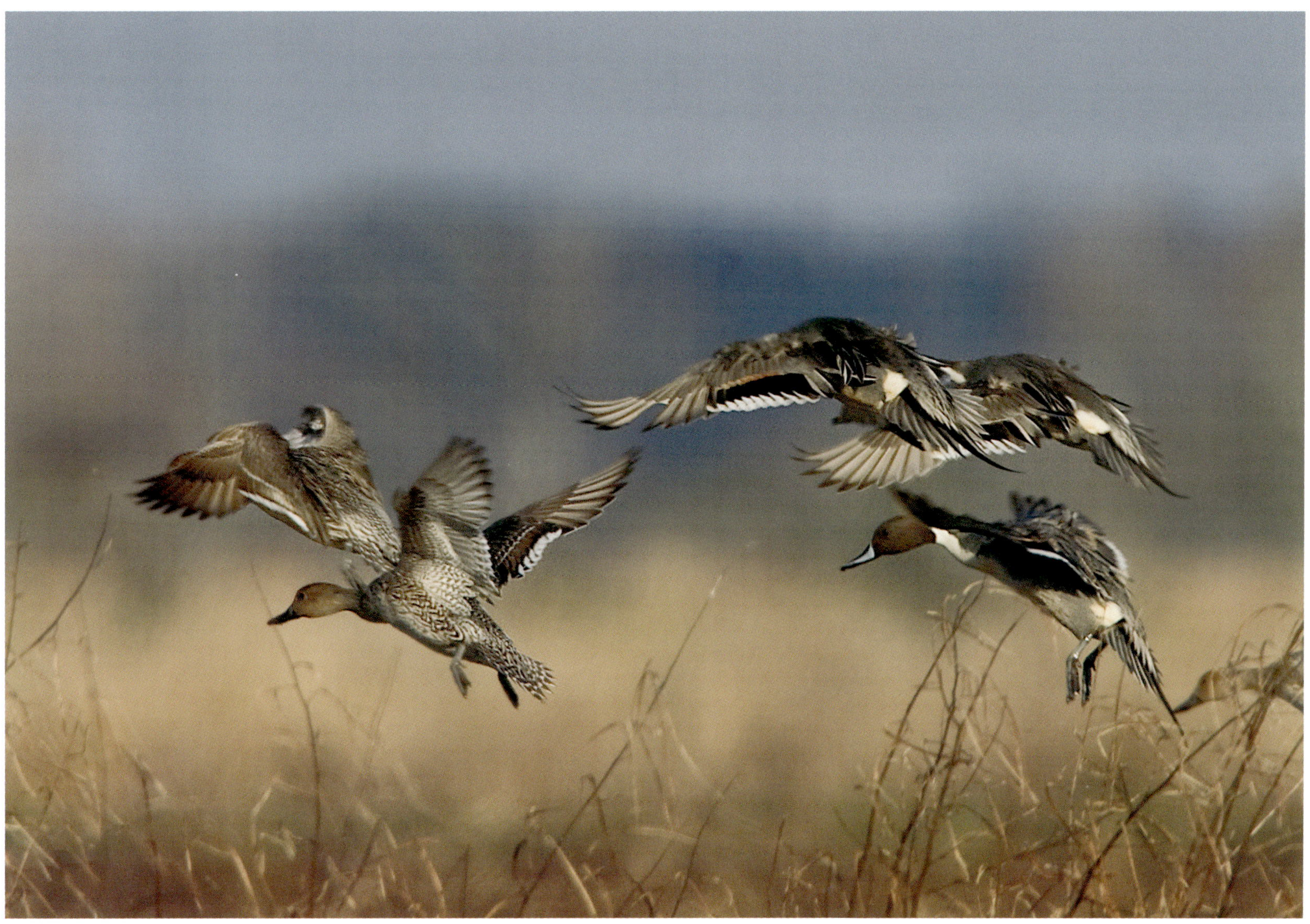

Male and female pintails coming in for a gentle landing in the marsh. (January 28, 2008)

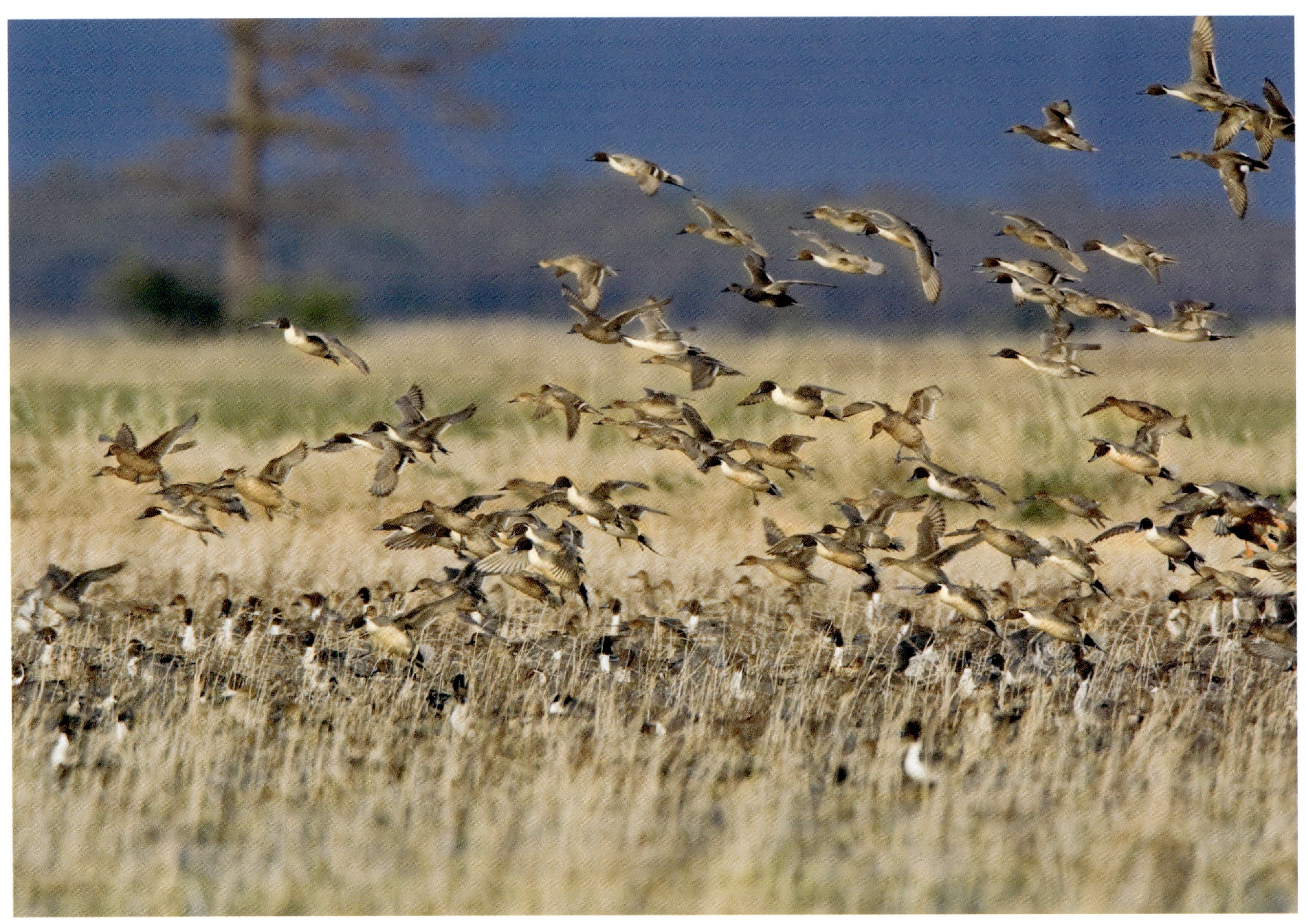

It was early New Year's day and a storm was brewing. Dark clouds were rolling in, and over my shoulder the sun lit up this huge flock of pintails as they flew over the wetlands in south Louisiana. A beautiful sight! (January 1, 2006)

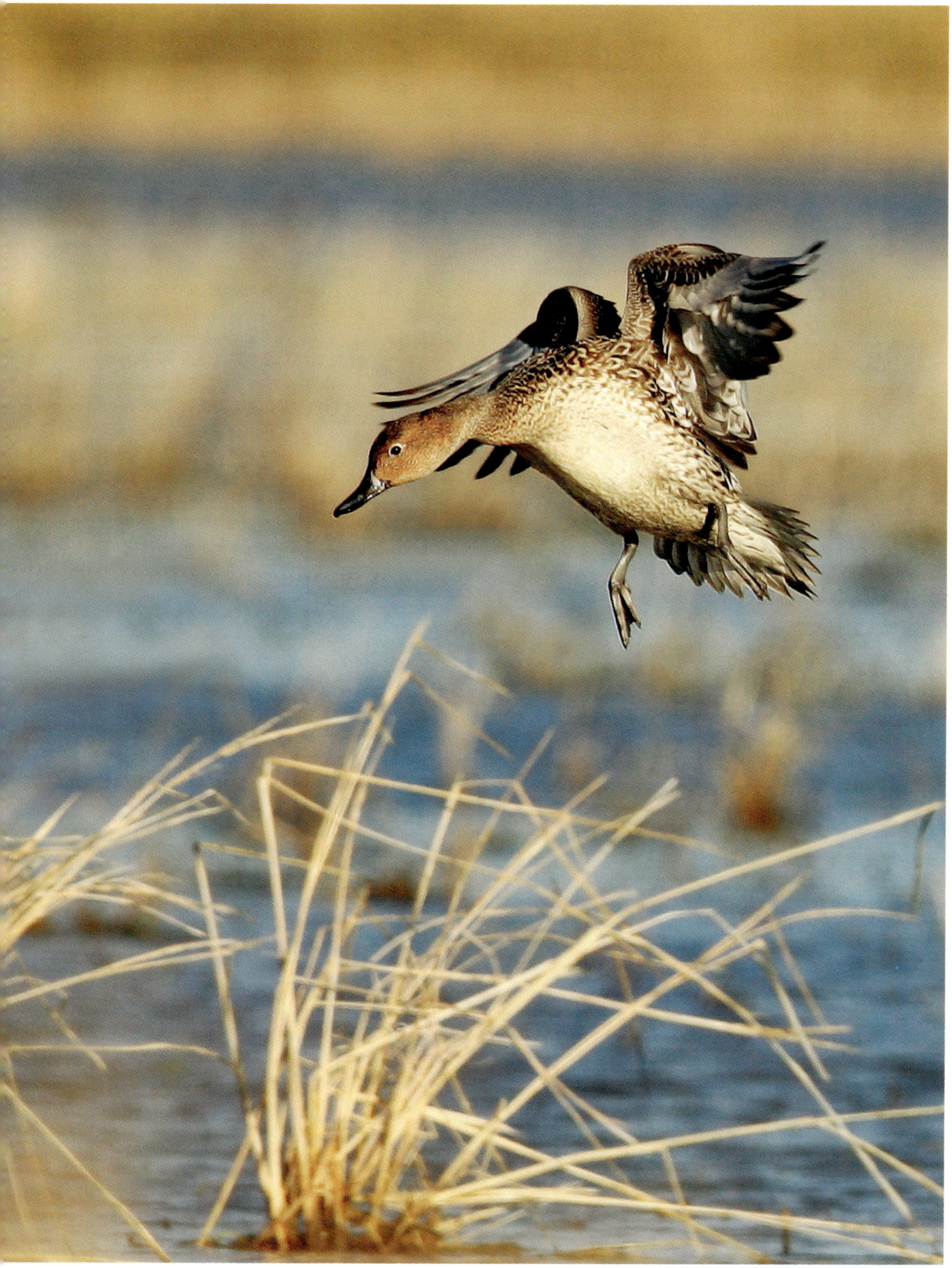

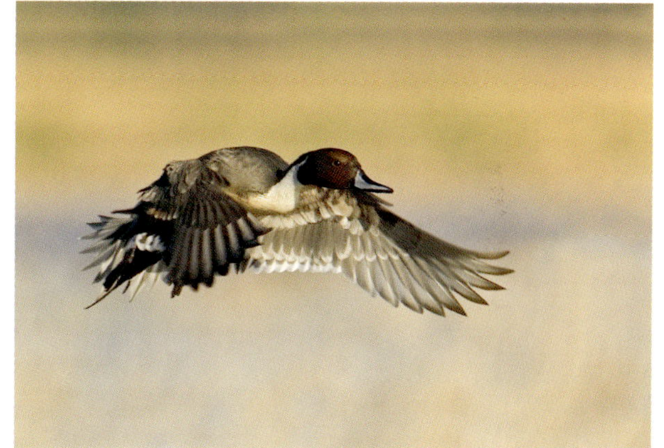

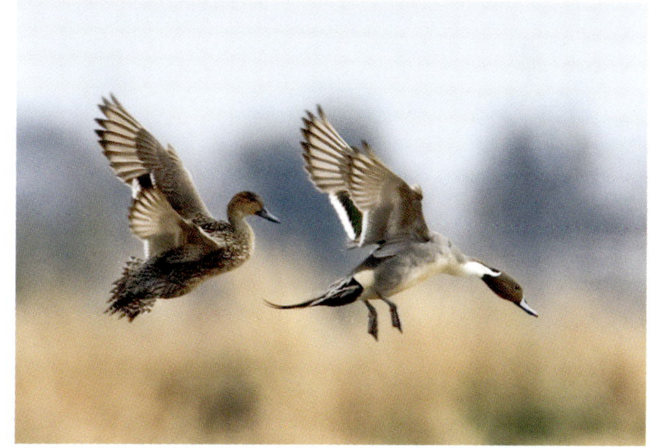

Above, right: Bull pintail on wing (December 27, 2005)

Below, right: This photograph illustrates the differences between female and male pintails. Note the distinct markings on the male. (February 3, 2008)

Left: Female pintail coming in (December 27, 2005)

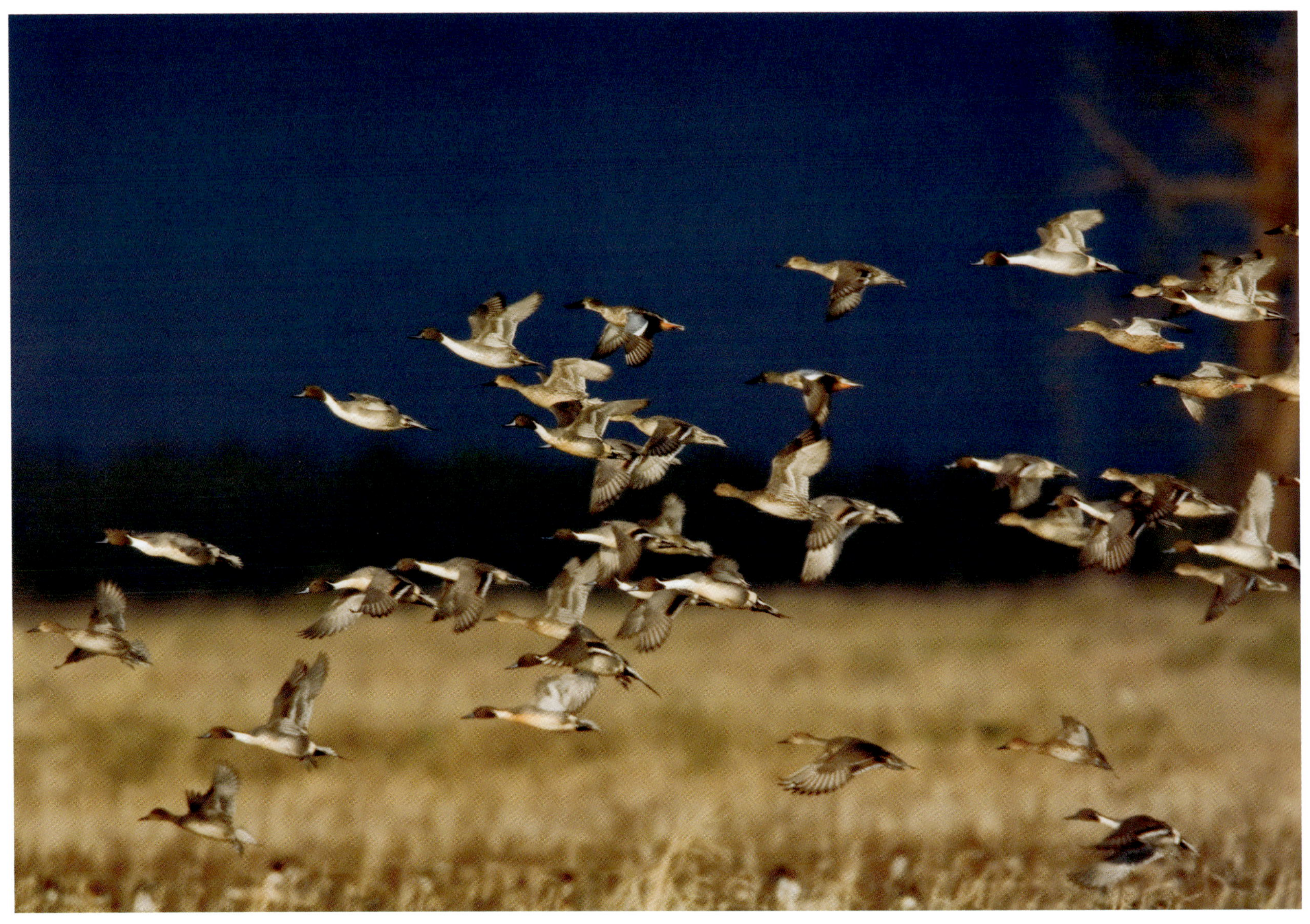

Above: Northern pintails are slim and long necked and have a distinctive silhouette. A fairly large duck, it gets its name from its long, pointed tail. The male is easily identified by its chocolate-brown, gray, and white markings. On the other hand, the female has mainly light brown plumage and a shorter tail. (December 25, 2005)

Facing page: A trio of pintails flying into the marsh (February 6, 2007)

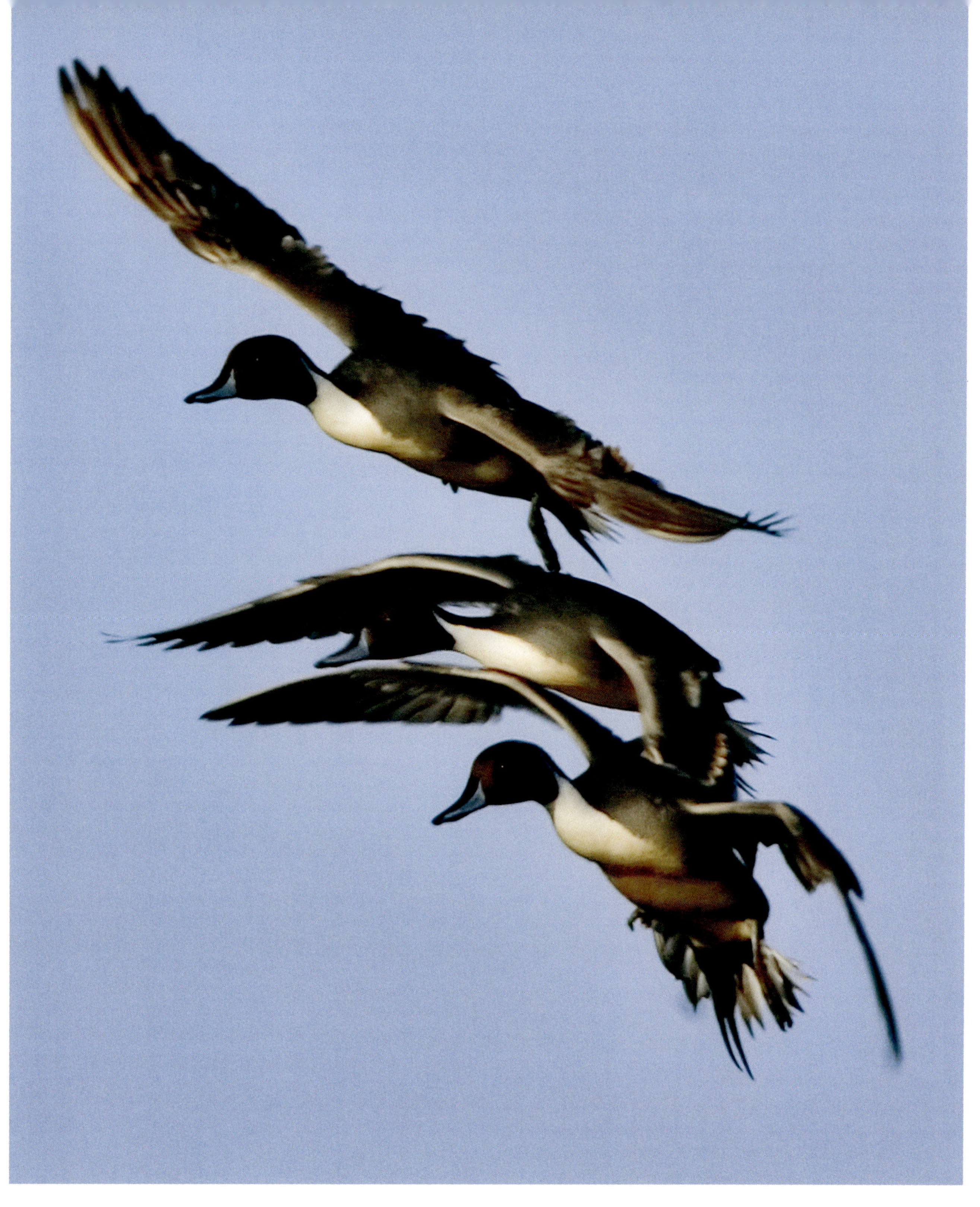

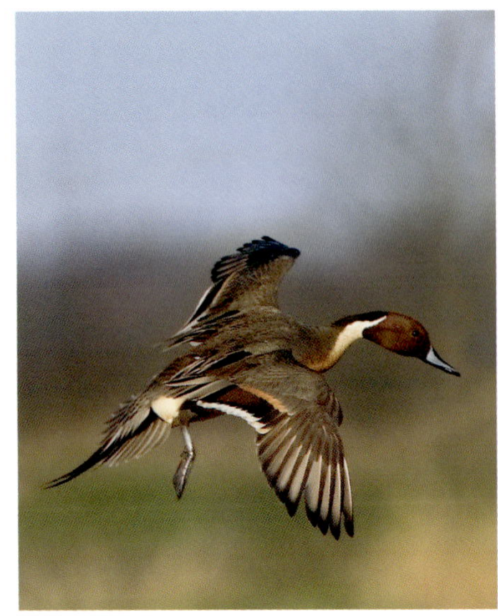

Above: As far as I'm concerned, this is a perfect specimen of a male pintail. (February 18, 2008)

Right, and facing page: These males are courting the lone female at center. (January 19, 2008)

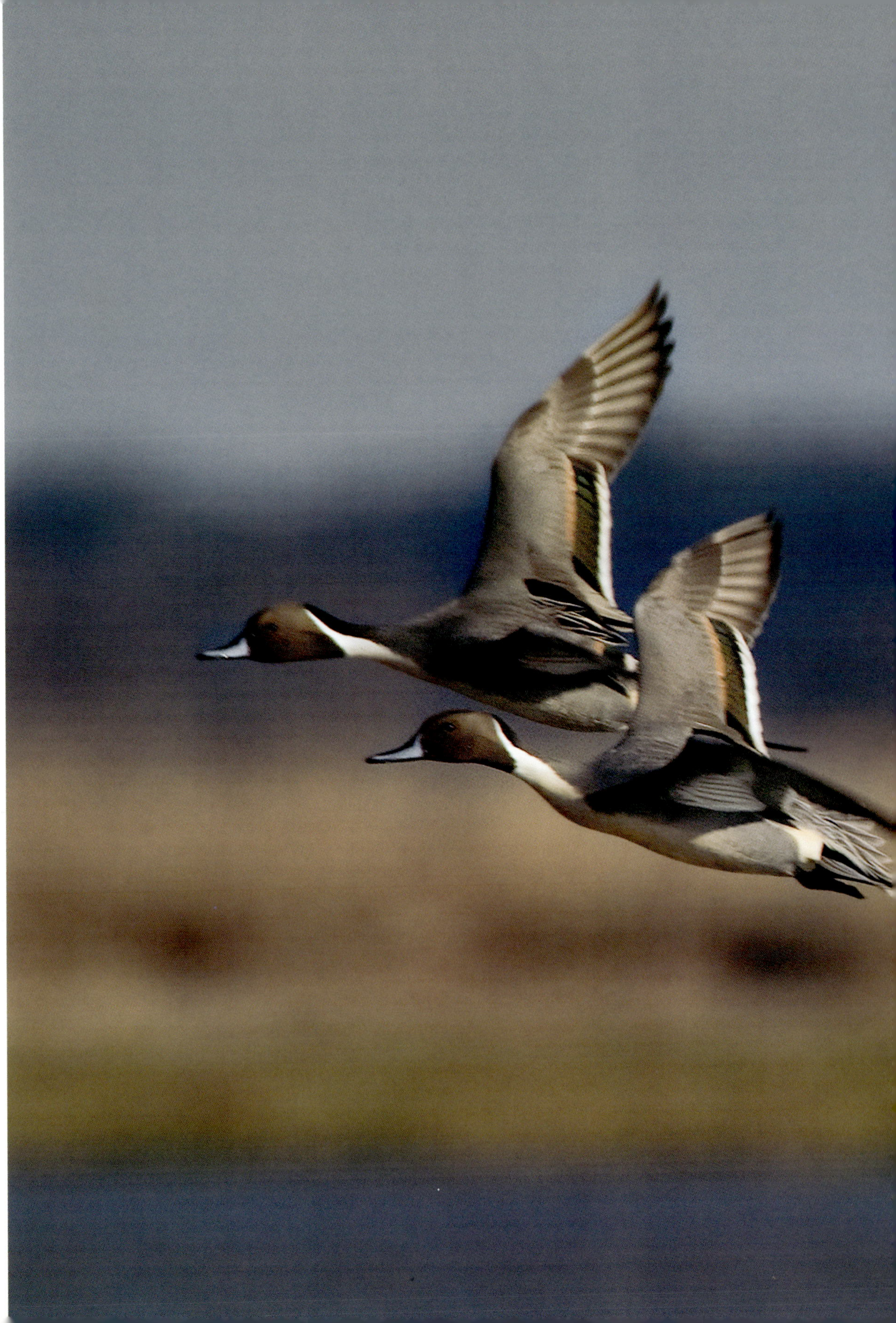

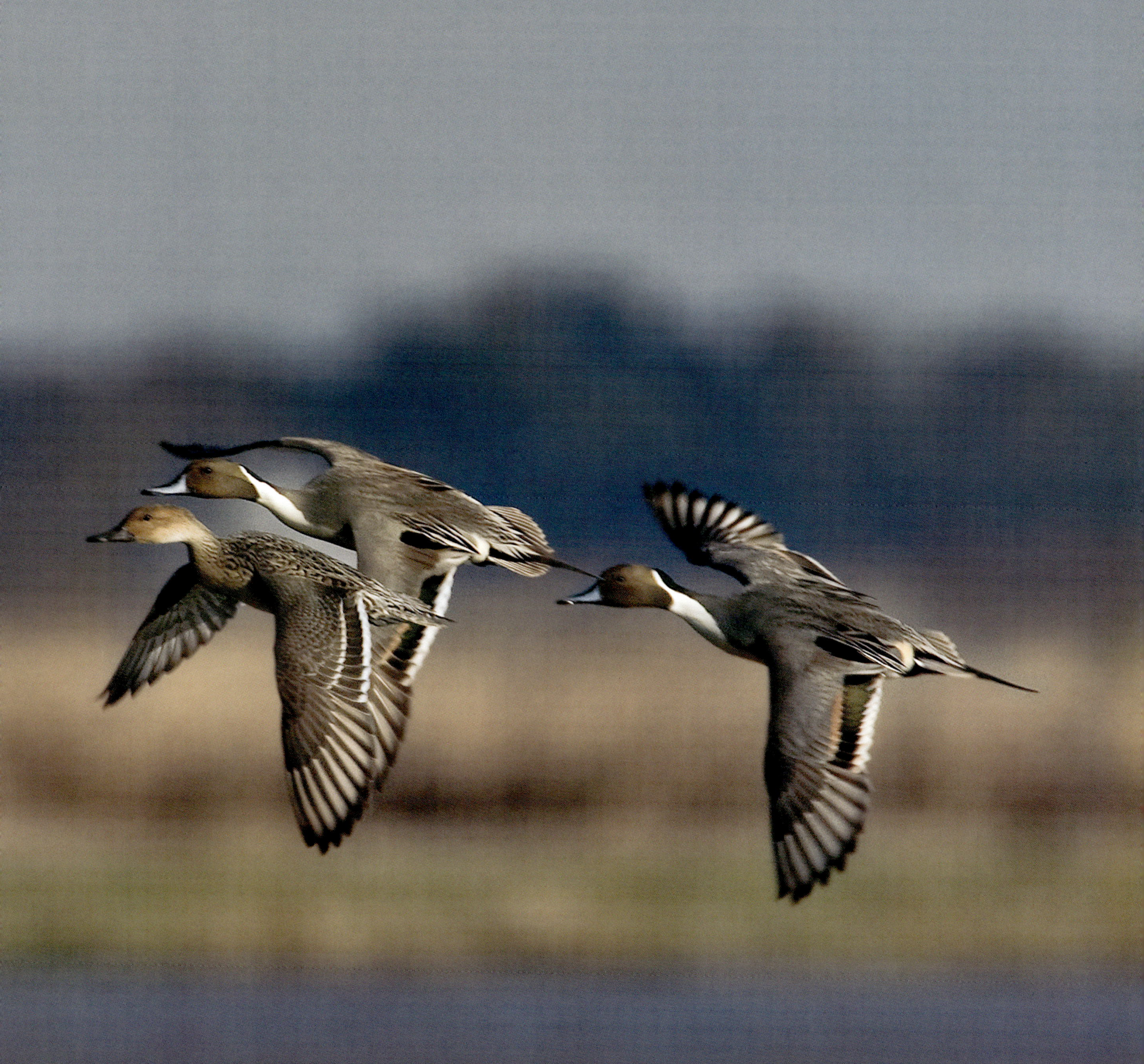

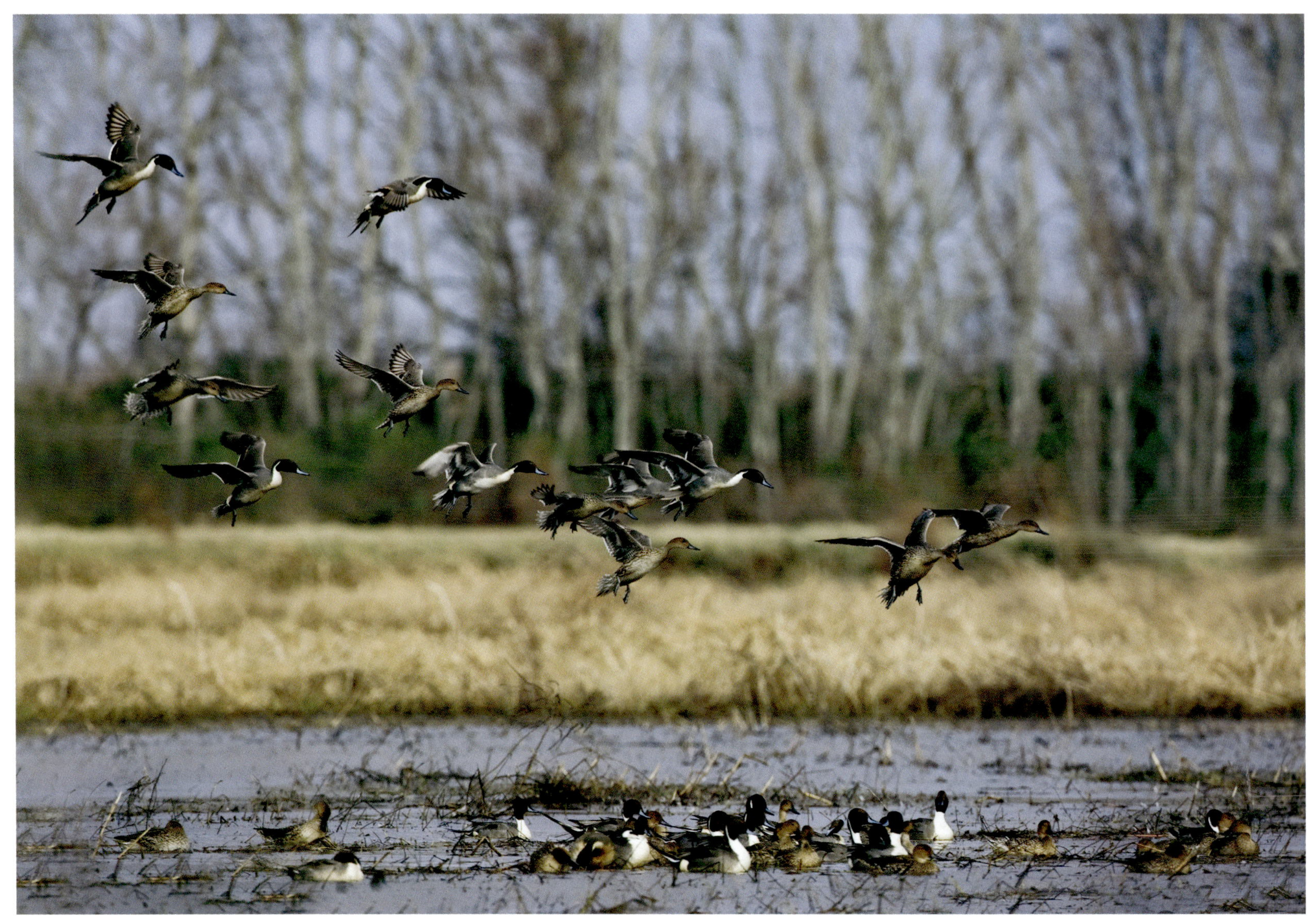

During the fall and winter months on their stopover in south Louisiana, thousands and thousands of pintails gather in shallow inland freshwater such as flooded agricultural land, where they feed on both plant and animal matter such as grain, aquatic insects, and crustaceans. (December 29, 2006)

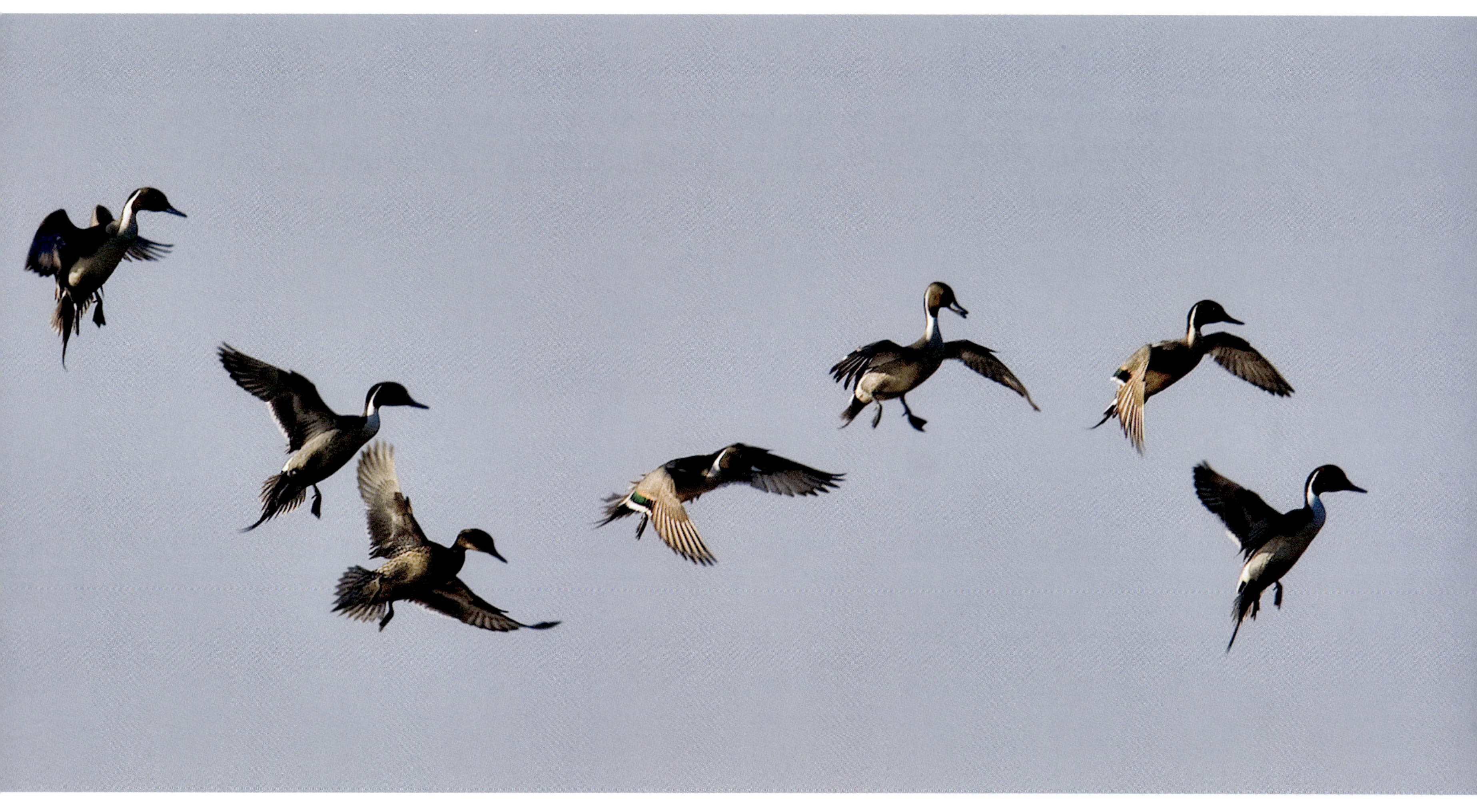

I have never seen another configuration like these pintails on the wing. They appear like musical notes dancing in the sky. (January 13, 2008)

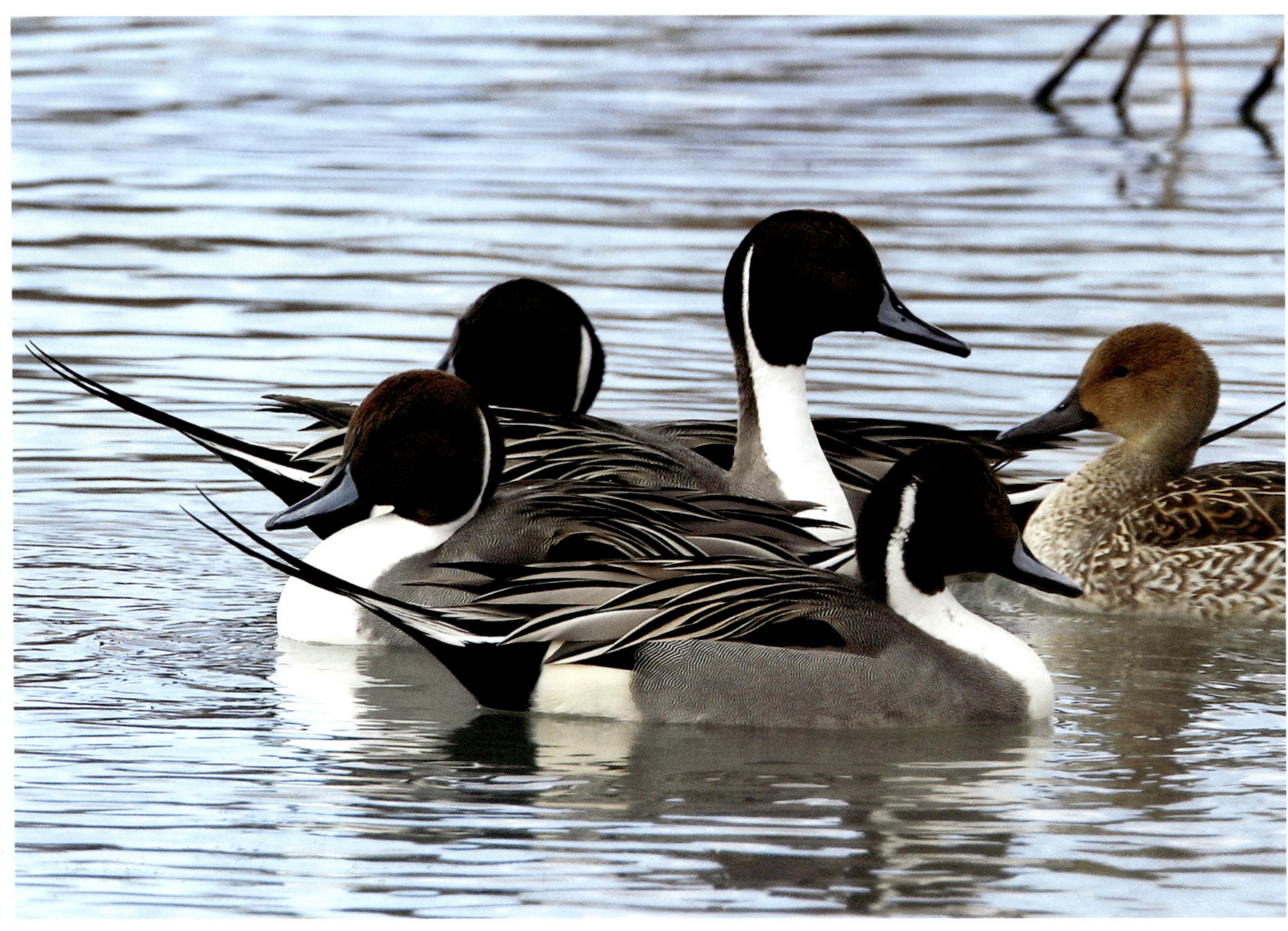

I couldn't have posed this better than nature did. The striking differences between male and female are incredible. (January 14, 2005)

MALLARDS

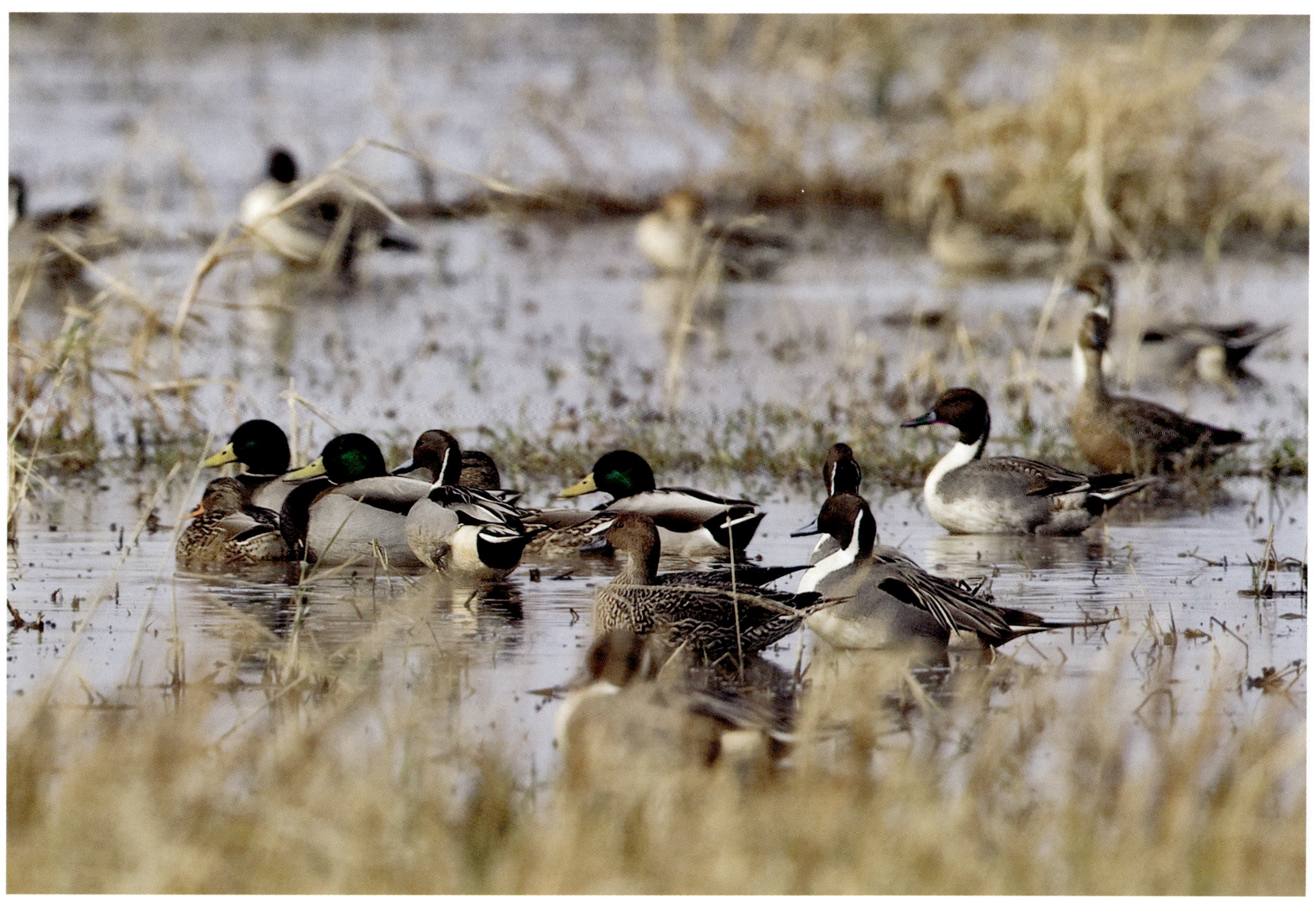

Mallards and pintails in the marsh at the Florence Club in south Louisiana. (December 30, 2005)

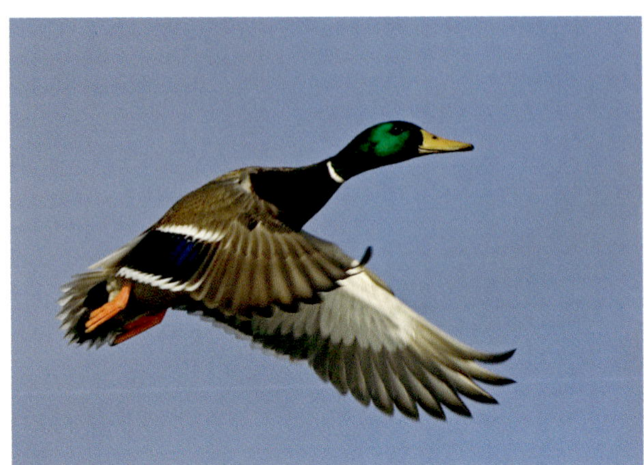

There are those who will tell you that mallards are some of the best eating ducks. I have to agree with them. Pretty bird—great taste." (December 29, 2006)

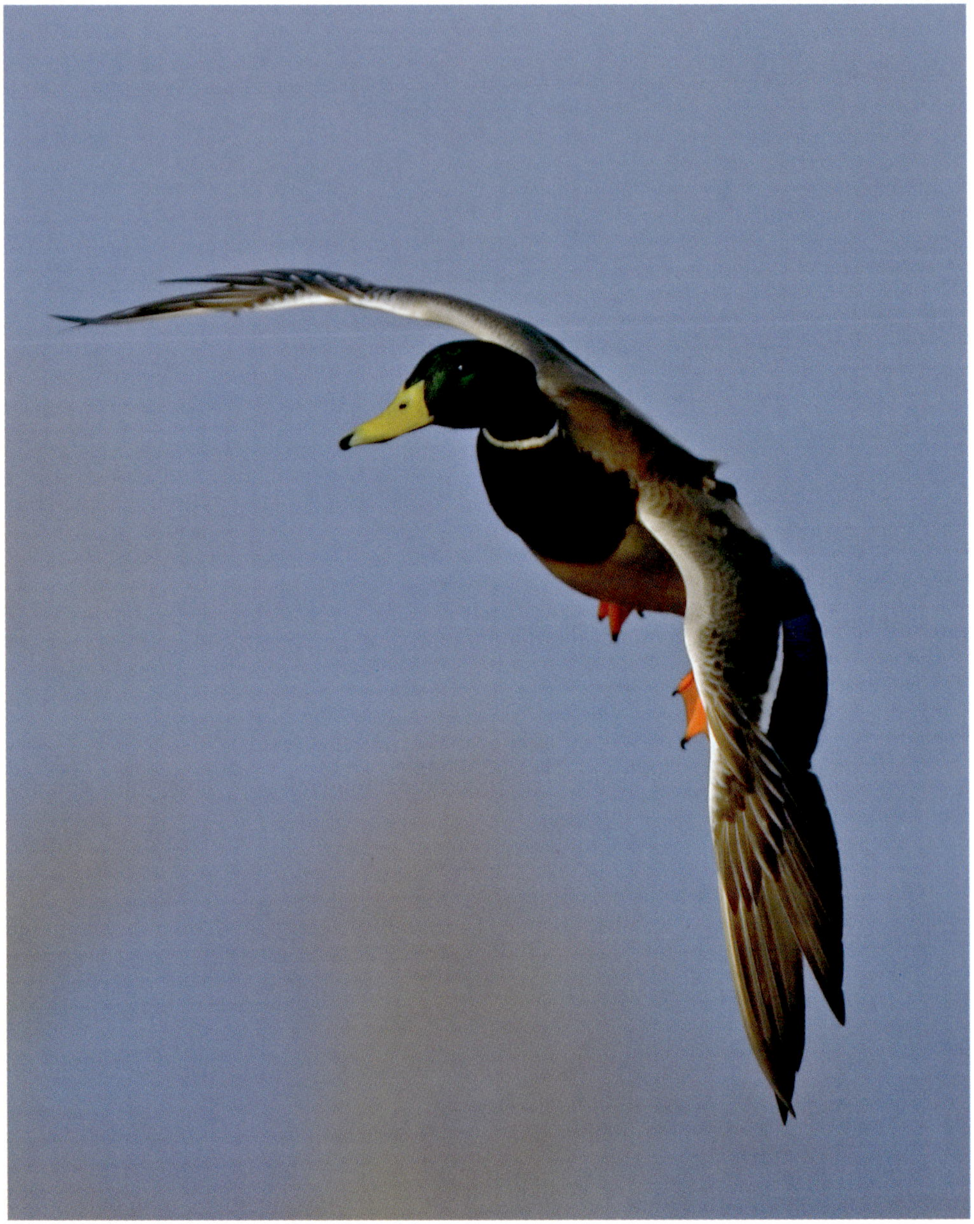

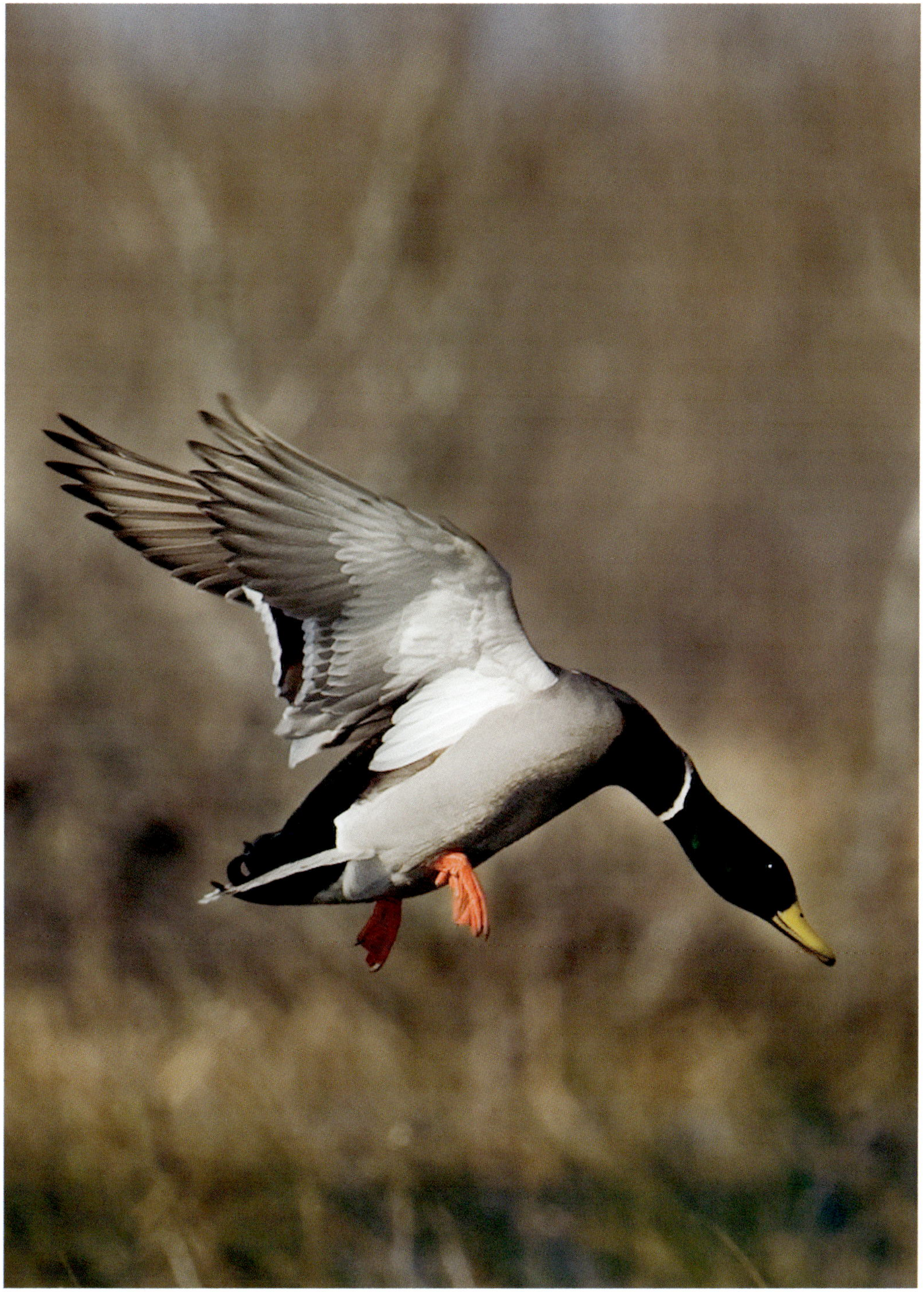

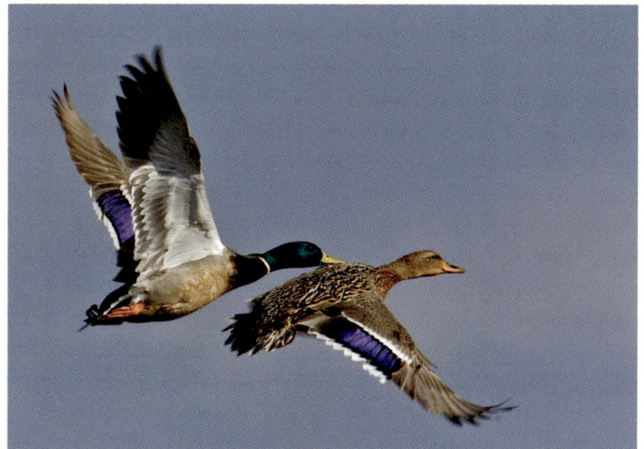

Above: By late February the plumage on this pair of mallards has filled out and is more intense than earlier in the migration period. (February 23, 2008)

Left: I've had the opportunity to photograph mallards all over south Louisiana, but it has been on the grounds of the Florence Club that I've been able to get the best shots. Mallard males, with their iridescent dark green heads, narrow white neck ring, and chestnut breasts, are striking birds to observe as they winter in the marshes before they take wing to begin their way north along the Mississippi Flyway. (January 28, 2007)

MOTTLED DUCKS

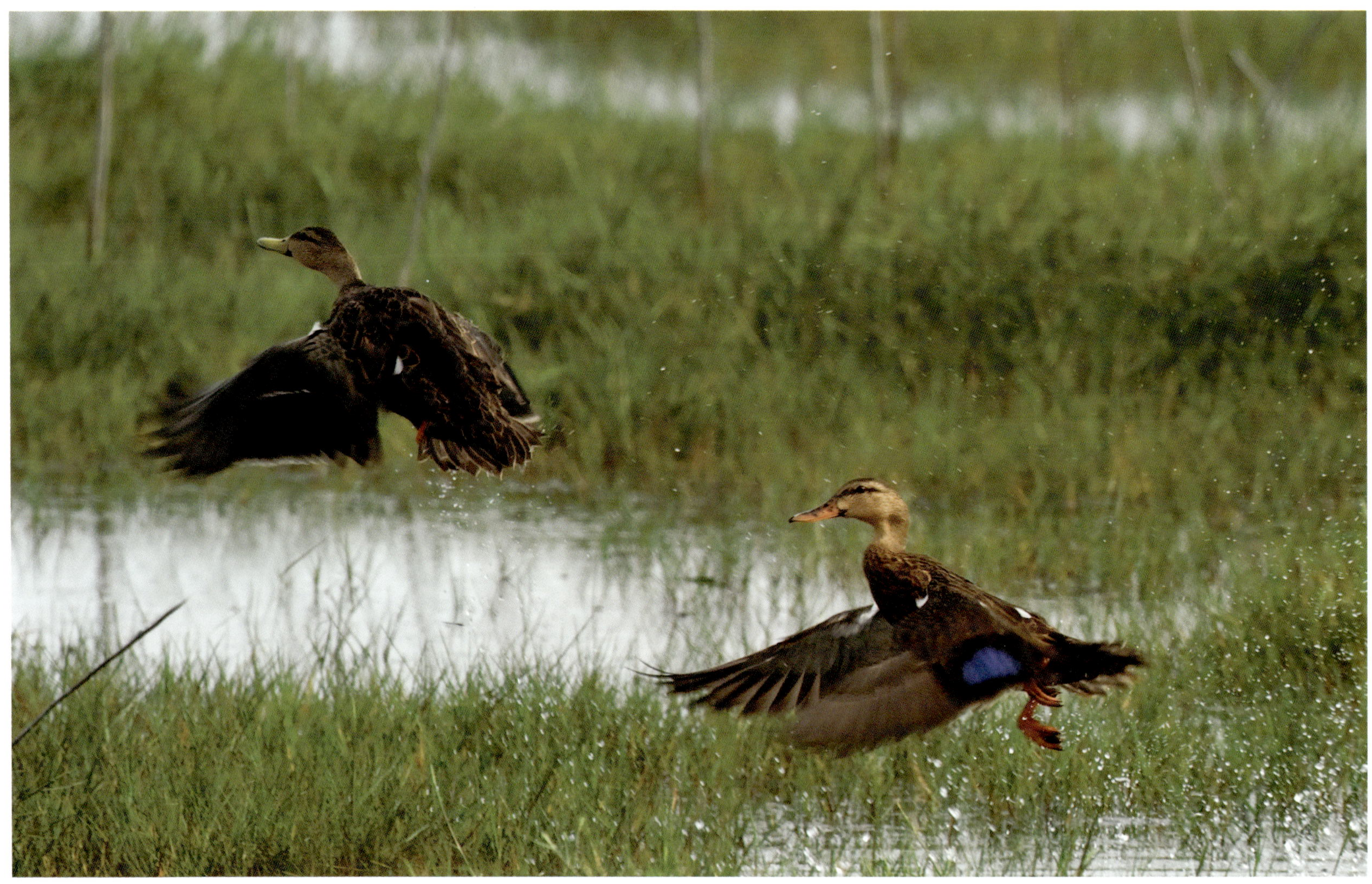

I often spend time at the Lacassine National Wildlife Refuge located in Cameron and Evangeline Parishes in southwestern Louisiana, where several hundred thousand ducks and geese winter in their natural habitat. It is there I found these mottled ducks, which are medium-sized dabbling ducks that breed in the coastal marshes. The adult mottled duck has a dark body, lighter head and neck, orange legs, and dark eyes and is not as attractive in color as a mallard, pintail, or teal. (September 2, 2007)

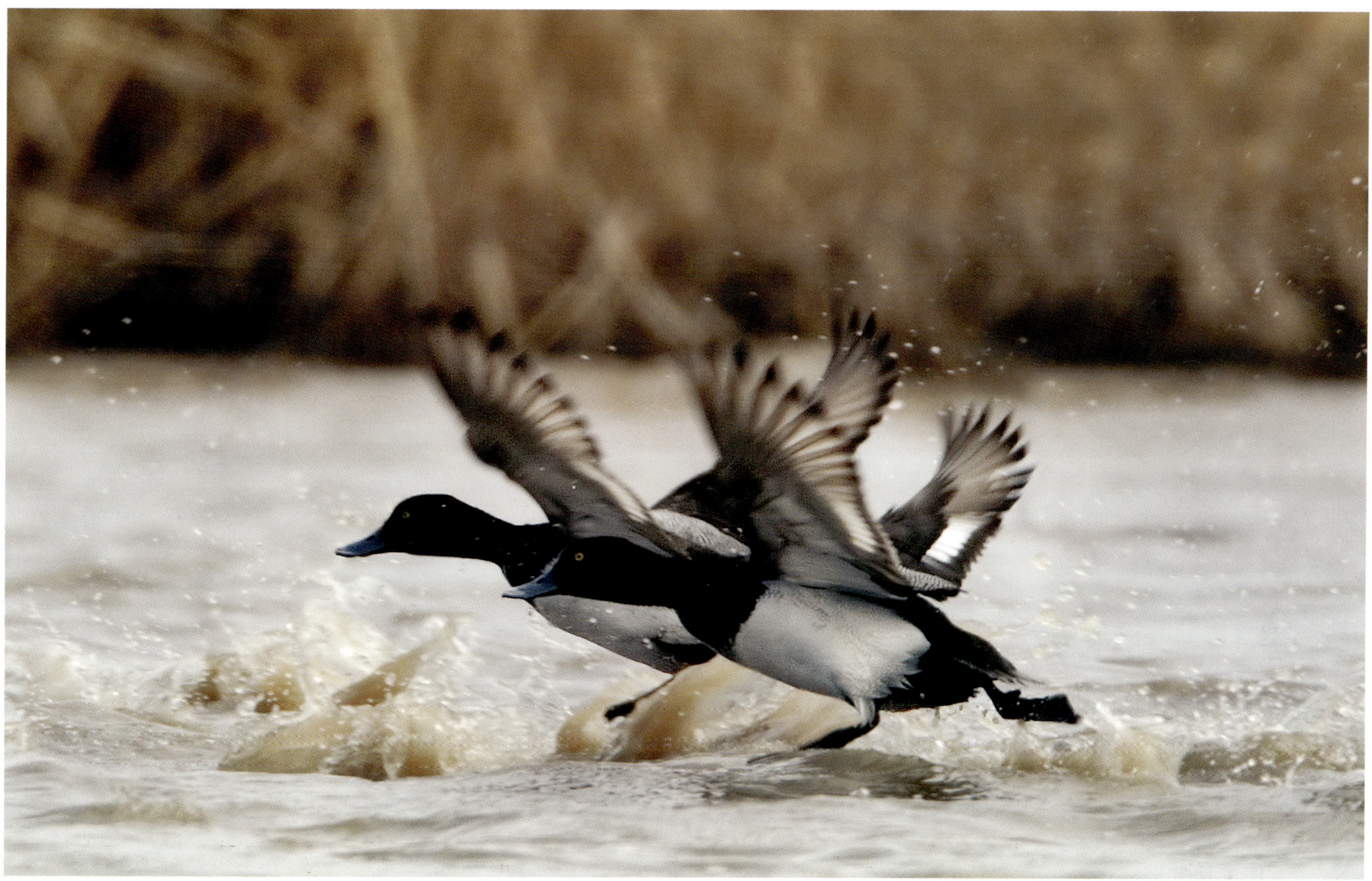

This pair of lesser scaups was peddling their way across a pond in south Louisiana. They are found only in North America and are the most abundant and widespread of the diving ducks. Very graceful. (February 10, 2005)

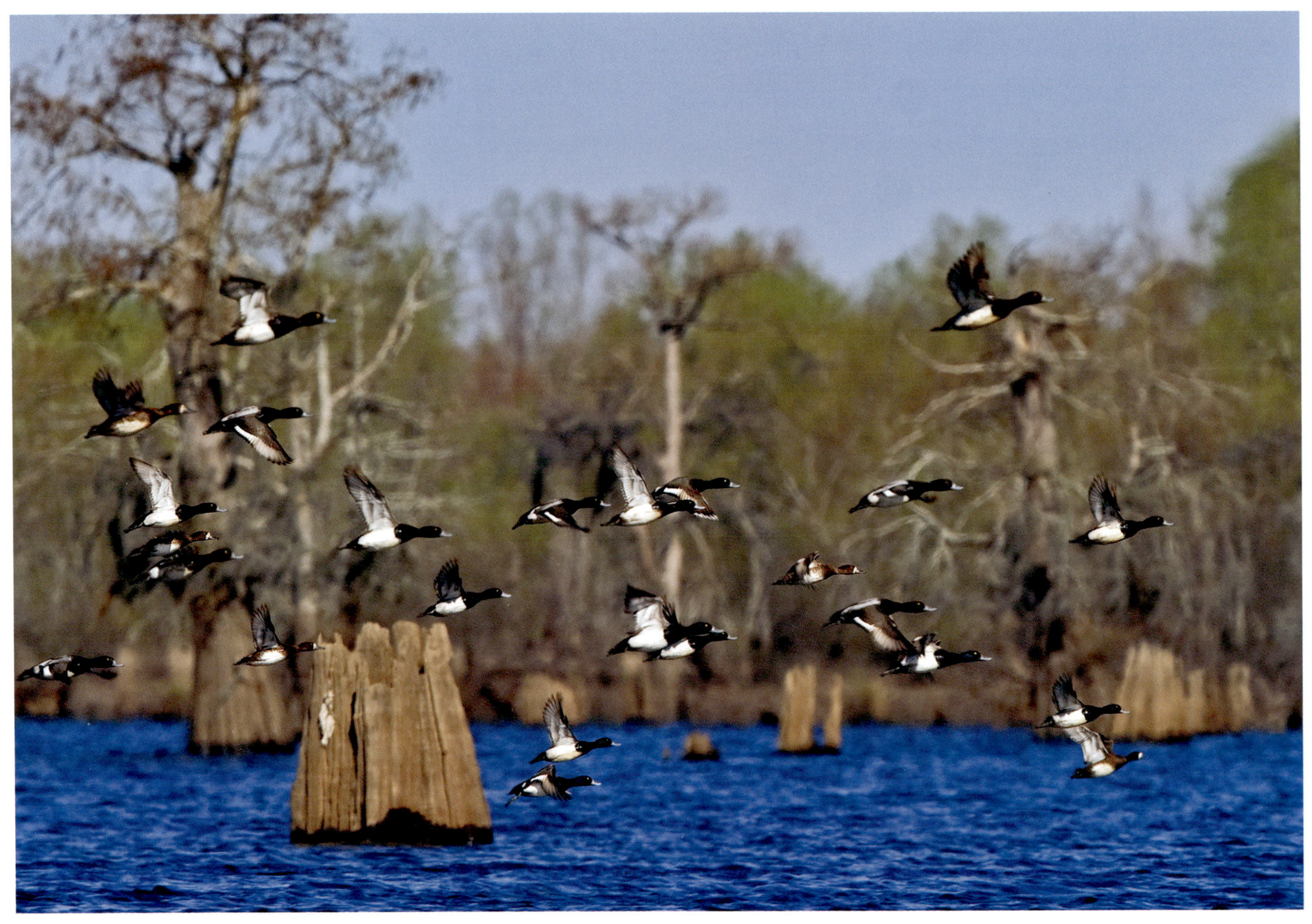

A flock of lesser scaups flying in the Atchafalaya Basin in March, just before the willows and bald cypresses leafed out. (March 3, 2007)

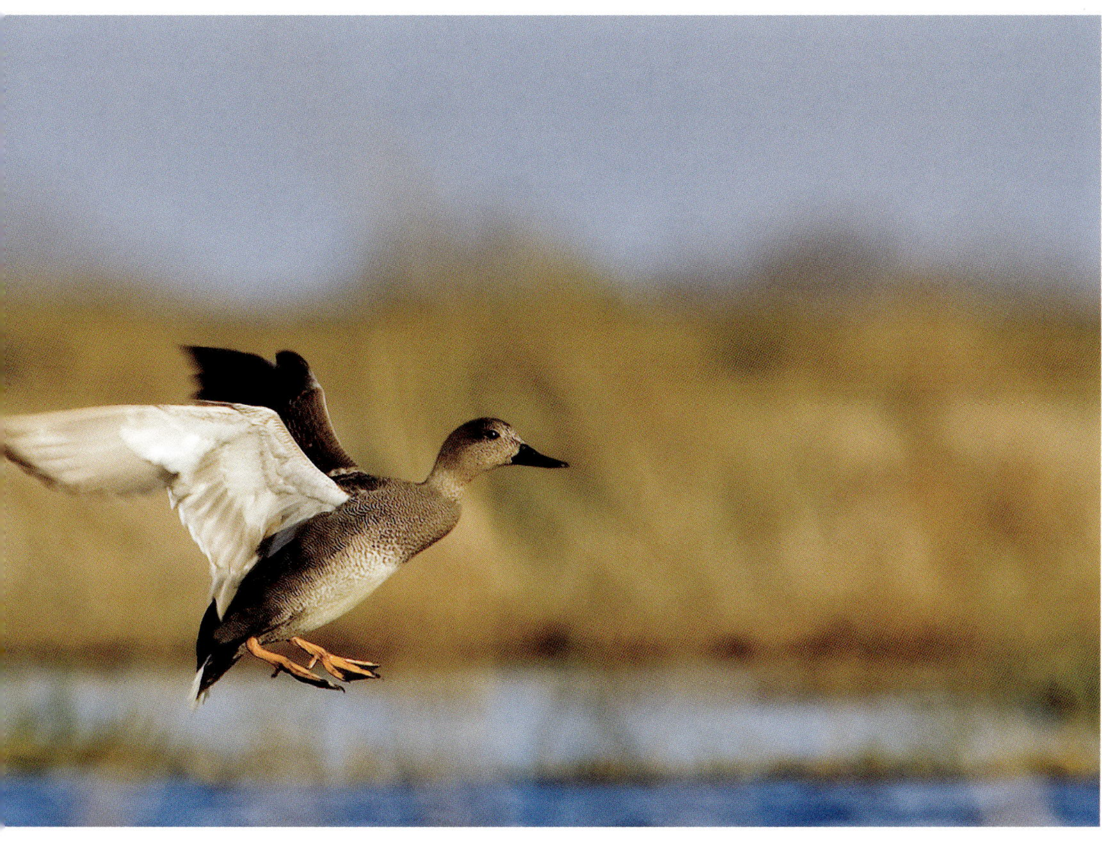

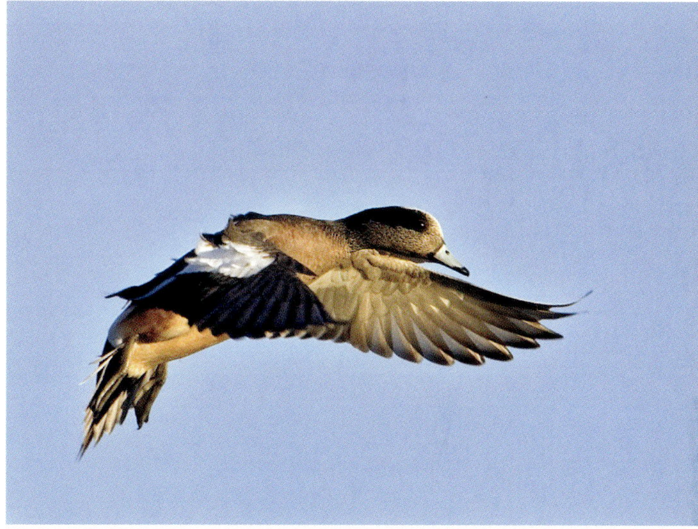

Left: The gadwall, or gray duck, is often called a Louisiana mallard in Louisiana. They're very plentiful but rather drab, like female mallards. (February 7, 2008)

Right: The American wigeon has some interesting markings. For instance, the male has a white forehead that resembles a bald head, which earned it the nickname of baldpate. I don't see them too often, but when I do, it's usually in the marshes where they feed by dabbling for plant food. (February 7, 2008)

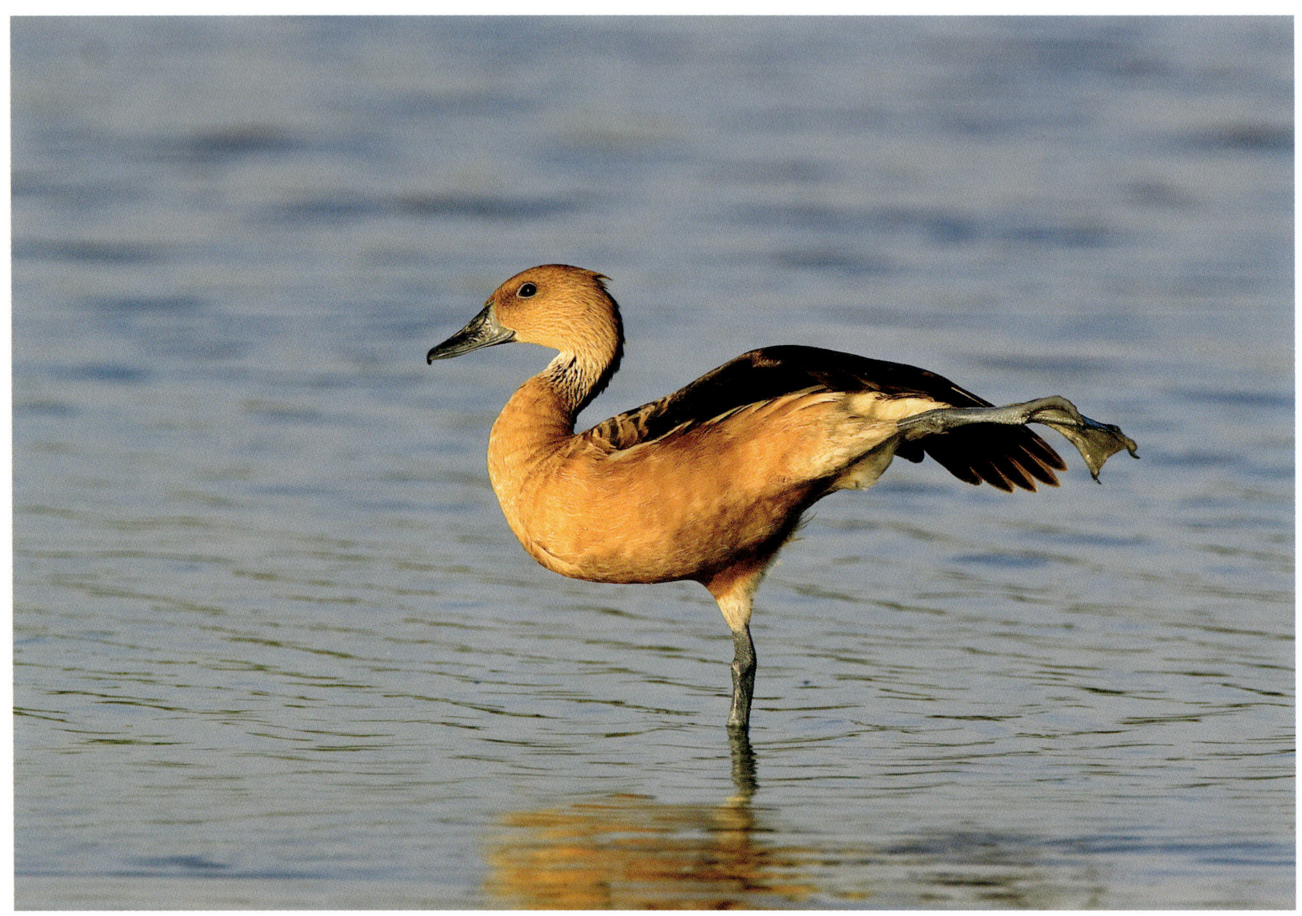

This fulvous whistling duck struck a pose in a rice field near Kaplan, Louisiana, and I couldn't pass up the shot. They are dabblers and pretty decent divers. (July 18, 2005)

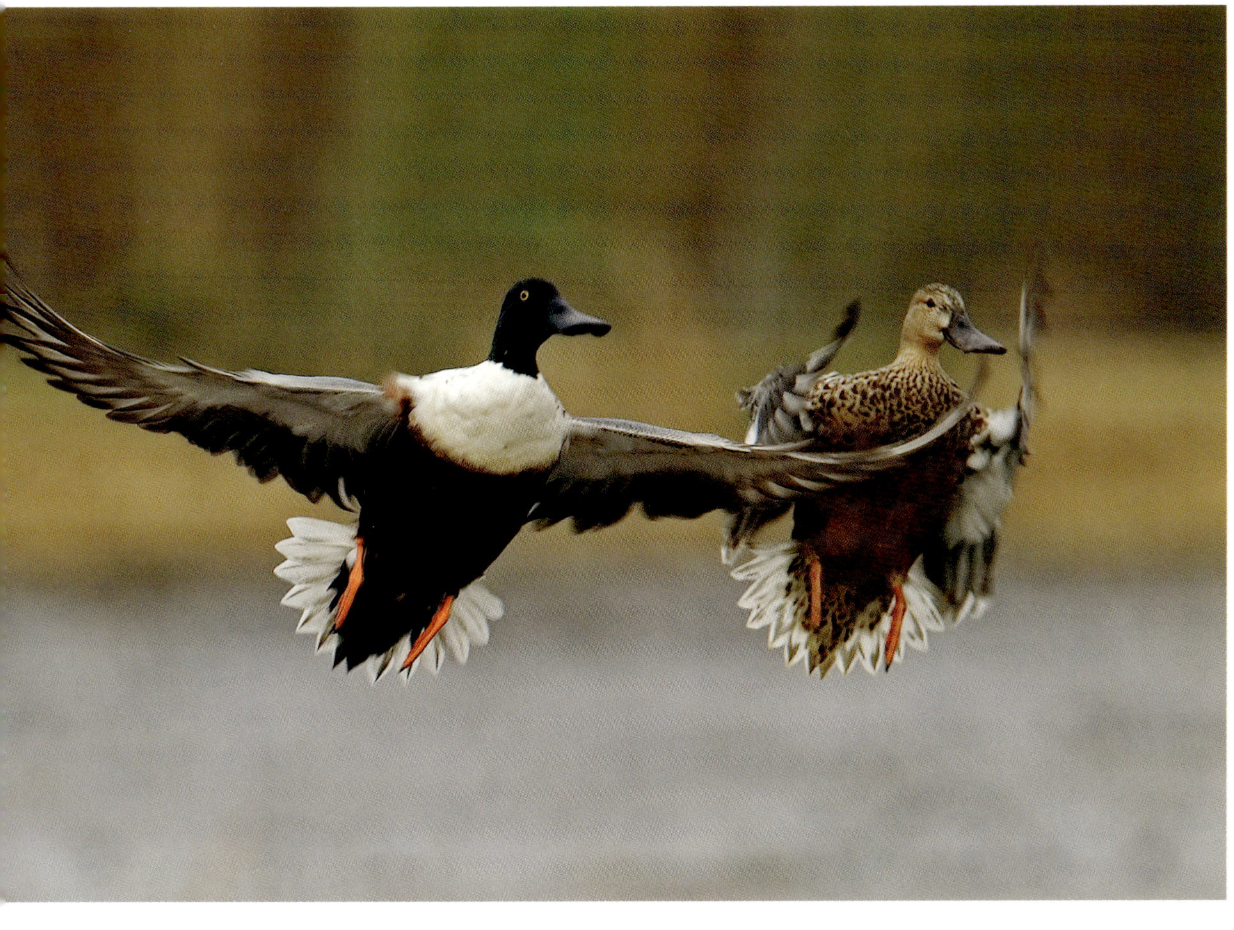

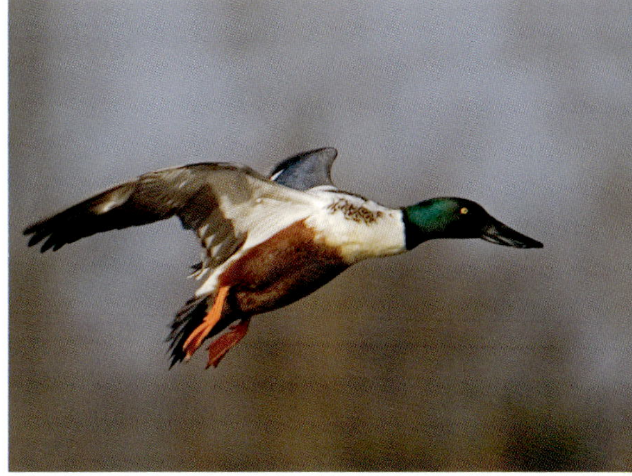

Above: Shovelers are also called spoonies because of their spatula-shaped bills. At times I think of them as being clumsy because of that, but they do have nice colorings. (December 23, 2006)

Left: Pair of shovelers. As usual, the female is less colorful and rather drab. (December 29, 2006)

WOOD DUCKS

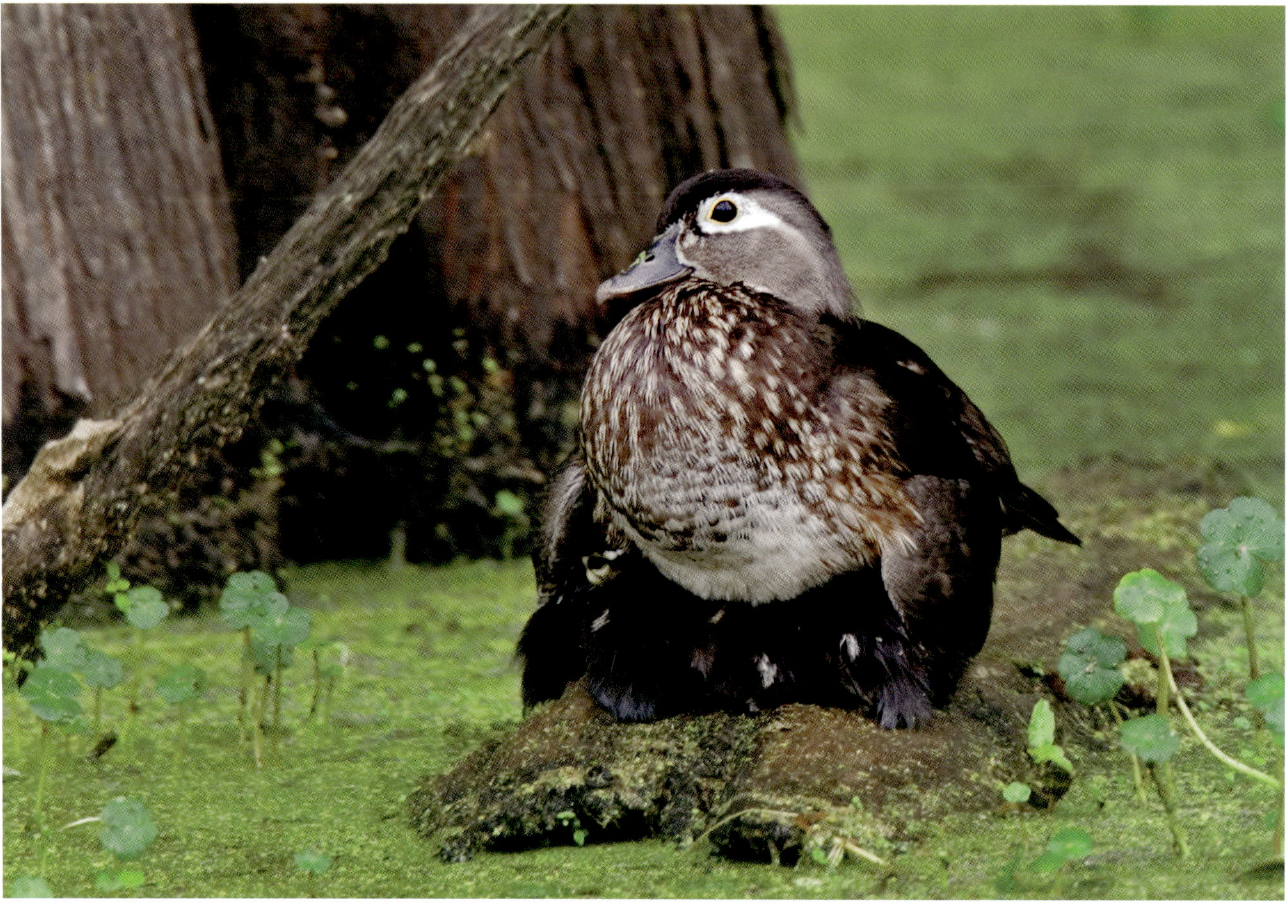

Darn, I love these wood ducks—so does just about everybody else who observes them. They are, without a doubt, the most beautiful of ducks. Although the male breeding ducks with their distinct coloring are by far the most striking, the females are also quite interesting. This female woodie and her baby ducklings are, well, cute—not a word I use lightly, but it fits, right? Once the ducklings hatch, they jump down from their nest and make their way to water. The mother calls them to her, but does not help them in any way. The markings on the ducklings are similar to the adult female—brownish-gray upper bodies with light gray cheeks, dark crowns, and red circles around the eyes. Most of the time I observe these colorful ducks in wooded swamps, like Lake Martin, or along the banks of bayous. Unlike most other North American ducks, the wood duck nests in trees or in special boxes that are provided by thoughtful duck-lovers if natural cavities for nesting are scarce. (March 12, 2007)

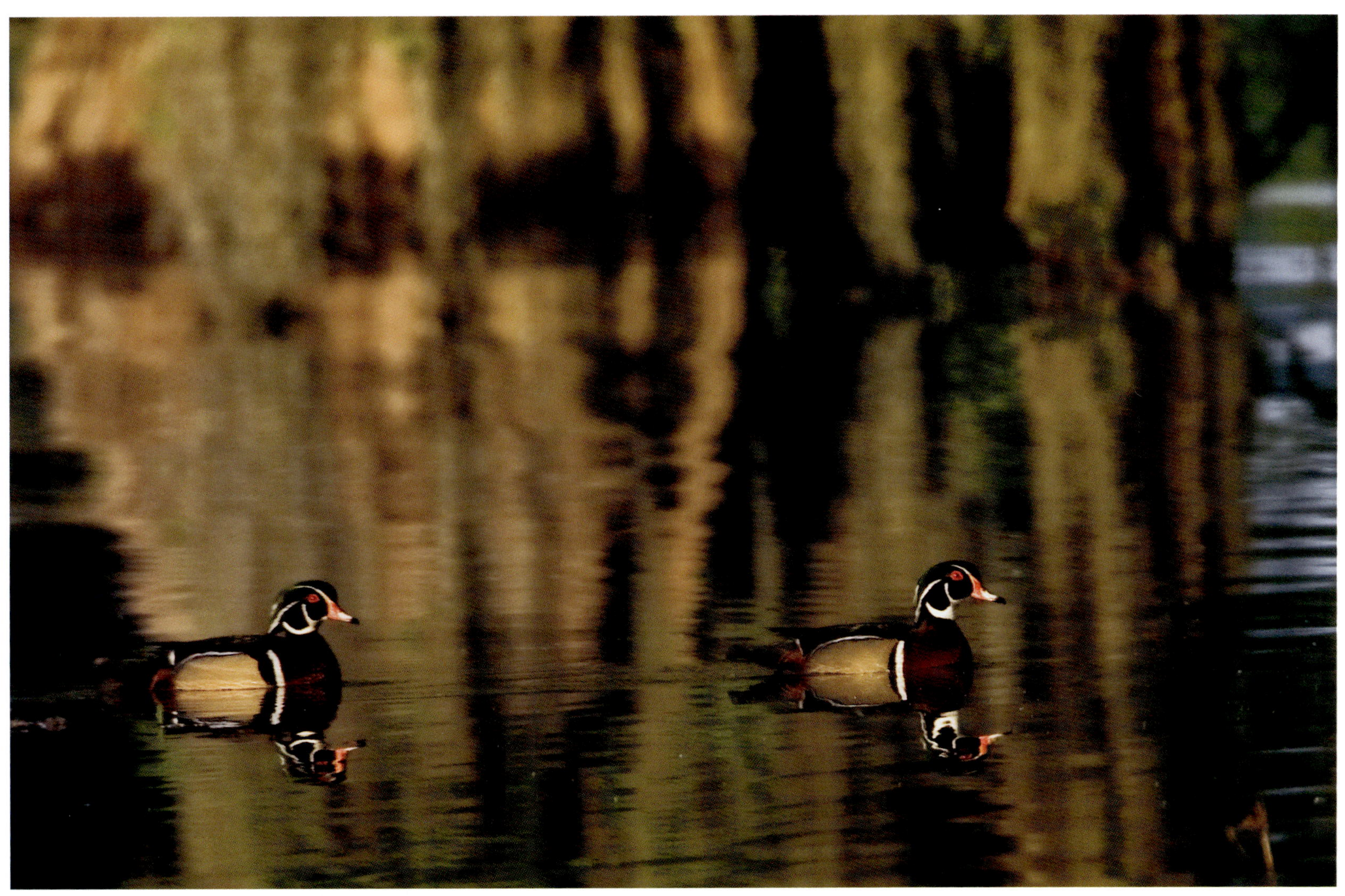

A beautiful mirror image captured at Lake Martin with the huge trunk of a bald cypress in the background (April 19, 2007)

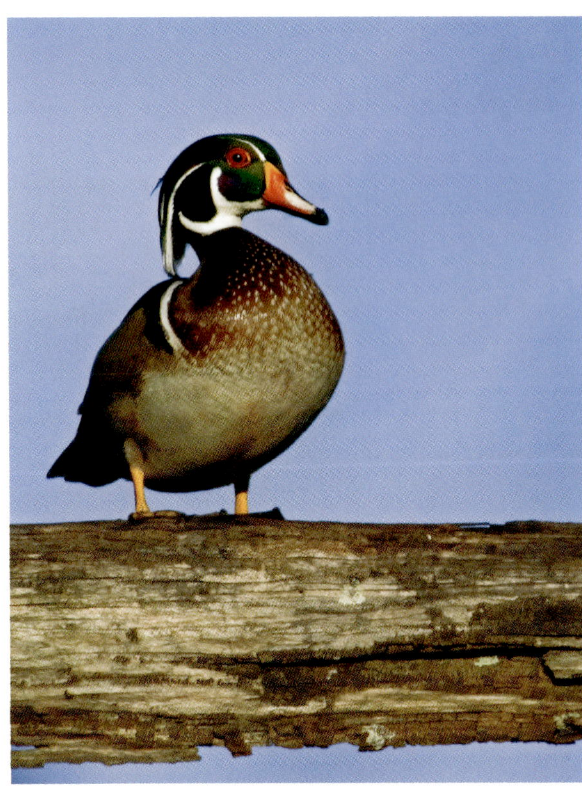

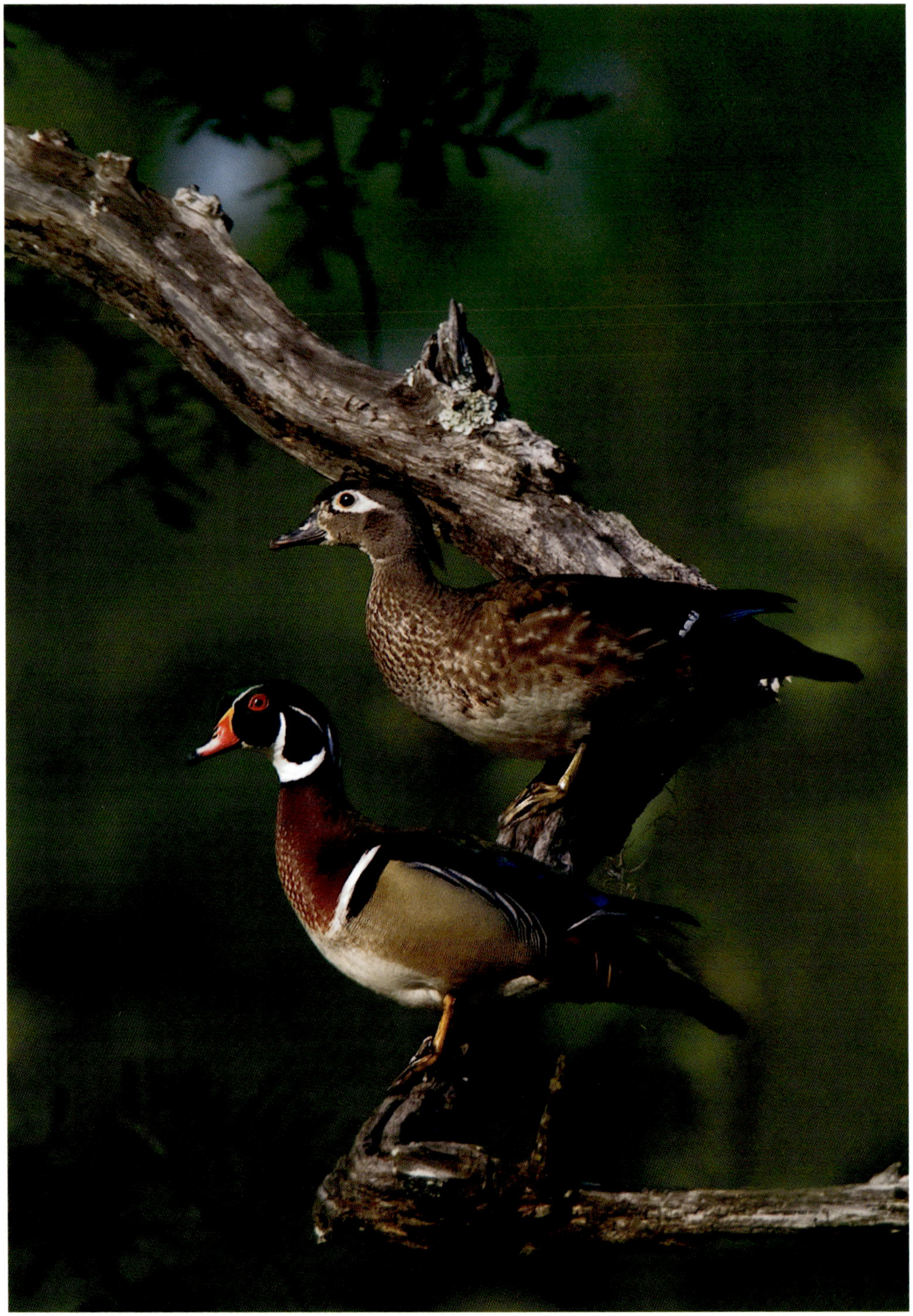

Above: You can see why I love a wood duck. Notice his crest, which looks like a slicked-back hairdo. What a dude! (February 11, 2005)

Right: A perfect pair—female and male—on a limb in the Atchafalaya Basin. (April 5, 2007)

GEESE
SPECKLEBELLY

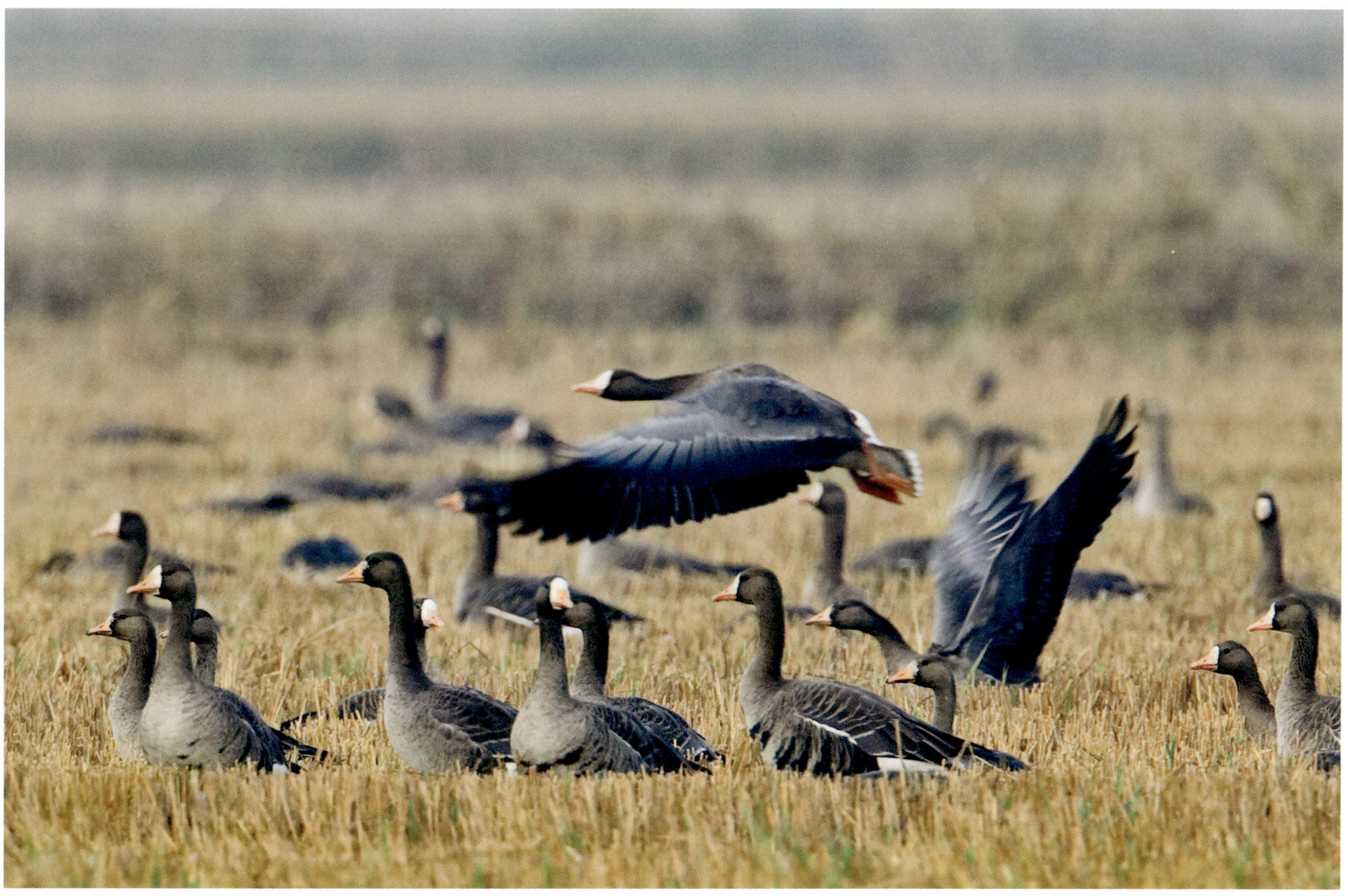

This image is a favorite of mine. The composition—the bird on wing and the others roaming around in a harvested rice field—depicts them right on. (November 5, 2005)

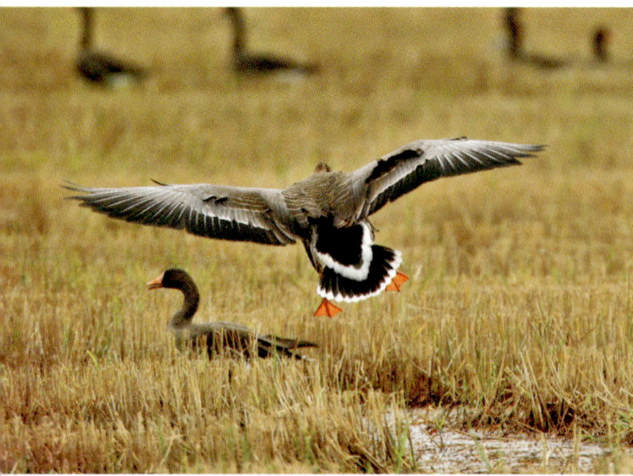

Above: I watched this big speck coming in for a landing and thought how much he looked like an airplane approaching a runway. (December 5, 2004)

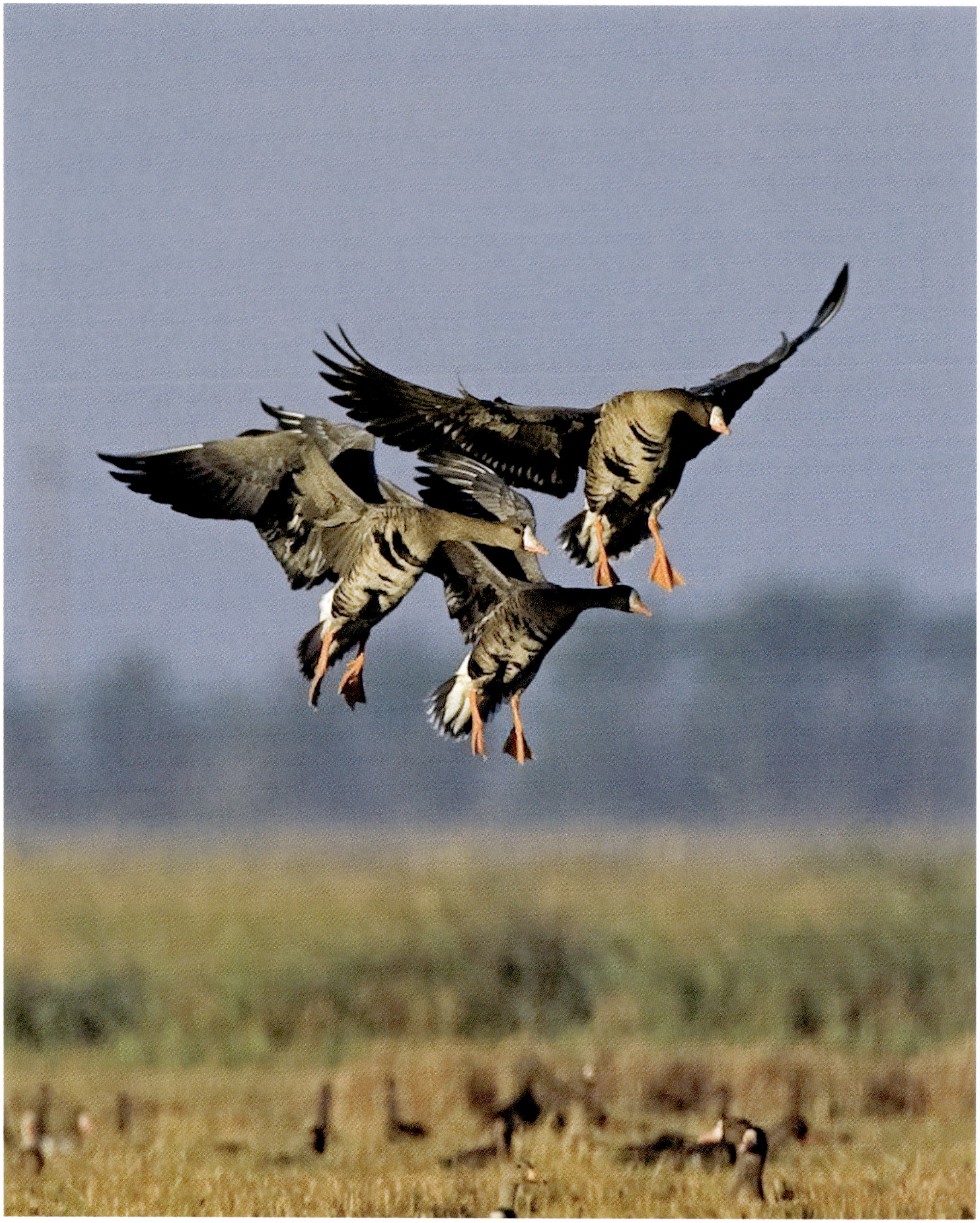

Right: The greater white-fronted goose, generally known as a specklebelly, is a favorite of hunters in Louisiana. The large birds are easily recognized by the black bars (stripes) across their large chests. I find them to be rather handsome birds to photograph because of their flight patterns and their elegant appearance. Here, three "specks" come in for a landing. They are big birds and exciting to watch in the marsh in south Louisiana. (October 23, 2005)

Facing page: Beautiful environmental shot in a rice field—the lighting was ideal. (November 5, 2005)

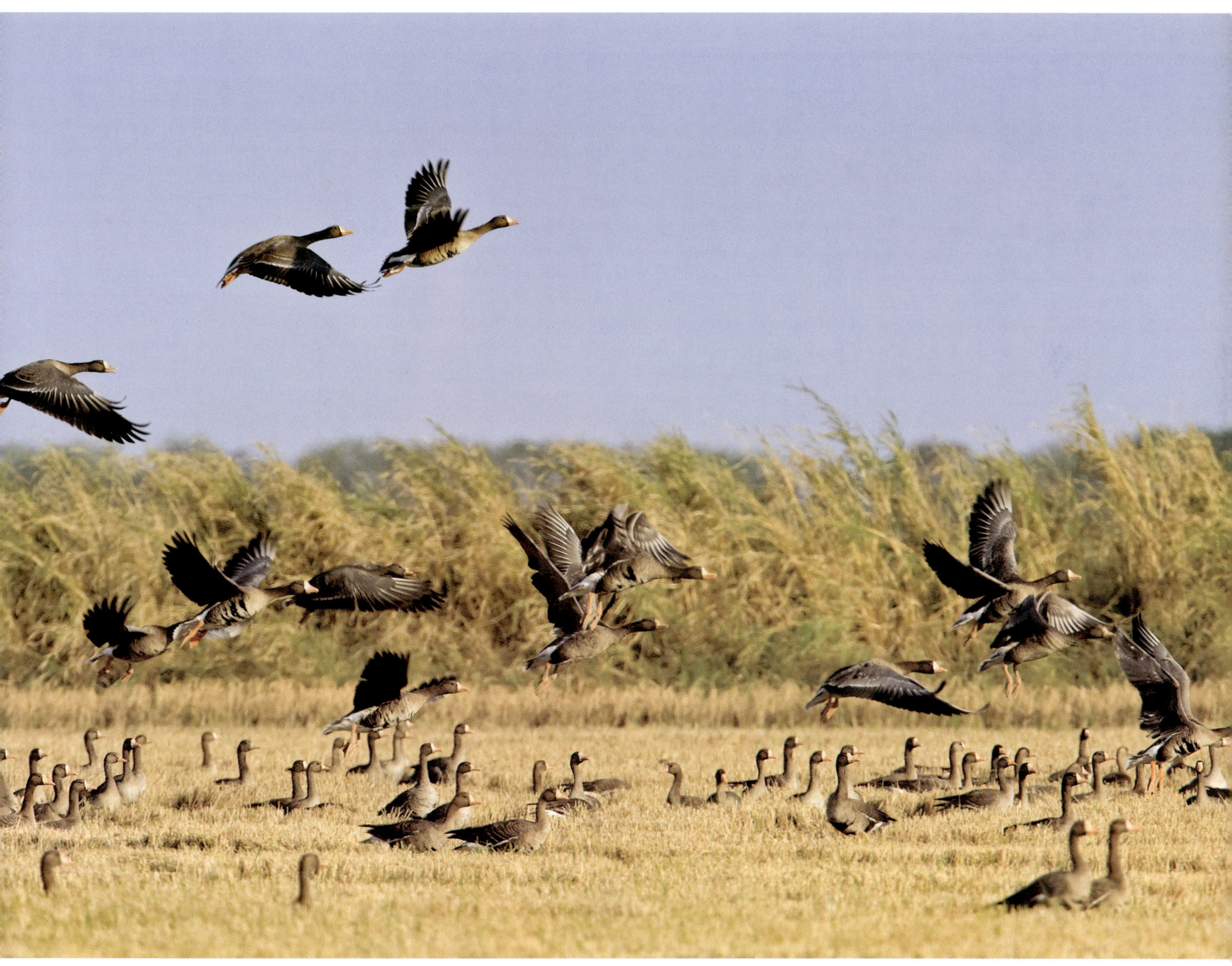

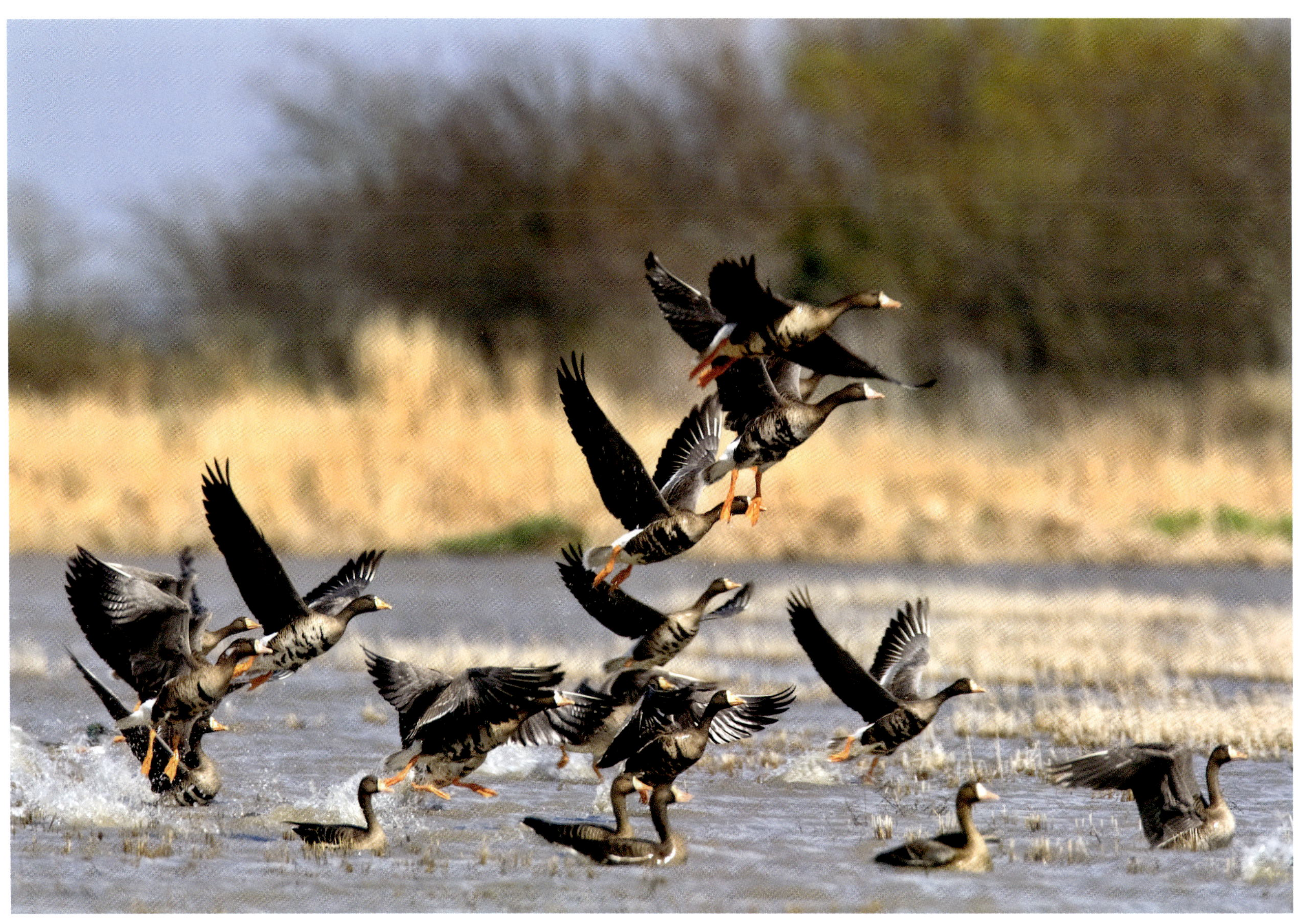

Taking off in the marsh, these specks were enjoying a fine, cool day without hunters to bother them. (February 16, 2008)

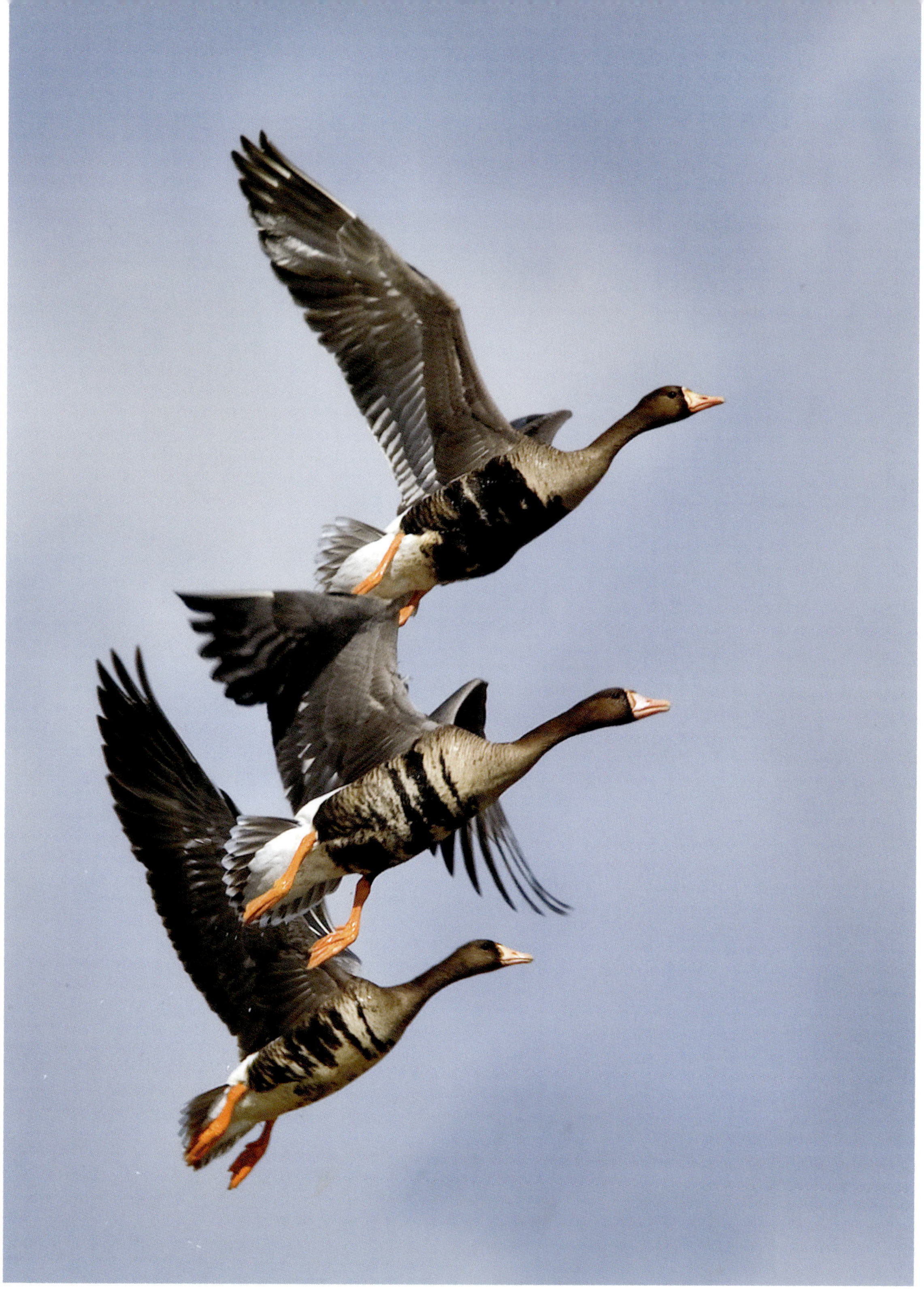

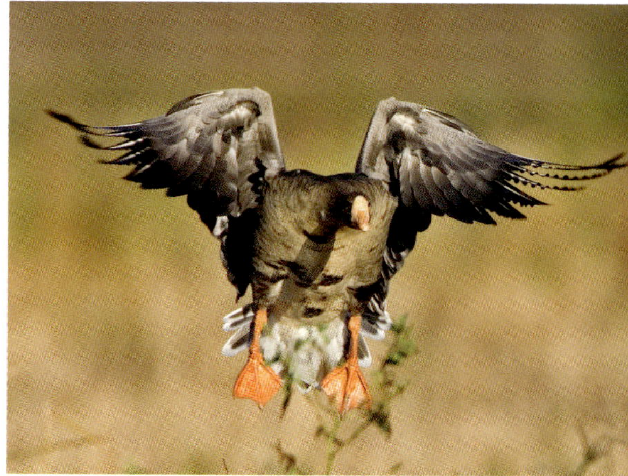

Above: As you can see this is a large bird, and some of our local hunters are apt to call speckle-bellies the "golden goose" because they're great to hunt and, when baked or roasted, are quite delicious. (October 29, 2006)

Left: This photo of a trio of specks on wing is one of my favorite shots. Notice the distinctive markings on the underbellies, the gracefulness of the wings, and the bright orange legs and beaks. (February 16, 2008)

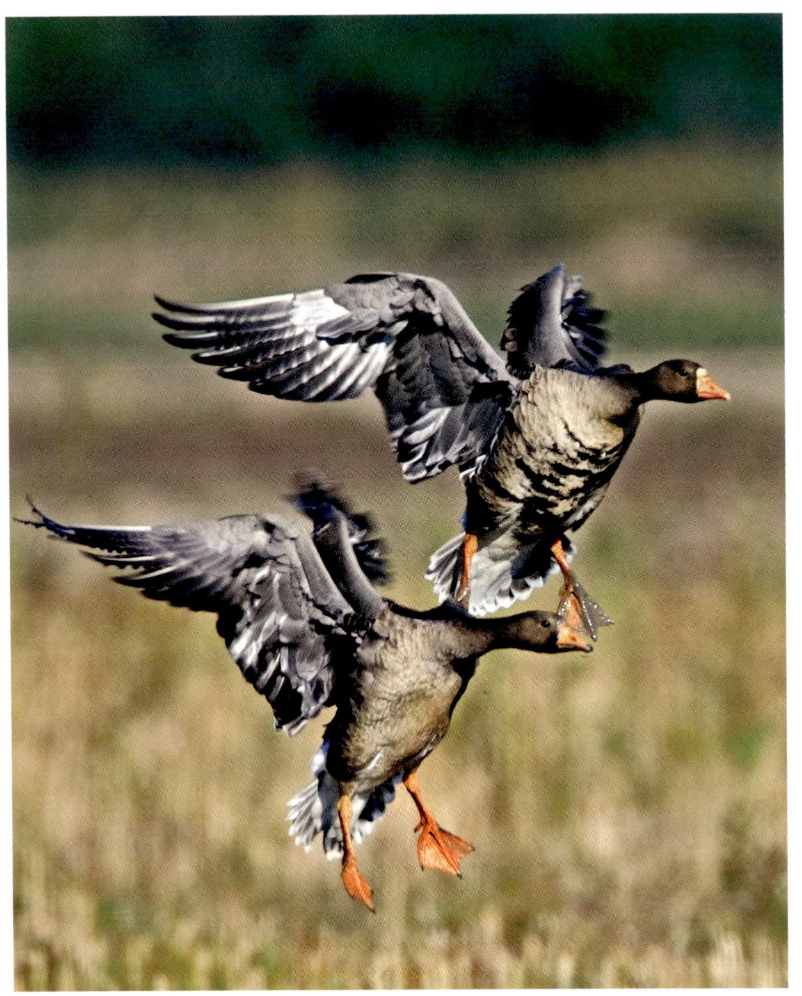

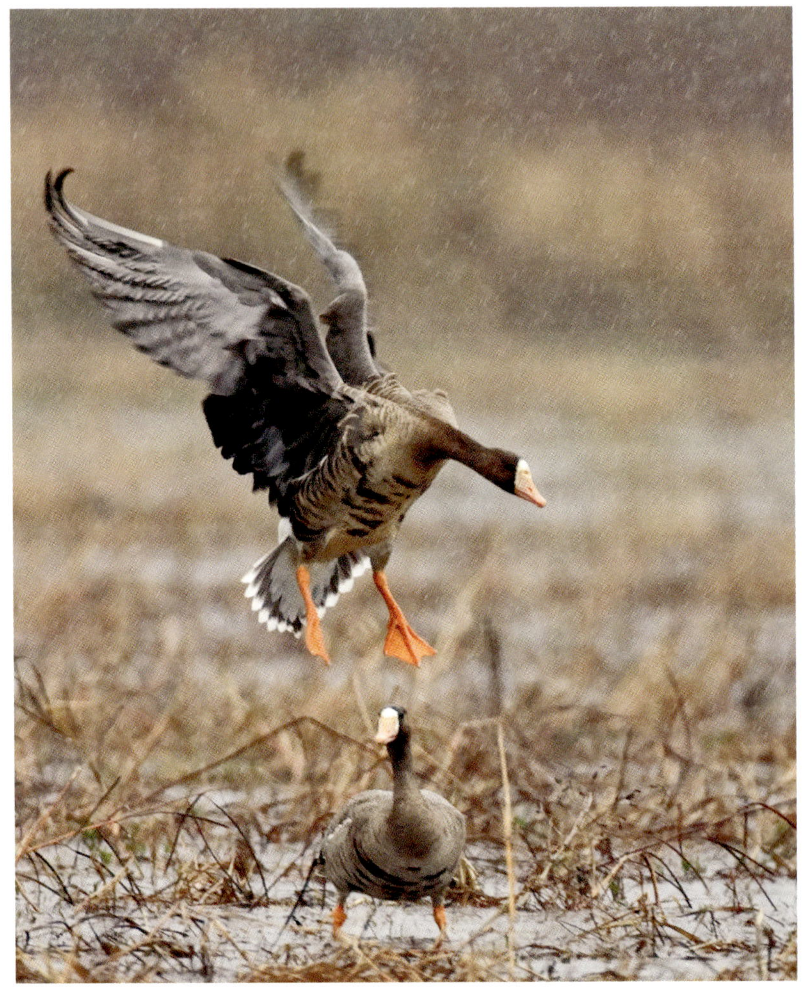

Left: An adult and first-year speck coming in to feed. (October 29, 2006)

Right, and facing page: These two photographs were taken while a gentle rain fell on the marsh. I like the soft texture of the rain in the photographs—beautiful. (November 18, 2007)

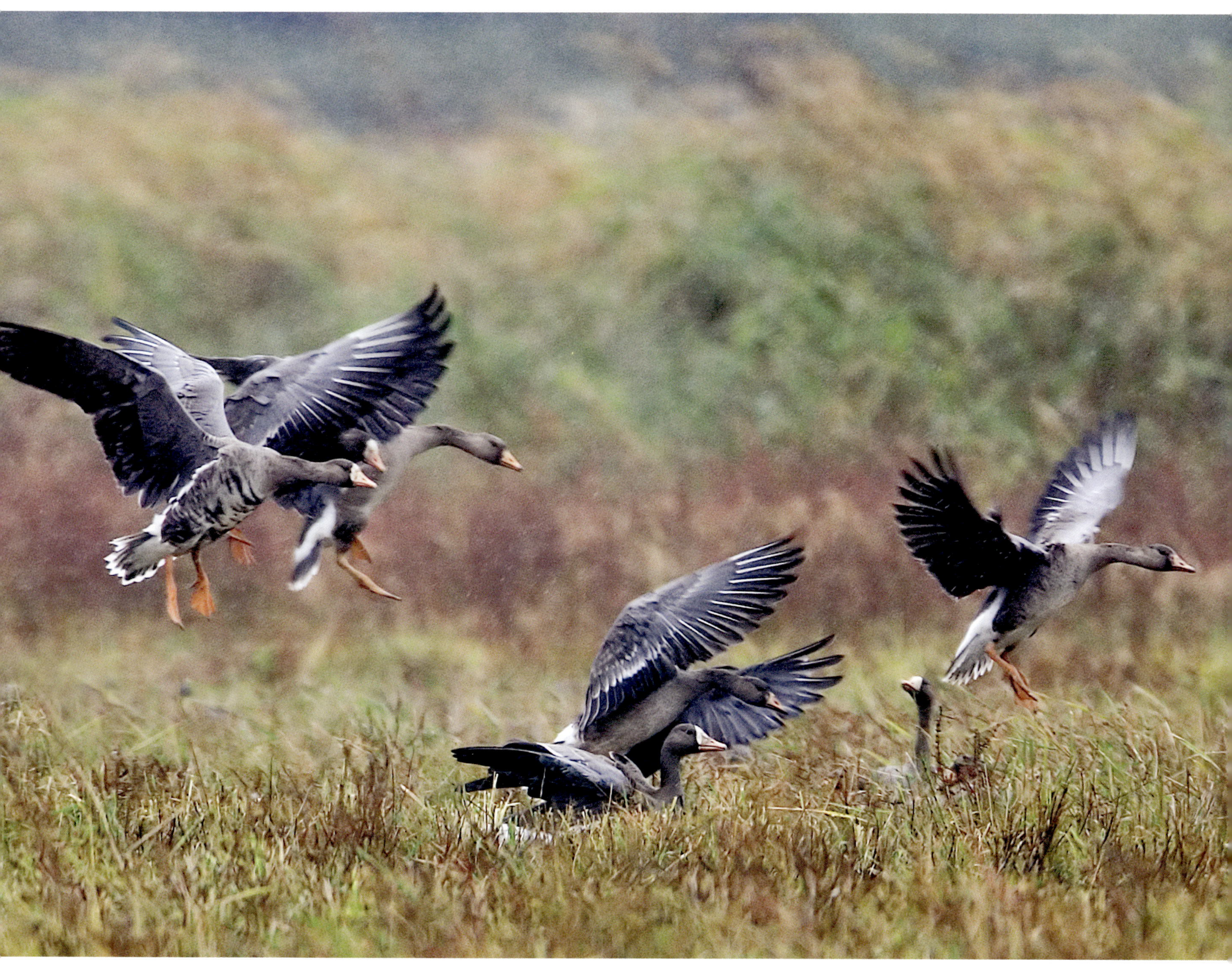

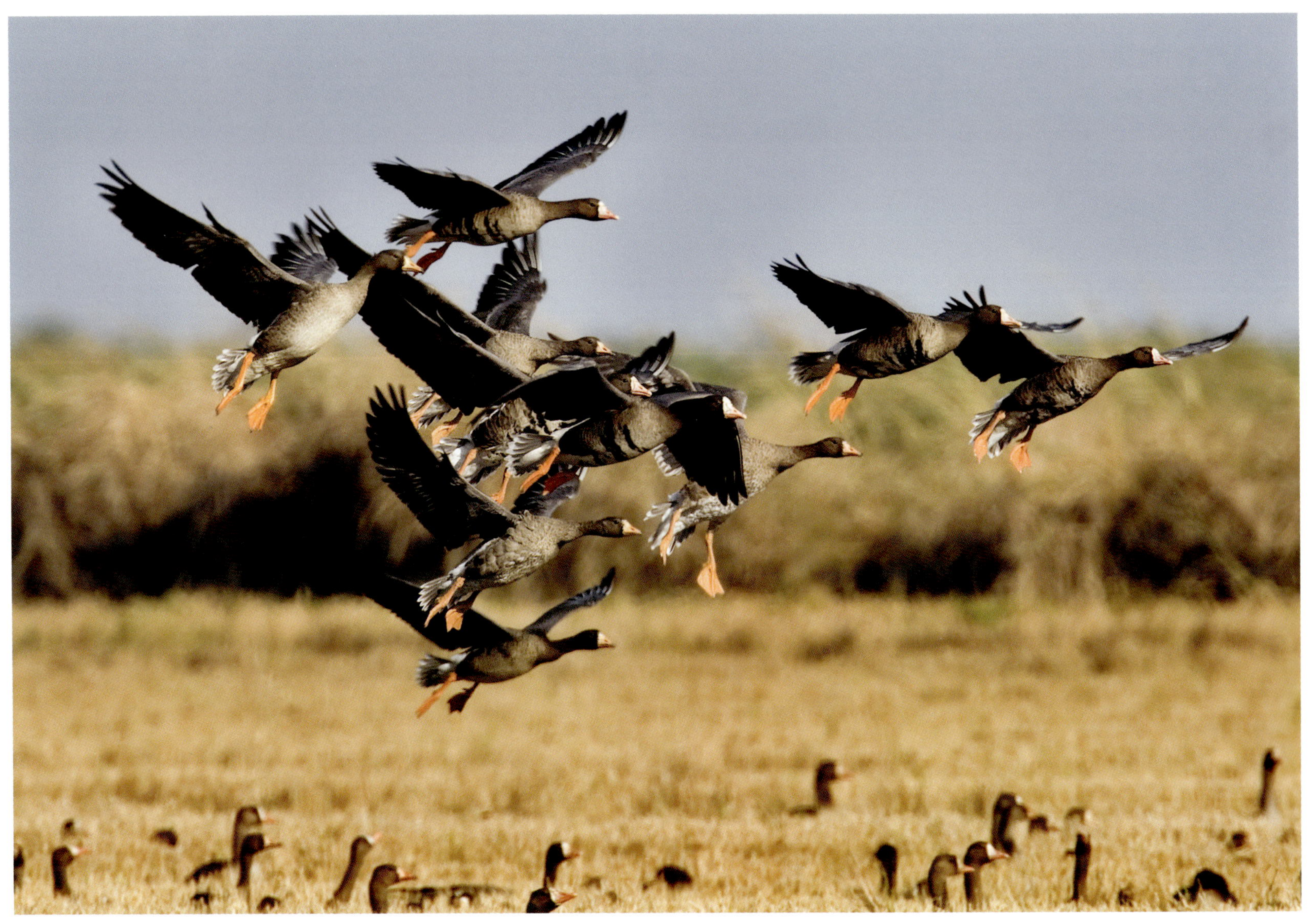

Note the stripes on the underbelly—sometimes I call them sergeants because of these markings. They have a very distinct call, and hunters are always practicing it on their goose calls. (November 6, 2005)

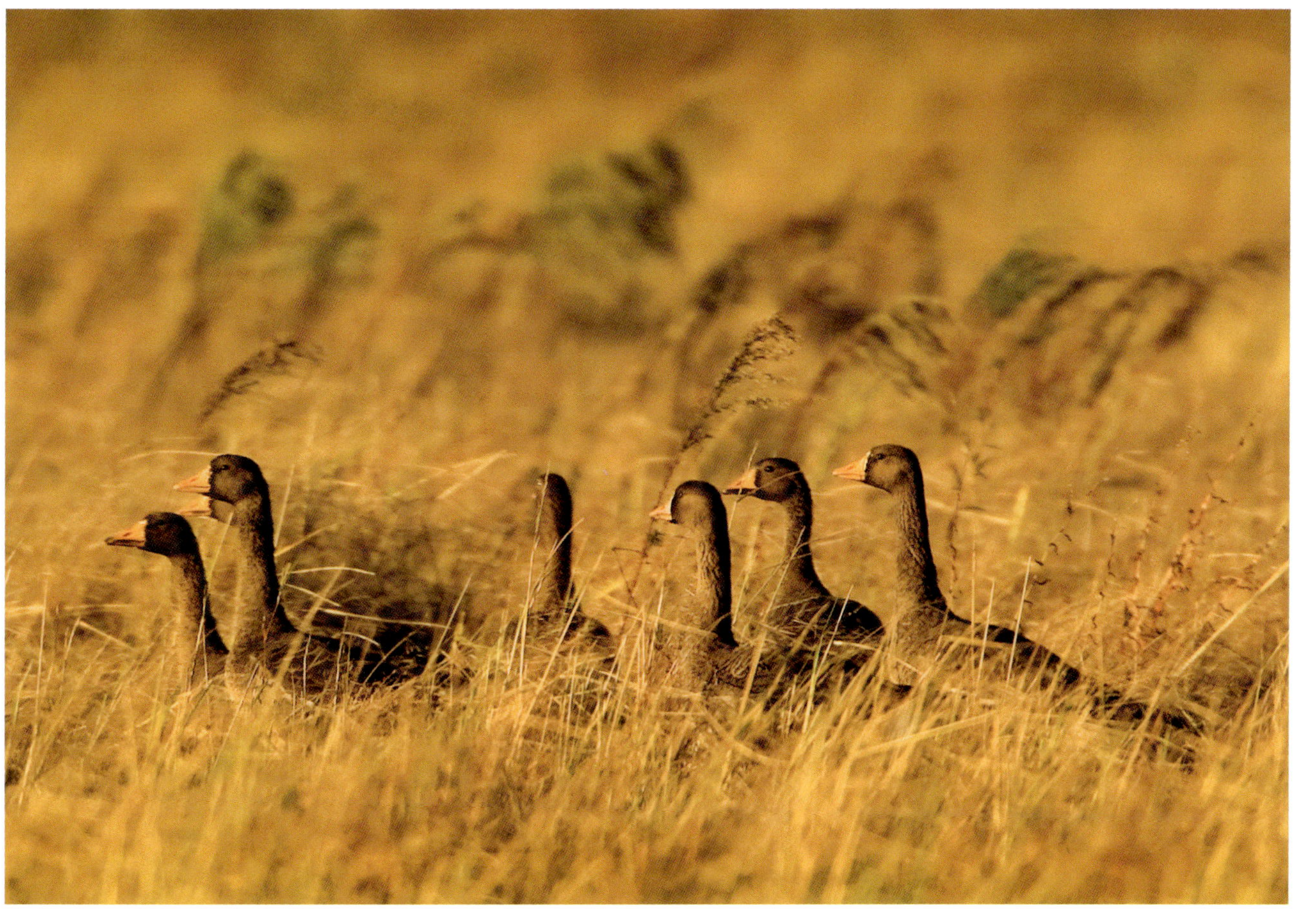

The sun was setting, and there was a golden glow on the marsh grass and on these specks. It looks like they were wondering from which way the predators were coming. (October 27, 2007)

CANADA GEESE

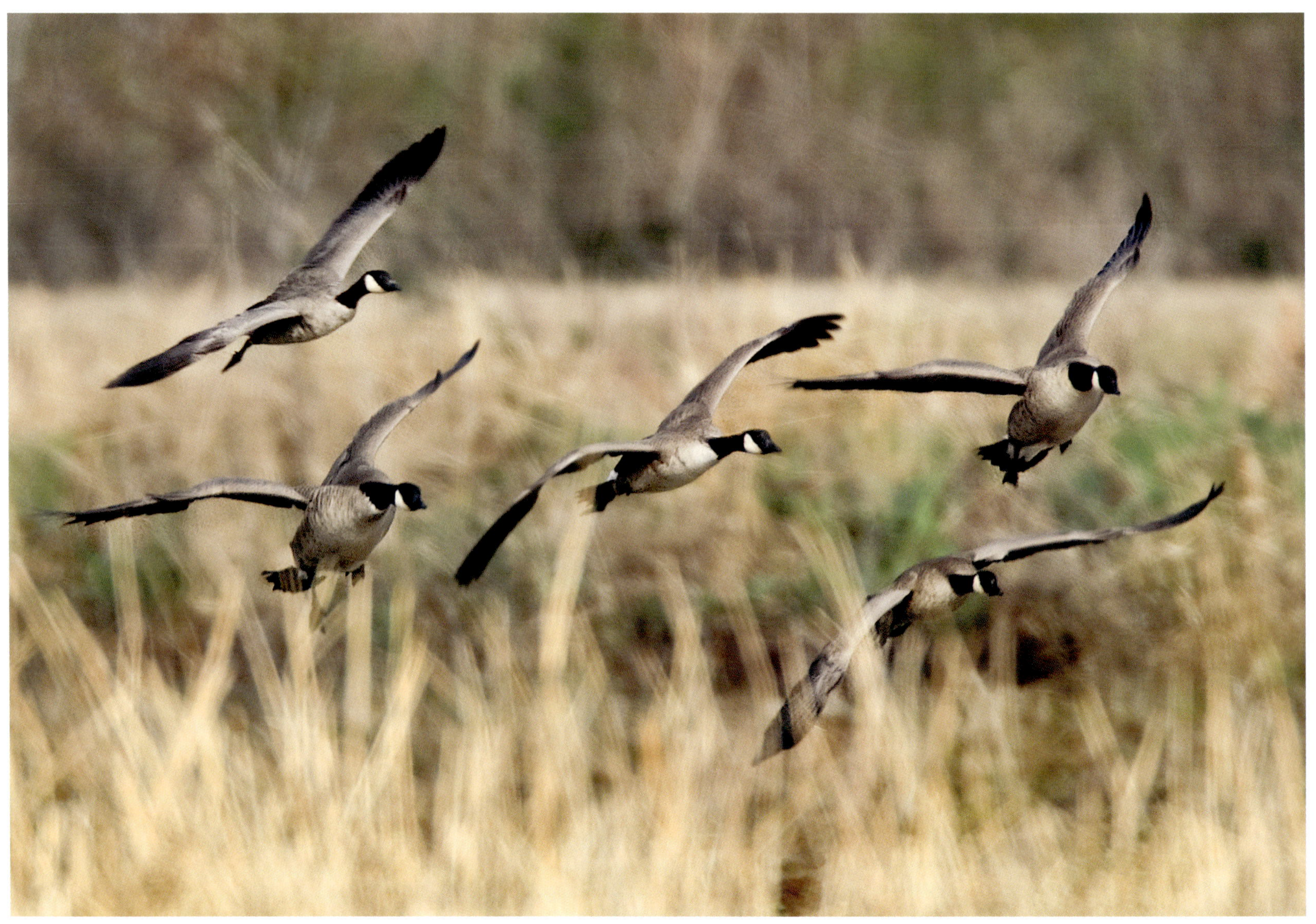

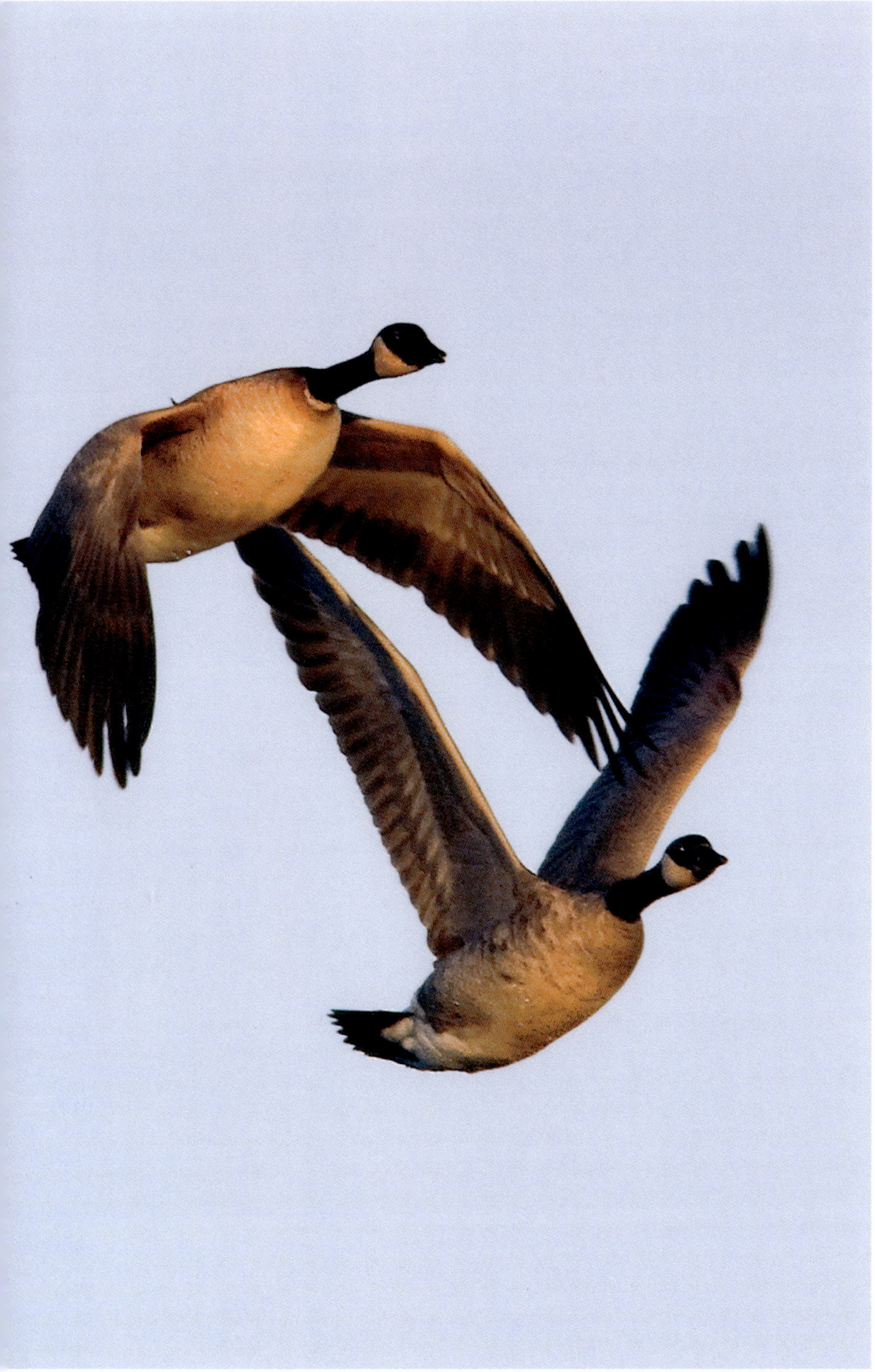

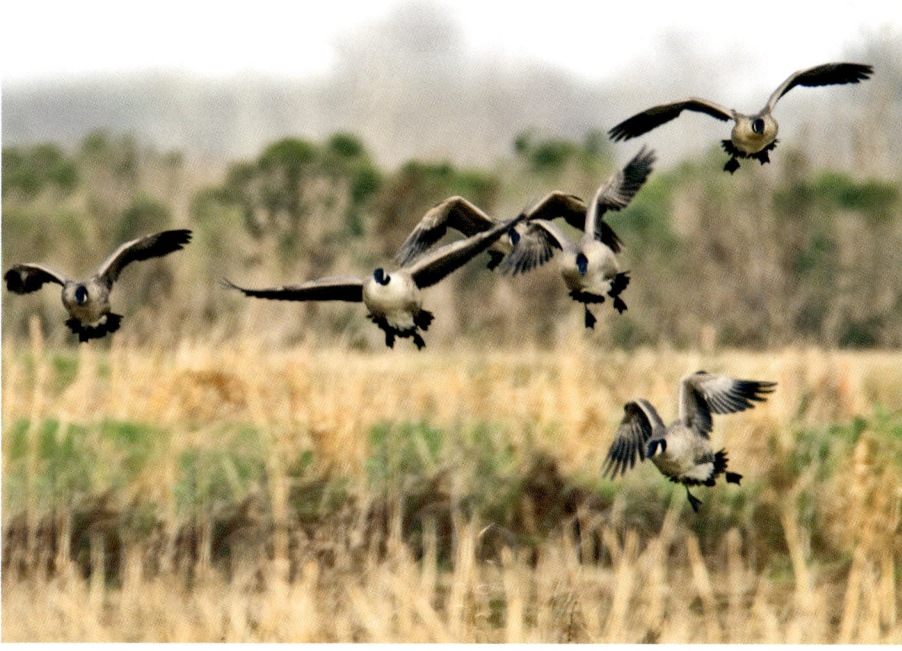

Above: These lesser Canadians are large birds with black necks and heads marked with bright, white cheek patches. (January 13, 2007)

Left: One Thanksgiving Day, I was out in the marsh and was just about to call it quits when these two Canadians flew overhead as if in a ballet. (November 22, 2007)

Facing page: Canada geese, usually called simply Canadians, are the most widespread and commonly-seen geese in North America. I can always tell when they are around because of their incredibly loud honking. (January 13, 2007)

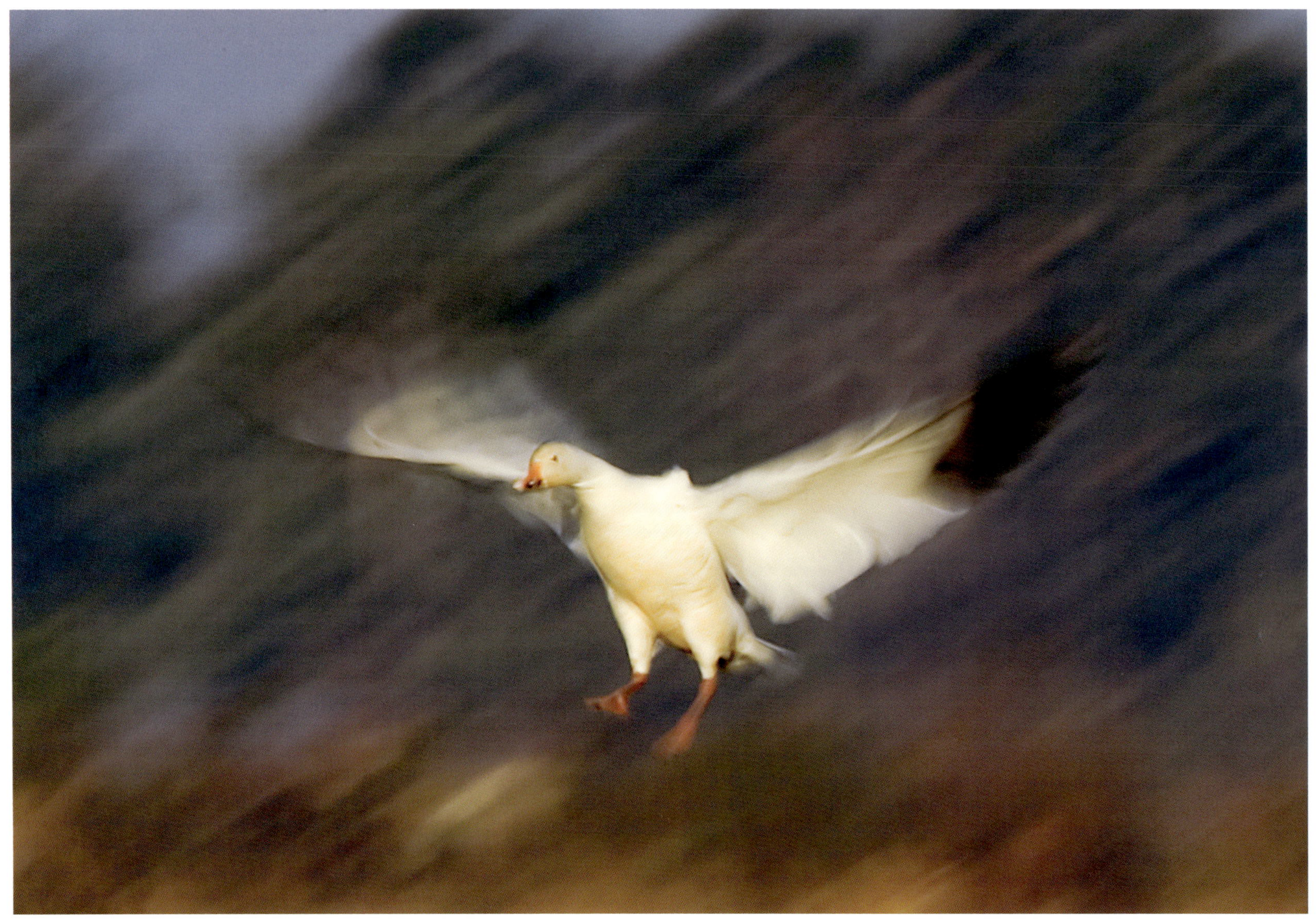

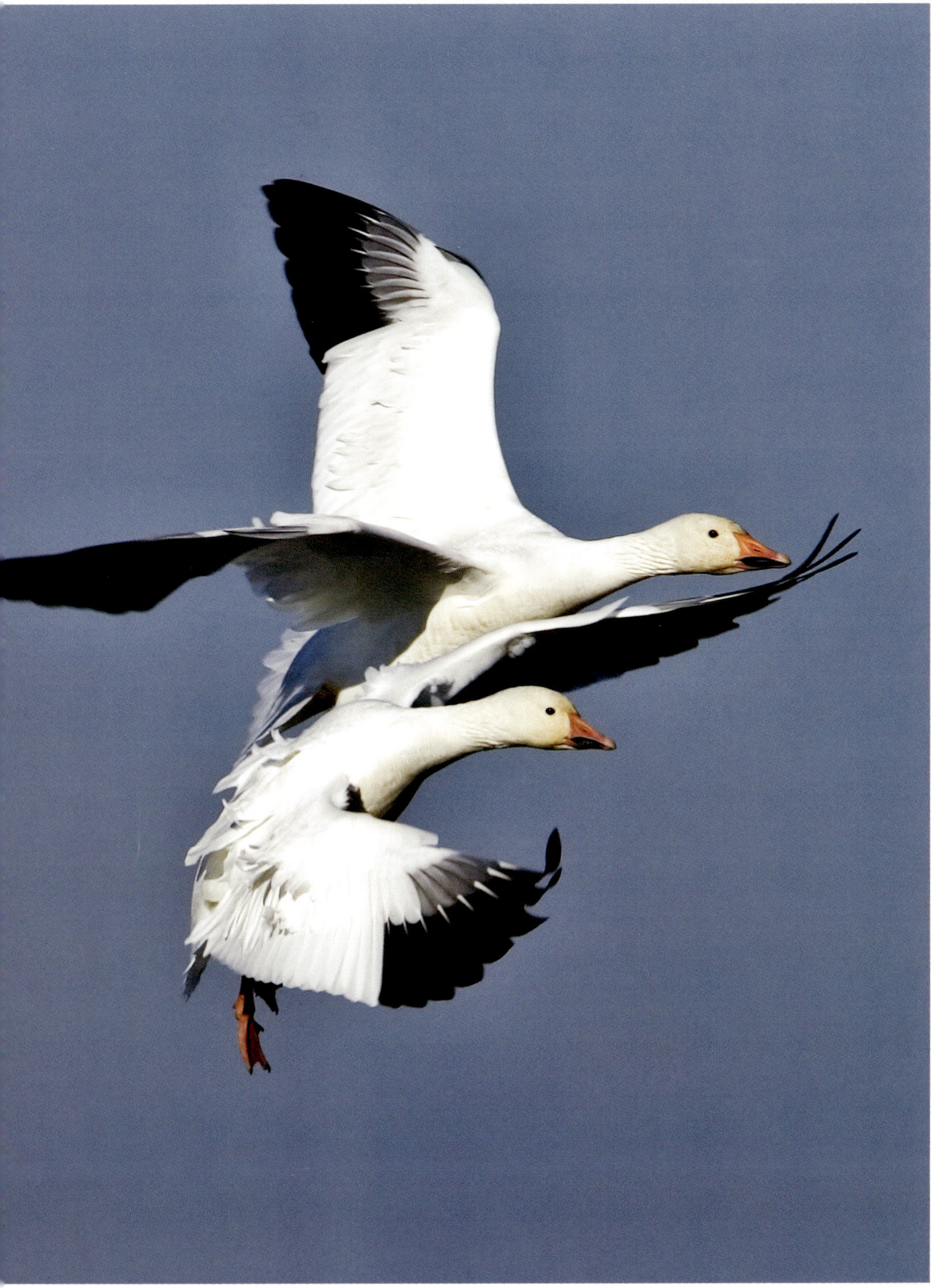

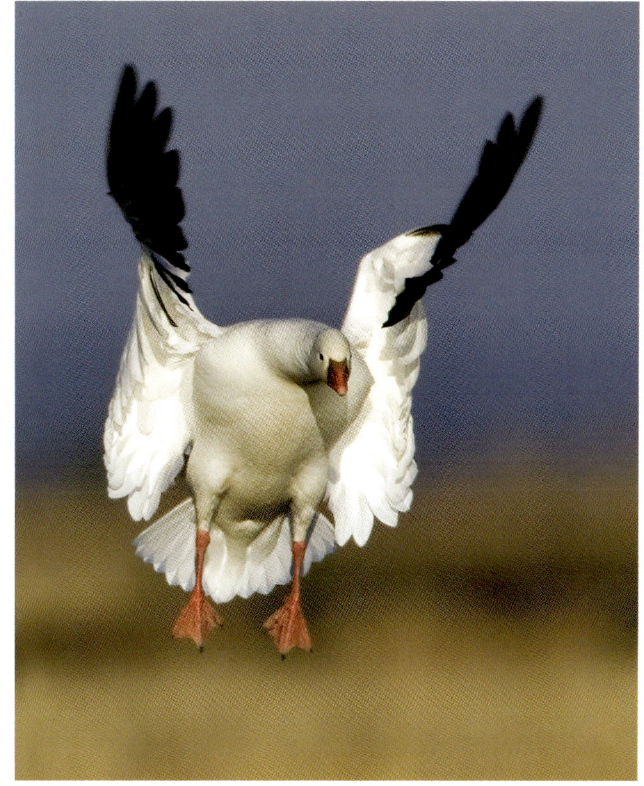

Above: I love this image. The large white body with the black-tipped wings is magnificent to see. (December 23, 2005)

Left: When I captured this image, I thought "yin and yang." (November 23, 2006)

Facing page: The snow goose travels south from the Arctic tundra in large, high-flying, noisy flocks that look like giant snowflakes. Among the white birds are also darker ones, which are usually referred to as blue geese. They are now recognized as a dark form, or a morph, of the snows. (November 23, 2006)

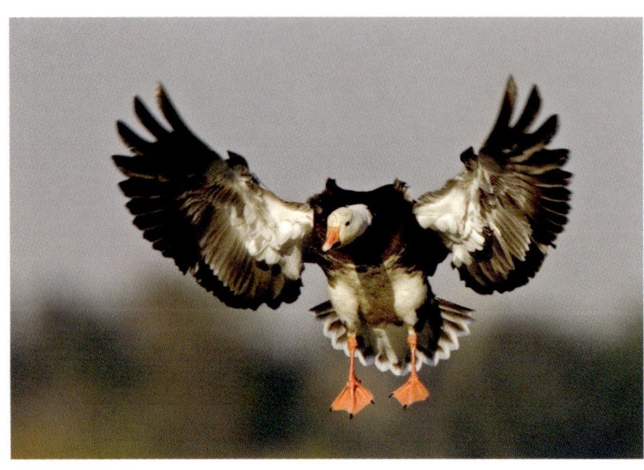

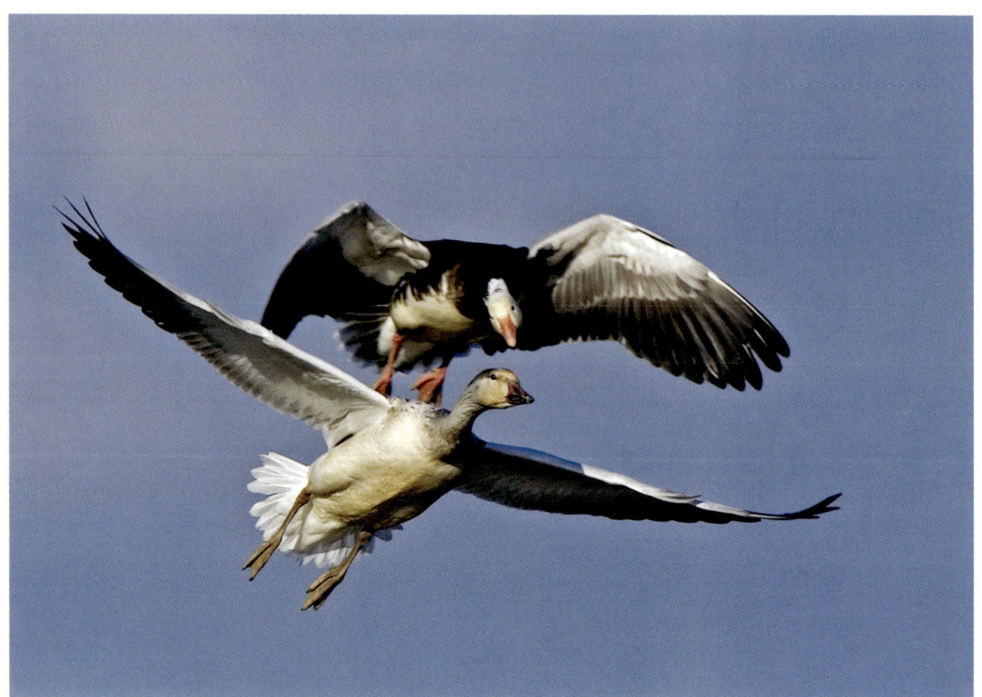

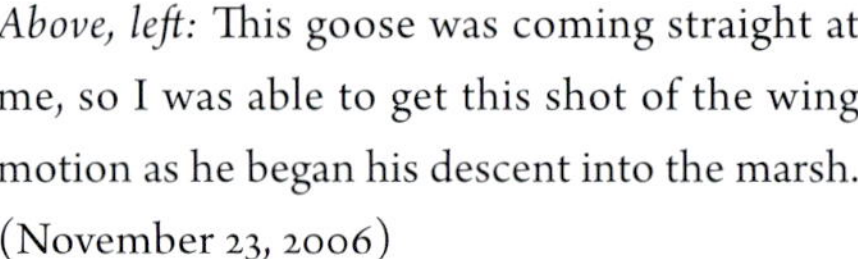

Above, left: This goose was coming straight at me, so I was able to get this shot of the wing motion as he began his descent into the marsh. (November 23, 2006)

Above, right: Lucky shot! A brown morph flying just above the white one. (November 23, 2006)

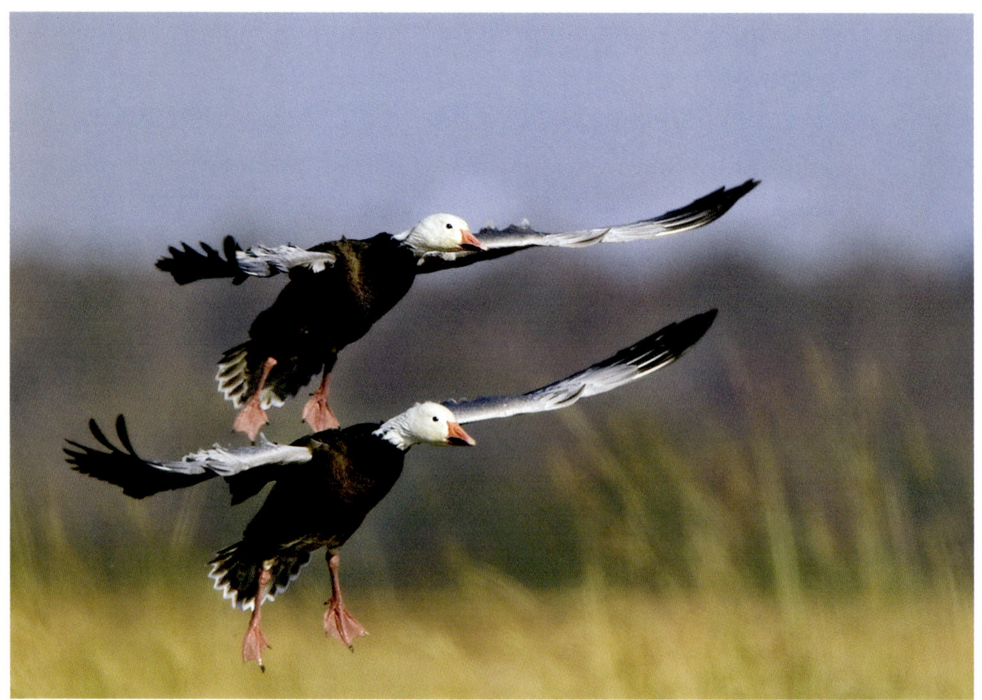

Right: Coming in for a landing, these two dark morphs looked like jets approaching a landing strip. Their wing feathers act much like an airplane's wings—the ruffling creates a drag, which regulates their landing into the wind. (December 23, 2005)

Facing page: There was a whole lotta honking going on as this flock of snows gathered in the marsh near Kaplan, Louisiana, on a very cold winter day. Notice the red band on the neck of the white snow goose. (December 30, 2005)

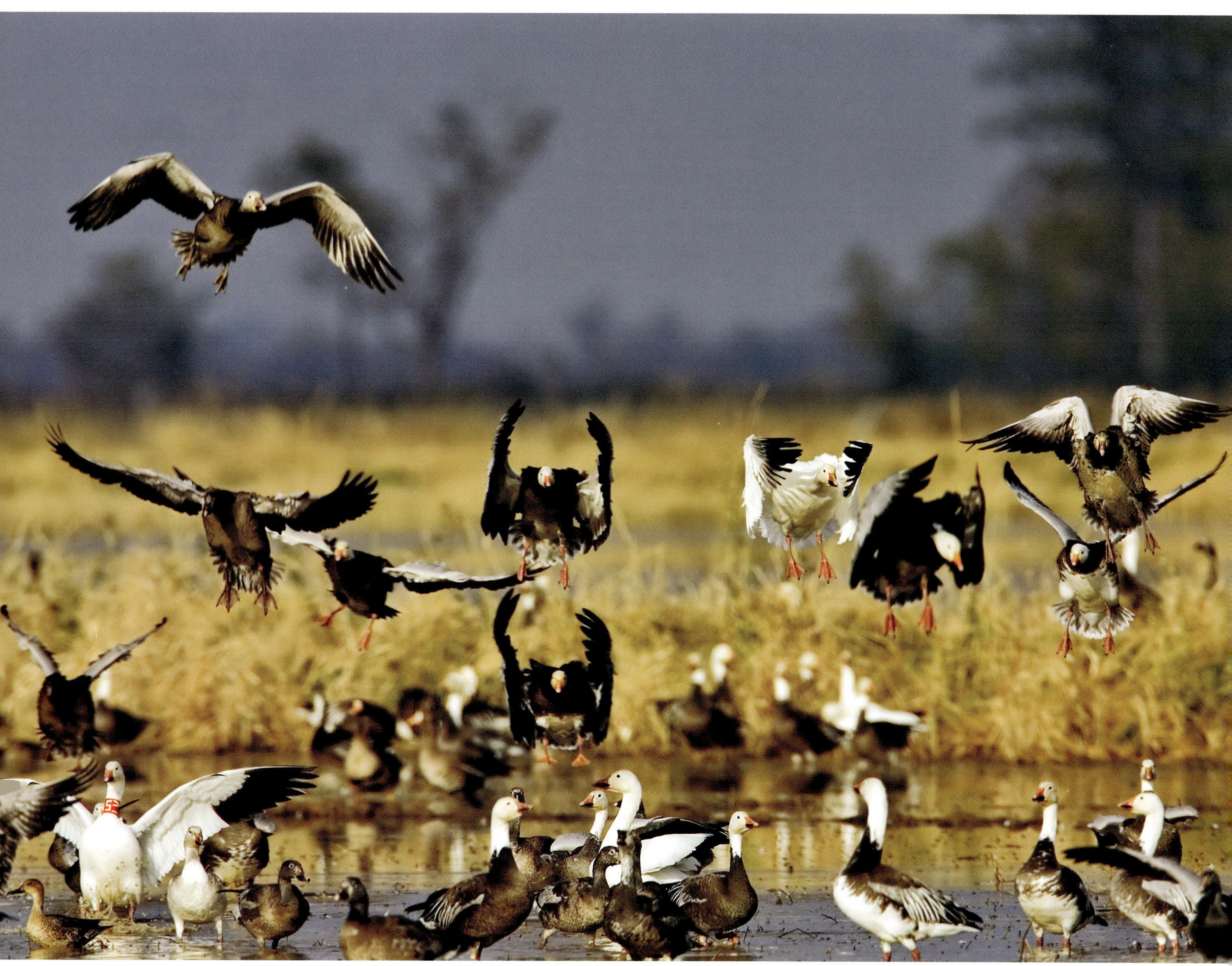

II

FROM FOOD FOR THE EYES TO SUSTENANCE FOR THE SOUL

MARCELLE BIENVENU

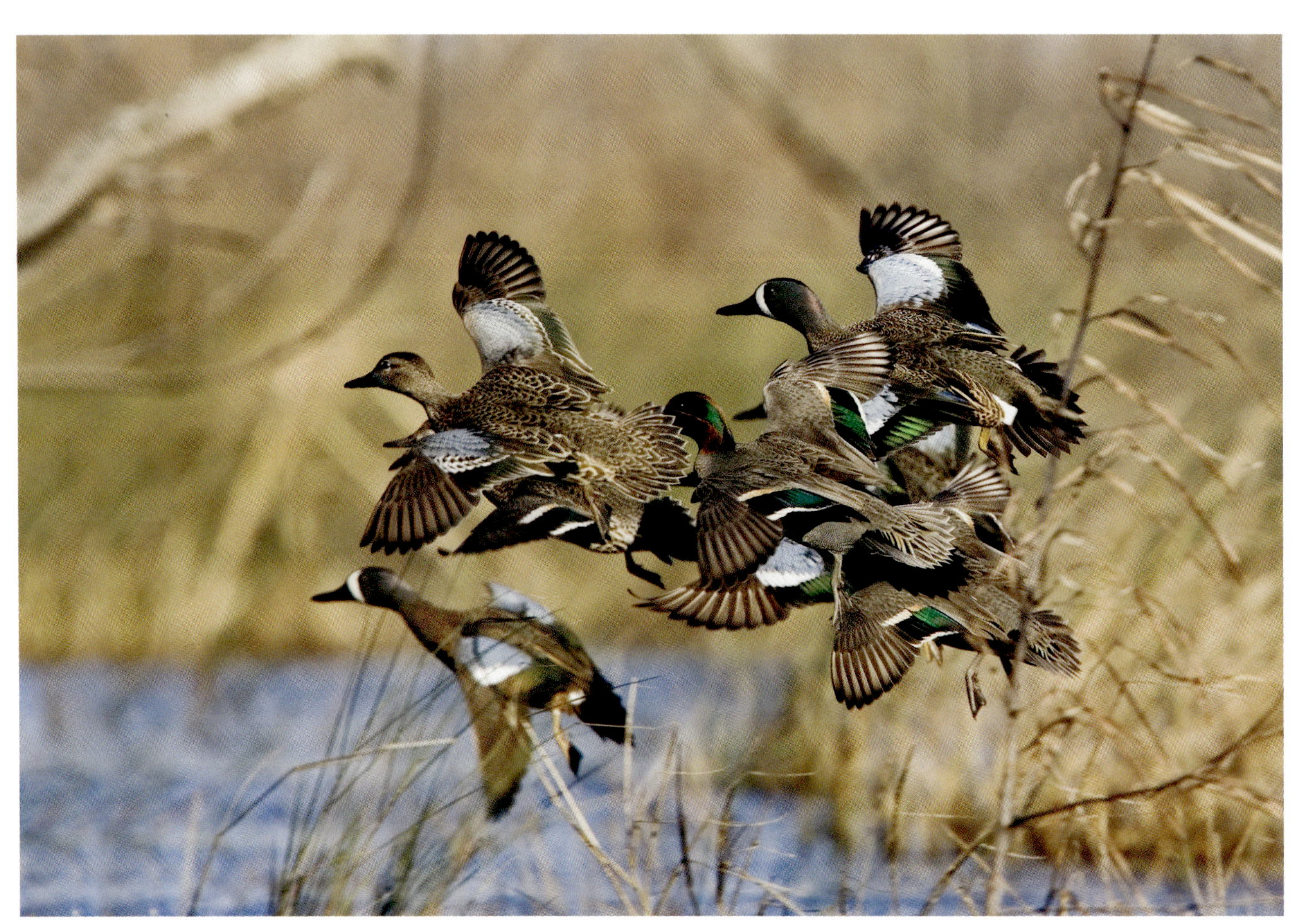

Charlie's stunning photographs capture the beauty and rich variety of birds, ducks, and geese that stop over in south Louisiana. For nature lovers and those with a passion for the outdoors, the photos are a feast for the eyes. Of course, game fowl also provide delicious physical nourishment as well. Cooking and eating the spoils of the hunt, either at the camp with pals or back home with family and friends, is one of the most important parts of the hunting ritual. It is no wonder that just about every hunter has his own repertoire of duck and goose recipes.

Louisiana has long been known as Sportsman's Paradise, and it's easy to understand why. Fish, shrimp, crabs, crawfish, and oysters abound in the thousands of miles of waterways that include bays, bayous, streams, lakes, and rivers. The Gulf of Mexico provides an even greater abundance of seafood.

But there is another reason why the state enjoys its nickname. Millions of ducks and geese from Canada fly along the Mississippi Flyway toward the Gulf of Mexico on their annual migration. During the fall and winter months, they spend their time in south Louisiana wetlands.

So it comes to pass that, as August arrives and bird hunting season approaches, Louisiana sportsmen are busily preparing for one of their favorite times of the year. Shotguns are cleaned and oiled, and probably a small fortune is spent on shells. The duck blinds are reworked to stand ready for that first day of hunting season. Decoys are retrieved from storage to be marked or tagged. Now it's just a matter of time before the hunters can go forth to their camps, get up before dawn, walk through the wind, rain, and mud, and then sit in a soggy, cold duck blind waiting for the birds to fly. For those who patiently sit and wait for the ducks and geese to come in, the reward is great.

I, too, am ready and waiting for the season to begin, because I enjoy the spoils of the hunt. I am quite fond of a roasted duck or a sausage and duck gumbo, or duck prepared in any number of ways for that matter. Growing up with a father and two brothers who were avid hunters, I learned at an early age the importance of a good hunting season. For instance, my family's Thanksgiving dinner has been for many years somewhat of a moveable feast—the reason being that the men in our family were such avid sportsmen that duck hunting season determined the day and time we sat down together to give thanks.

Many times we gathered on the Wednesday night before Turkey Day for our Thanksgiving repast so Papa and my brothers could head out in the wee hours the next morning to get to the blinds for an early hunt. Sometimes they didn't return for several days. But then there were times when they would depart on Wednesday and come back late Thanksgiving Day, and more often than not duck, instead of a turkey, was our bird of the day.

In fact, many of our meals throughout the winter season revolved around ducks or geese. There were roasted ducks, goose and oyster gumbos, duck and sausage jambalayas, as well as baked specklebellies, cooked long and slow and served with wild rice dressing and cauliflower au gratin.

Every year, when hunting season approaches, I recall how Papa so enjoyed going to his hunting camp with his sons and friends. He especially relished the duck and goose hunting season—fall and winter—in south Louisiana. I remember many times Papa rushing from his newspaper office, crashing through the kitchen door as though a herd of wild horses were after him, shouting with glee, "A cold front is on the way. Perfect duck-hunting weather!"

Mama, my siblings, and I knew the routine. Papa would go directly to the hall closet for his "grip." Mama would throw down mothball-scented blankets kept in an overhead storage closet. My brothers would gather shotguns and shells from the gun cabinet, while my sister and I would stuff gear into the tattered suitcase. By then, Papa was pulling on his long johns with one hand and stuffing shells and duck calls into the pockets of his hunting jacket with the other. Within five minutes, Papa was climbing into his old red pickup truck and, with a grin on his face, shouting, "I'll see you when I see you!"

That meant not to look for him until either he had shot his limit or the weather had turned into one of those clear bluebird days so common after a cold front moves through. It was awfully quiet in the kitchen after his departure. But upon his return (whenever it was), the hullabaloo returned as well. The slamming of the truck doors announced his arrival. He would crash through the kitchen door, this time proudly presenting his ducks or geese, a mess of bloody and feathered birds!

He would take his ducks or geese out to the backyard where he had a special area set up for cleaning fish and plucking waterfowl. Whistling while he worked and with an ice chest of cold beer at his elbow, he happily went about his task.

Then he and Mama would discuss the preparation. Sometimes the birds were slowly baked on a bed of onions, bell peppers, celery, and *tompinambours* (also known as sunchokes or Jerusalem artichokes), until they were tender and a wonderful gravy simmered in the pot. Other times there was a gumbo to be made, with the addition of *andouille* sausage and perhaps a handful of oysters thrown in at the end of the cooking time. On cold and rainy winter nights, there wasn't anything better!

There were also the times his hunting buddies and their families joined us at the table, and the children and ladies dutifully listened to the hunting tales. I remember thinking that one day I was going to go on a hunting trip to experience these adventures firsthand. I often wondered what was so magical about the times these men spent together in usually cold and primitive quarters.

I could only imagine where the hunting camp was located, although I knew that it was near Gueydan, a small community in Vermilion Parish. (In Louisiana counties are called parishes.) A seemingly desolate area lying between the marshes and the Gulf of Mexico, Vermilion Parish is actually a place of teeming wildlife—fish, crustaceans, alligators, and waterfowl. Long before the first brisk north wind of a cold front moves into these lush lowlands, flocks of green-winged teal, mallards, and pintails can be seen flying overhead in loose V formations. By the time the cold winter winds blow through south Louisiana, the ducks are joined by the honking blue and snow geese and specklebellies (fondly called the golden goose by hunters because of their delectable full, wide breasts) on the feeding grounds of the marsh.

To most males of south Louisiana, hunting is an important ritual of manhood. Even those who are not passionate about hunting will find themselves part of a group that heads to the camp on any given Friday afternoon during hunting season. In my book *Who's Your Mama? Are You Catholic? And Can You Make a Roux?* I asked a young man about coming of age in regards to hunting. I offer you his narrative.

There are several rites of passage that every young man in south Louisiana must go through en route to manhood. Eating raw oysters, killing a buck, and mastering the art of frogging are, of course, all part of that ritualistic experience. There is one ritual, however, that many consider to be the most sacred of all—cooking supper for a group of men at the camp. Unlike making love for the first time, if a south Louisiana boy fails this test, he many never be asked to do it again.

For example, I remember hearing a television anchorman ask his audience what they remembered about November 22, 1963. My answer immediately sprang to mind. That was the day that my Aunt Tootie made the best turtle sauce piquante that I've ever tasted. I was humbled when I heard the anchorman continue. November 22, 1963 was the day President John F. Kennedy was assassinated. I was a mere child then, so I forgave myself.

In case you haven't caught on to the food association, let me further explain.

One day a friend of mine came to my office to ask me if I wanted to go goose hunting with him at Shot's camp in Lake Arthur. I was excited about the proposition, but rather than envisioning graceful flights of specks and snows, I wondered what we would eat the night before the hunt. Being a stickler for details, I began to plan a menu. First, I scanned my brain for a reference point. Like a newly-made slab of hogshead cheese, a thought congealed in my mind.

I remember back to that cold December night when I crossed the sacred bridge that separated the men from the boys. It was at Goat Romero's camp in Kaplan. The men had gone out for an afternoon hunt leaving me, a fifteen-year-old boy, with two feathered French ducks with which to make supper. I poked around the ice chests and pantry, searching for familiar ingredients to make a gumbo. I knew from a reliable source that a meal at the camp is incomplete unless it includes at least four starches. With this in mind, I accompanied my duck, oyster, and andouille gumbo with rice, potato salad, hot French bread, and baked sweet potatoes.

After the last bites of the supper were washed down with a hearty red wine, I knew that the meal was a success and that I had entered the bonds of manhood, for Mr. Goat said out loud, "Son, tu n'est pas un petit bêbè. Tue es un grand homme maintenant." (You are no longer a baby, you are a grown man now.)

I have returned to his narrative many times when I've been asked to write a food feature on cooking wild fowl in hopes of being inspired despite not having participated in a real goose hunt.

I finally did realize a lifelong dream of actually "going to the hunting camp" thanks to a dear friend, Patrick Caffery, Jr., of New Iberia, Louisiana. He called me one year during the last week of goose hunting season and invited me to accompany him and his buddies on their last goose hunt of the year. I was ecstatic but a little uncomfortable.

"Patrick, are you sure those guys want me there? I don't want to infringe on what I have long perceived as a male-only adventure," I questioned.

"No, I talked with them all, and they said it was okay with them," he responded.

On the appointed day, Patrick picked me up in his pickup truck, not unlike Papa's of long ago, and stowed my canvas bag containing a pair of khaki pants, a denim jacket, a flannel nightgown, rubber boots, and heavy wool socks I pinched from my husband's closet. I owned no camouflage pants, hats, gloves, or jacket, but I felt certain we could pick some up on the way down to the camp if my buddy thought it was necessary.

We bumped along the rural back roads as the sun dipped in the western sky. Patrick gave me the latest weather forecast that promised ideal conditions for the next day (a cold front was moving in and a low cloud cover was expected). We stopped halfway to the camp for a cold beer. Patrick told me that this was part of the ritual. The beer went down easily, and I was soon just about as excited as my partner.

When we arrived at the camp, which was nothing more than two house trailers arranged together to form an L, a light mist was falling. I noted a couple of outbuildings that I later learned housed assorted hunting gear, decoys, and a washer-dryer combination.

When we emerged from the pickup, I saw several men laughing and drinking, what else but cold beer. I noticed also that a big butane burner with a large boiling pot was ready at hand. Victor Huckaby, the owner of Victor's Cafeteria in New Iberia (frequented by author James Lee Burke for home-style meals), greeted me with a firm handshake. A big burly fellow, he explained that my sleeping accommodations, complete with my own bathroom, were to be in the smaller of the two house trailers.

"And Marcelle, I'm washing the sheets now," he explained as he pointed to the sloshing washing machine in the shed.

I got out my flask of scotch, and soon we were all sitting around the boiling pot in which Victor was going to boil crawfish, some of the first of the season. I listened attentively while the men discussed shotgun shells, stalking deer, and the great weather forecast for the next day.

After our supper of boiled crawfish, I was shown to my room where my bed was made up with clean sheets (with a duck motif), the neat but tiny bathroom had clean towels, and the walls were adorned with lots of Playboy centerfolds. On a table Victor had laid out my hunting outfit, evidently scavenged from the closet. I had camouflage pants (large enough to fit a giant), a heavy insulated camouflage jacket, and some camouflage gloves. No hat, but I did find a khaki Pensacola Yacht Club cap in my suitcase, left from a previous adventure.

I fell asleep before my head hit the pillow. During the night I could hear a gentle rain on the roof, and barking Labs, in their kennel right outside my window, woke me at 3 a.m. I slept fitfully until 6:30 a.m. when Patrick knocked at my door bearing a mug of strong, hot coffee.

"Be ready in 30 minutes. We have to go eat breakfast," he said.

I brushed my teeth and combed my hair. No makeup and no perfume. Thank goodness I'm not vain.

In 35 minutes our group was seated at a small café in Gueydon chowing down on huge biscuits the size of cat heads, slabs of fried ham, eggs over easy, and buttery grits. Now that's what I call a big-girl breakfast! We made our Creole goodbyes as several camouflaged gentlemen helped themselves to more coffee and set up for a domino game.

It was cold and misty when we arrived at the rice fields. According to the men, this was ideal weather. I was given a bucket to sit on in a clump of grass where I blended in quite well with my camouflage outfit. In fact, I could hardly find myself once I got settled! And all I could think of for a minute or so was, please don't let me have to go to the bathroom. I didn't see anything that would serve as an outdoor toilet, and I couldn't bear the thought of having to take off all my clothes in the cold and wet!

Then the fun began. The hunters were strategically placed in other areas around the rice fields, and they began their calls. Soon there were specks, snows, blues, and all sorts of waterfowl flying overhead. I must say that I was giddy with excitement every time geese were spotted coming our way. And I was also quite impressed with the goose calling the guys did. In no time everyone had shot their limit. The Labs were sent to retrieve, and all of us stomped along the rice field levees to the pickup trucks where we had a cold beer while we relived the past two hours.

Now I understand the camaraderie of hunters! Sure, it was cold sitting on those buckets, but the exhilaration of the hunt was something that I had never experienced. Listening to the unique call of the specks as they flew overhead and the sound of shotguns was unforgettable. And there I was with the guys! I was a little tired and very cold, but hey, it was quite an adventure.

A little short of noon, we finished packing our gear, picked up the geese from the lady who cleans them, and headed home. One more stop, though, for a link of hot boudin tucked into a piece of crusty French bread and another cold beer!

And here then is a collection of recipes from Louisiana hunters and their families. The recipes are not exact, because everyone has his or her methods as well as personal taste. We hope that you will make them your own by experimenting with different herbs and spices and by using the recipes as a guideline to create your own.

Enjoy!

Krazy Al's Duck Gumbo

Contributed by **AL BROUSSARD**, Loreauville

Al is known far and wide for cooking for a crowd—anything from fried catfish to gumbo. Call your friends and invite them over for this delicious duck gumbo.

MAKES 7 ½ GALLONS OF GUMBO

3 roasting hens, each about 4 ½ pounds
4 wild ducks or 2 specklebelly geese
Tony Chachere's Original Creole Seasoning, garlic powder, and cayenne pepper to taste
2 ½ pounds all-purpose flour
1 quart vegetable oil
2 gallons hot water
5 pounds smoked sausage, cut crosswise into ¼-inch slices
2 pounds tasso, diced
20 yellow onions, peeled and chopped
18 green bell peppers, seeded and chopped
6 bunches green onions, chopped

Place hens and waterfowl in an electric roaster oven and bake at 250 degrees overnight (about 8 hours) or until the meat is falling off the bones. Reserve the broth. Debone the meat and cut into 1 ½-inch cubes. Season generously with Tony's seasoning, garlic powder, and cayenne pepper.

Combine the flour and oil in a large, heavy pot or Dutch oven over medium heat. Cook, stirring constantly, to make a very dark roux. Add the hot water, reserved broth, sausage, tasso, and chopped onions, bell peppers, and green onions. Simmer at a gentle boil until the roux is cooked, about 1 ½ hours.

Add the chicken and duck meat and enough water to fill the pot ¾ of the way up and simmer for about 1 hour. Adjust seasonings if necessary.

Serve in bowls with steamed white rice.

Chafing Dish Ducks

Contributed by **ANNETTE BARTON**, Wilson

This is a delightful appetizer to put out before dinner. Annette says both men and women love this preparation.

Ducks of your choice
Salt and pepper
Worcestershire sauce
Apples
Onions
Celery
Red wine

Preheat the oven to 350 degrees.

Clean and season ducks generously with salt, pepper, and Worcestershire sauce. Stuff each duck with an apple and an onion quarter and a 3-inch piece of celery. Close and secure the cavities with small skewers or toothpicks.

Place the ducks in a roasting pan and add ¼ cup dry red wine per duck. Bake, basting often with the pan drippings, until the ducks are so tender the meat is falling off the bones.

When tender, remove the ducks from the oven and cool. Discarding the stuffing, remove the meat from the bones and shred. Add the shredded duck to the pan drippings. (Add a little chicken broth if needed). Serve hot in a chafing dish with small party rolls or assorted party crackers.

A NOTE ON INGREDIENTS

Cajun Stuff-It Capsules are available at some grocery stores and supermarkets in south Louisiana or at www.cajunbrands.com. Cajun seasoning mixes, andouille, and many other specialty ingredients can be found at www.cajungrocer.com.

Baked Wood Duck

Contributed by **ANNETTE BARTON**, Wilson

Wood ducks are relatively small, but you can certainly substitute larger ducks, such as mallards. Annette suggests serving rice dressing, black-eyed peas, and squash casserole with the ducks. Oh, and maybe a salad and, of course, wine.

MAKES 6 SERVINGS

6 wood ducks, dressed, rinsed in cool water, and patted dry
Salt, cayenne pepper, and freshly-ground black pepper to taste
6 apples, seeded and quartered
2 onions, quartered
6 pieces celery (each about 3 inches long)
¼ cup bacon grease or olive oil (more if needed)
All-purpose flour
¼ cup chopped green bell peppers
¼ cup chopped red bell peppers
1 ½ cups chopped yellow onions
½ cup chopped celery
Low-sodium chicken broth
½ cup dry sherry or red wine
1 cup chopped green onions
1 pound white button mushrooms, wiped clean, stemmed, and sliced
¼ cup chopped parsley

Preheat the oven to 350 degrees.

Season the ducks generously with salt, cayenne pepper, and black pepper. Stuff the cavity of each duck with the quartered apples, onions, and celery in equal amounts. Secure the cavities with small skewers or heavy-duty toothpicks.

Heat the bacon grease or olive oil in a large, heavy pot or Dutch oven over medium-high heat. Coat each duck with flour and brown evenly on all sides in the hot grease. Add more bacon grease or olive oil as needed. Transfer the ducks to a platter and set aside.

Add about 2 tablespoons flour to the grease in the pan and reduce the heat to medium. Whisk constantly to make a dark brown roux.

Add the chopped bell peppers, onions, and celery. Cook, stirring, until they are soft and lightly golden, about 6 minutes.

Return the ducks to the pot and add enough chicken broth to cover them completely. Cover and bake until the ducks are tender, about 1 ½ hours.

Add the dry sherry or red wine, green onions, and mushrooms and cook until the ducks are very tender, about 30 minutes longer. Add the parsley and serve immediately.

Emergency Wood Duck Meal

Contributed by **JOE REGARD**, New Iberia

Joe says this is a great recipe when you don't have time to thaw frozen ducks, or if you just shot some teal and you want a meal in a hurry. Drink a couple of beers or some wine while the ducks cook.

MAKES 4 TO 5 SERVINGS

½ cup apple juice
3 medium-size onions, sliced
½ teaspoon chopped garlic
4 frozen wood ducks or 5 teals
Salt and cayenne pepper to taste

Put the apple juice, onions, and garlic in a 2-gallon pressure cooker. Season the ducks with salt and cayenne pepper. Add the ducks to the pressure cooker, put the cooker on medium heat, and cook until steam begins escaping, about 55 minutes.

Remove the ducks (they will be fully cooked) and serve with rice, cornbread, and sweet potatoes.

The Best Duck or Goose Recipe

Contributed by **JOE REGARD**, New Iberia

Joe says to follow the recipe exactly for the best results.

Duck or goose
Whole milk
Salt and other seasonings to taste
Peanut oil or cooking spray

Remove the duck or goose breasts from the bone and slice crosswise into ½-inch-wide pieces (a little thicker than a pencil). Soak the breasts in whole milk for two hours or longer in the refrigerator. Remove the breast pieces, pat dry, and season to your taste. Coat the pieces with peanut oil or cooking spray.

While the breast pieces are soaking up the seasoning, put a cast-iron skillet on a burner and turn the heat to high. Do NOT oil the skillet. After 3 minutes the skillet should be 400 degrees.

Have a spatula, a warm but not hot (about 100 degrees) plate, and enough aluminum foil to cover the plate at the ready.

You will cook these pieces only 1 minute and 40 seconds; so take careful note of the time. Put 8 to 10 pieces in the skillet. They will tend to stick a little, so turn to sear on all sides. Do not cook one second over 1 minute and 40 seconds. You may want to cook less after testing the first batch!

Remove from skillet, place on the warm plate, cover with foil, and let sit for 7 minutes.

Serve immediately with toothpicks or on a warm plate with the rest of the meal.

Harvey's Sausage-Stuffed Roasted Duck

Contributed by **HARVEY GAUTHIER**, St. Martinville

Harvey and his family own a grocery store in St. Martinville and specialize in making all kinds of fresh sausages, so it was natural to use fresh pork sausage in his duck recipe.

MAKES 4 SERVINGS

4 teals, dressed, rinsed in cool water, and patted dry
Salt and cayenne pepper (or your favorite Cajun seasoning mix) to taste
1 pound fresh pork sausage, cut into 3-inch pieces
1 medium-size yellow onion, peeled and quartered
3 tablespoons vegetable oil
1 ½ cups chopped onions
1 cup chopped green bell peppers
1 cup chopped celery
2 (14-ounce) cans chicken broth

Preheat the oven to 350 degrees.

Season the ducks, inside and out, with salt and cayenne pepper or Cajun seasoning. Stuff each duck cavity with a piece of sausage and a quarter of onion.

Heat the vegetable oil in a large, heavy pot or Dutch oven over medium-high heat. Add the ducks and brown evenly on all sides. Transfer the ducks to a platter and set aside.

Reduce the heat to medium and add the chopped onions, bell peppers, and celery and cook, stirring, until the vegetables are almost caramelized, about 15 minutes.

Return the ducks to the pot, add the chicken broth, and cover. Bake, turning the ducks several times in the gravy, until tender, about 2 hours. Adjust seasoning if necessary.

Remove the ducks and let sit for 5 to 10 minute before carving. Serve over steamed white rice with gravy.

Duck, Fresh Pork Sausage, and Mirliton Gumbo

Contributed by **CHEF PATRICK MOULD**, Lafayette

It's the crack of dawn, thirty-two degrees. A stiff north wind is blowing, and a light mist is falling. You ask why I have a smile of on my face? Duck season is open.

Understand that I'm not an avid hunter. I didn't grow up going out to the blind. I'm an occasional hunter but all it takes is once to be hooked. Part of the allure is just being miles away from so-called civilization and the hustle and bustle of city life. No cell phone, no television, and if you're lucky, you might get some guys to join in a poker game and enjoy some good sipping whiskey.

One of my all time favorite things to eat is teal in a sauce rouille, what Cajuns call a rusty gravy. Teals are the best eating ducks around, and the recipe is so simple. It is nothing more than a few teals, lightly seasoned and browned in a Dutch oven in a little oil. Add a little chopped onions, maybe some chopped garlic, and continue to brown the ducks. Add some water, continue to cook until the water has evaporated and the ducks and onions begin to brown, again basting the ducks throughout the cooking process. Add more onions and repeat the process over and over until the ducks are tender. What you end up with is this incredibly rich, dark gravy. This cooking method allows the true flavor of the ducks to shine, which is the ultimate compliment to any ingredient.

Another one of my favorite ways to enjoy duck is in a gumbo. This recipe has a little twist to it—adding some par-boiled mirlitons (or chayotes as they are sometimes called) into the gumbo. The crunch of the mirlitons is a nice compliment to the tenderness of the duck.

If you don't have a hunter in the family, don't worry, I've used domesticated ducks before. If you are using wild ducks, you'll need the equivalent of 5 to 6 pounds of duck for the recipe, and you'll have to cook the ducks longer to tenderize them. The length of time will depend upon the toughness of the ducks. You will also have to increase the chicken broth by 2 cups.

MAKES 6 TO 8 SERVINGS

1 domestic duckling (5 to 6 pounds) or wild ducks to equal 5 to 6 pounds, cut into serving pieces
2 tablespoons Worcestershire sauce
4 teaspoons Tony Chachere's Original Creole Seasoning
1 ½ teaspoons hot sauce
1 teaspoon granulated garlic
1 teaspoon granulated onion
2 quarts chicken broth (plus 2 cups if using wild ducks)
1 cup chopped onions
½ cup chopped celery
½ cup chopped bell peppers
1 tablespoon minced garlic
½ cup dark roux
3 bay leaves
1 pound fresh pork sausage
2 large mirlitons, peeled and cut into medium-size cubes and cooked until slightly tender in boiling water
¼ teaspoon salt
¼ cup sliced green onions
8 cups cooked rice

Season the ducks with the Worcestershire sauce, 3 teaspoons of Tony's seasoning, 1 teaspoon hot sauce, the granulated garlic, and granulated onion. Store in an airtight container in the refrigerator for 6 to 8 hours.

Preheat the oven to 400 degrees.

Place the ducks in a baking pan and roast for 45 minutes. Remove the ducks from the pan and drain off any fat that has accumulated.

In a large saucepan over medium heat, combine the chicken broth, half of the onions, the celery, and the bell peppers. Add the roux, the remaining hot sauce, the bay leaves, the unsliced fresh sausage, and the roasted ducks.

Bring to a boil, reduce the heat to medium-low, cover the pot, and simmer for 30 minutes.

Remove the cooked sausage, cool, and cut into ½-inch slices. Set aside.

Add the remaining onions, celery, bell peppers, and the garlic. Cover and simmer for an additional 30 minutes.

Add the sausage, mirlitons, and salt. Continue to simmer uncovered for 15 minutes. Cover and cook for 15 minutes longer. Stir in the green onions and serve over rice.

Roasted Teal

Contributed by **BURTON E. CESTIA, JR.**, New Iberia

Burt and his wife, Mary, along with their three children often spent Thanksgiving week at this duck camp near Gueydan when the kids were young.

"We rather roughed it, but it was always a lot of fun. Mary gathered whatever wildflowers were in bloom or used driftwood and branches she found on the property for the centerpiece on the table. We enjoyed roaming around the marshes during the day and marveled at the incredible sunsets, but cooking our Thanksgiving dinner together was always the highlight of our stay. This is one of our favorite duck recipes," says Burt.

MAKES 4 SERVINGS

4 teals, dressed, rinsed in cool water, and patted dry
Cavender's All Purpose Greek to taste
Tony Chachere's Original Creole Seasoning to taste
1 ½ Granny Smith apples, seeded and quartered
½ cup raisins
½ cup pecan halves
Olive oil
1 cup chopped green bell peppers
1 ½ cups chopped green onions
1 cup chopped celery
6 carrots, peeled and cut crosswise into 1-inch slices
8 to 10 small new potatoes
¼ cup chopped green onions, for garnish

OPTIONAL INGREDIENTS:
Ground cinnamon
Orange or mandarin slices
Walnuts

Season the ducks, inside and out, generously with the Greek seasoning and Tony's seasoning. Stuff the duck cavities with equal amounts of apples, raisins, and pecans. Place the ducks in a large, heavy pot or Dutch oven over medium heat and brown evenly on all sides, adding a small amount of olive oil to help the browning process depending upon the amount of fat on the ducks.

When the ducks are well browned, transfer them to a platter and set aside.

Reduce the heat to medium-low and add the bell peppers, green onions, and celery and cook, stirring, until the vegetables are translucent, about 8 to 10 minutes.

Periodically scrape the bottom of the pot lightly with a square-ended wooden spoon to loosen the browned bits on the bottom of the pot to create a dark brown gravy. A little water may be added periodically to help the process.

Return the ducks, breast down, to the pot and add enough water to cover completely. Bring to a gentle boil over medium-low heat and then cover the pot. Check occasionally and add more water for the loss caused by the cooking process. Turn the ducks when adding liquid. Cook until the ducks surrender and are fork tender, about 2 hours. Remember the ducks have to surrender! Add the carrots and potatoes and cook until they are fork tender.

Serve over wild rice. Garnish with the green onions.

Optional suggestions:

Add ground cinnamon to taste when seasoning the ducks. Rather than the apple, raisin, and pecan mixture, use orange or mandarin slices and walnuts.

Lane's Stuffed Duck Breasts

Contributed by **LANE LAMAIRE**, Lafayette

Lane's friends and family brag that these are fabulous as appetizers. Bet you can't eat just one!

MAKES 24 TO 32 PIECES

12 to 16 deboned duck breasts
1 (8-ounce) bottle Italian dressing
Onion powder, garlic powder, and seasoned salt to taste
1 (8-ounce) package cream cheese
1 small jar sliced pickled jalapeño peppers
1 pound thick bacon slices, cut crosswise in half
1 ½ cups grape jelly
1 ½ cups Stubb's Original Bar-B-Q Sauce

Cut the duck breasts into 2-inch cubes. Combine the duck pieces, Italian dressing, onion powder, garlic powder, and seasoned salt in a bowl. Cover and refrigerate for 2 days.

When ready to prepare, drain off the marinade mixture and reserve. Set aside.

With a sharp, pointed knife, make a slit in each of the duck cubes. Insert a slice of cream cheese into each slit. Place a slice of jalapeño in the center of each bacon slice and top with a duck cube with the slit facing down. Wrap the bacon around the duck cube and secure with a toothpick.

Arrange the bacon-wrapped duck cubes in a shallow bowl and pour in the reserved marinade, covering the duck cubes evenly.

Combine the grape jelly and the Stubb's in a bowl and whisk to blend. Set aside.

Heat the grill to medium-high. Place the bacon-wrapped duck cubes on the grill and turn often until the bacon is cooked and crisp and the duck breast is cooked to medium or medium-well, depending on personal taste.

Remove from the grill and baste with the jelly–barbecue sauce mixture. Serve immediately.

Teal Stuffed with Sausage

Contributed by **BRENDA SMITH**, Lafayette

MAKES 8 SERVINGS

8 teals, dressed, rinsed in cool water, and patted dry
Lemon-pepper seasoning
Seasoned salt
Accent Flavor Enhancer or MSG
4 links venison and pork sausage
Cajun Power Garlic Sauce
Worcestershire sauce
Lea and Perrins Marinade for Chicken
½ cup corn oil
4 medium-size onions, chopped
1 celery rib, chopped
2 medium-size green bell peppers, seeded and chopped
2 garlic cloves, chopped
4 links duck and chicken sausage, cut crosswise into 2-inch slices

Season the teals with lemon-pepper seasoning, seasoned salt, and Accent. Store in an air-tight container and refrigerate overnight or 8 hours.

When ready to cook, remove the teals from the refrigerator.

Cut each venison and pork sausage link in half lengthwise. Insert a half link of each of the sausages in the cavity of each teal. Sprinkle the teals generously with the Cajun Power sauce, Worcestershire sauce, and Lea and Perrins marinade.

Heat the corn oil in a large, heavy pot or Dutch oven over medium-low heat. Add the teals and brown evenly on all sides, turning often, for 20 to 30 minutes. Transfer the teals to a platter and set aside.

Add the onions, celery, bell peppers, and garlic. Cook, stirring, until they are soft and golden, about 8 to 10 minutes. Return the teals to the pot and add the duck and chicken sausage, arranging them in between the teals. Add enough water to just cover the teals.

Cover and simmer until the ducks are tender, about 1 ½ hours, adding more water if the gravy gets dry.

Serve warm.

Spoonbill Breast Roll-Ups

Contributed by **ODON L. "DONNIE" BACQUE**, Lafayette

Many people don't eat spoonbill, scaup, or other non-quality ducks, because they believe there is no way to make them tasty. This recipe will make a believer out of the biggest skeptic and can be used with "quality" ducks as well.

Duck breasts based on number of guests

2 tablespoons each of finely chopped onions, green bell peppers, and celery per duck

1 tablespoon pepper jelly per duck

Sliced jalapeños

Bacon slices cut in half lengthwise

Breast a spoonbill or other duck, removing all the skin. Split the 2 breasts in half, then cut a pocket in each of the 4 halves. One duck will make 4 roll ups, and I serve 2 rollups per person.

Put the onions, bell peppers, and celery in a small bowl and add the pepper jelly. Heat the mixture in the microwave on high for 1 minute; mix well.

Open the duck breast pocket that you made and stuff with one jalapeño slice, a teaspoon of the vegetable mixture, and another jalapeño slice. Roll up the breast, wrapping ½ slice of bacon around it, securing with a toothpick. Cook on a barbecue pit on high heat until rare to medium-rare. Do not overcook.

Remove from the grill, cut the rollups into thirds, and serve with Jezebel sauce.

Jezebel Sauce

MAKES 3 CUPS

1 cup apple jelly

1 cup pineapple-orange marmalade or pineapple preserves

1 (6-ounce) jar prepared mustard

1 (5-ounce) jar prepared horseradish

¼ teaspoon pepper

Beat the apple jelly in a mixing bowl at medium speed with an electric mixer until smooth. Add the remaining ingredients and beat at medium speed until blended. Use immediately or store in an airtight container in the refrigerator for up to 1 week.

Fried Ducks or Geese

Contributed by **ODON L. "DONNIE" BACQUE**, Lafayette

Donnie says that he and his pals have enjoyed fried turkeys for years and thought that ducks or geese might also benefit from this preparation.

Ducks or geese

Cajun Injector Creole Garlic Marinade

Apples, oranges, or onions

Cajun seasoning

Vegetable or peanut oil

Clean and rinse ducks (or geese) in cool water inside and out. Pat dry with paper towels. Inject with Cajun Injector Creole Garlic Marinade.

Stuff the cavity with a quarter of an apple, orange, or onion. Season the outside well with your favorite Cajun seasoning.

Heat vegetable or peanut oil in an electric fryer to 375 degrees. Put the birds in the fry basket and carefully lower the basket into the hot oil. Fry for 5 minutes per pound. Remove from the hot oil and let rest for a few minutes before carving.

Pot Roasted Ducks

Contributed by **ODON L. "DONNIE" BACQUE**, Lafayette

Donnie, who hunts mainly in the Pecan Island area in southwestern Louisiana, says that you can use any "quality" duck, such as teal, mallard, pintail, or wood duck for this recipe.

MAKES 6 TO 8

5 to 6 ducks (depending on size), dressed, rinsed in cool water, and patted dry
4 bacon slices, cut into 1-inch pieces
1 cup equal parts chopped bell peppers, onions, and celery
Cajun Stuff-It Capsules
Cajun Injector Creole Garlic Marinade
Cajun seasoning (your favorite)
Apples, oranges, or onions (quartered for stuffing cavity)
Vegetable oil
Flour
Additional bell peppers, onions, and celery (optional)
Mushrooms (optional)

Preheat the oven to 300 degrees.

Make a slit along the breastbone of each duck and insert a piece of bacon, a tablespoon of the vegetable mixture, and 1 or 2 of the Cajun Stuff-It Capsules, then seal with another piece of bacon. Repeat on other side.

Inject the ducks with the Creole Garlic marinade and then season with Cajun seasoning mix. Stuff the cavity of each duck with a quarter of an apple, orange, or onion.

Put about 2 tablespoons oil in the bottom of a large, heavy pot (preferably cast-iron) or Dutch oven. Put the ducks in the pot, breasts down, cover, and bake for 1 hour. Turn the ducks over and cook, covered, for 1 hour longer.

Remove the ducks and thicken gravy by adding a tablespoon or two of flour, whisk to blend, and stir until the gravy thickens to your taste. You can also add more bell peppers, onions, and celery to the gravy for more flavor and texture. Donnie happens to be a gatherer of chanterelle mushrooms, which he likes to add to the pot, but you can use canned or fresh stems and pieces of white button mushrooms.

Serve over rice with baked sweet potatoes as a side.

Charlie III Duck Breasts

Contributed by **CHARLES HOHORST III**, Lafayette

Charlie III is the son of the photographer of this book. He swears that this recipe is one of the best around. He's right!

MAKES 12 SERVINGS

12 deboned duck breast (any species will do)
1 (16-ounce) bottle Dale's Seasoning
1 pound thick bacon slices
1 pound cream cheese or brie (or your favorite cheese), cut into thin slices
Sliced jalapeno peppers or sliced peppers of your choice
Toothpicks
Salt and cayenne pepper to taste

Marinate the duck breast in Dale's Seasoning for 2 days in the refrigerator. (If Dale's is not available, use your favorite marinade.)

Lay three bacon strips close together on a platter. Place one duck breast at the end of the bacon strips. Place a piece of cheese and a few pepper slices on top of duck breast. Take another duck breast and place on top of peppers and cheese. Roll the bacon until the duck breast becomes a roll. Secure with toothpicks.

Sprinkle the roll with salt and cayenne pepper. Prepare the grill for low-to-medium heat. Place the rolls on direct heat and cook for about 20 to 30 minutes. Be sure to cook all sides. Serve immediately.

Smoked Mallards

Contributed by **CHARLES HOHORST III**, Lafayette

MAKES 6 TO 8 SERVINGS

2 to 4 whole dressed mallards, DO NOT REMOVE SKIN
Cajun Injector Creole Garlic Marinade
Konriko Creole Seasoning
Pure cane syrup

With an injector syringe, inject ½ ounce of the marinade into each breast. Season the mallards generously with the Creole seasoning. Place the mallards, breast-side up, in a water smoker with hickory wood chips or Tabasco wood chips. Smoke for 1 hour. Baste the breasts with the syrup, and then smoke the mallards for an additional 1 to 1 ½ hours.

Kirk's Duck Glacé

Contributed by **KIRK SIEBER**, New Iberia

Kirk is a fisherman, a hunter, and a person who enjoys cooking whatever he brings in from the water or the woods. He experimented with the glacé—a dish usually made in south Louisiana using chicken, beef, veal, or pork—made with duck. Delicious! The gelled duck meat makes a great party offering to serve with party crackers or toasted French rounds.

MAKES 1 LARGE MOLD OR SEVERAL SMALL ONES

8 large ducks, such as mallards or 3 specklebelly geese
Cajun seasoning
1 cup water
2 tablespoons vegetable oil
½ cup finely chopped onions
½ cup finely chopped green bell peppers
½ cup finely chopped celery
4 garlic cloves, finely chopped
4 envelopes Knox gelatin
2 chicken bouillon cubes
1 tablespoon Kitchen Bouquet or other browning sauce (optional)
2 tablespoons minced fresh parsley leaves (optional)

Preheat the oven to 350 degrees.

Season the ducks generously with Cajun seasoning. Place the ducks in a large roasting pan and add the water. Cover and bake until the ducks are very tender, about 3 hours.

Remove the ducks from the oven and cool completely. Reserve the broth from the roasting pan and set aside. Debone the ducks and either shred the meat or chop it finely.

Place the duck meat in a heavy, deep saucepan with 4 cups of the reserved broth over low heat. If you don't have 4 cups, add enough chicken broth to make 4 cups total.

While the duck cools, heat the vegetable oil over medium heat and add the onions, bell peppers, celery, and garlic. Cook, stirring, until the vegetables are soft and lightly golden, 6 to 8 minutes. Add this mixture to the duck meat and broth.

Increase the heat to medium, bring the mixture to a gentle boil, and simmer for 15 minutes. Add the gelatin and bouillon cubes and season to taste with more Cajun seasoning. If using, add the Kitchen Bouquet, for color, and the parsley.

Pour the mixture into a large, lightly oiled 4-cup mold or several smaller ones. Cover and chill until the mixture sets, 3 to 4 hours.

When ready to serve, remove the glacé from the mold and serve chilled with party crackers or toasted French rounds.

Note: Once the glacé has set, it can be covered securely with plastic wrap or aluminum foil and frozen. When ready to serve, allow the glacé to defrost before unmolding.

Johnny Beyt's Pot Roasted Ducks with Turnips

Contributed by **JOHN L. "JOHNNY" BEYT III**, New Iberia

Johnny is not only an avid sportsman, he is also a great cook and bon vivant. Here he shares one of his duck recipes and the recipe for his favorite drink.

Says Johnny, "You will find that this is a great way to spend a long, cold, wet afternoon at the camp. It is recommended that when one begins preparations for this meal an Old Fashioned should be served. Also on occasion, during the cooking process one should renew the Old Fashioned being careful not to over serve."

Old Fashioned

MAKES 1 SERVING

1 old fashioned glass
Ice
Bourbon
Simple syrup
Maraschino cherries and their syrup
Angostura bitters
Orange slices

Fill the glass to the brim with clear, crushed ice. (Do not use refrigerator ice.)

Add bourbon of choice (a good blend Crown Royal works great) until the glass is a little over half full. Add 2 teaspoons simple syrup and 1 teaspoon of the syrup in a jar of maraschino cherries. Add 2 dashes of Angostura bitters. Squeeze the juice of a slice of orange into the drink, add the orange slice, and muddle with a spoon, stirring for 30 to 45 seconds. Garnish with a maraschino cherry on a stem.

Sip and RELAX!!

Pot Roasted Ducks with Turnips

MAKES 4 SERVINGS

2 large ducks (mallards) or 4 small ducks (teals), skin on
Salt and cayenne pepper to taste
¼ cup vegetable oil
4 medium-size onions, coarsely chopped
2 celery ribs, finely chopped
1 green bell pepper, seeded and chopped
2 to 3 garlic cloves, chopped
⅓ cup dark roux
1 cup dry red wine (more or less to taste)
5 medium-size turnips, peeled

Season the ducks with salt and cayenne pepper. Heat the oil in a large, heavy pot (preferably cast-iron) or Dutch oven over medium-low heat. Add the ducks. You want to slowly brown the ducks evenly on all sides, keeping the pot covered, but turning the ducks often for about 1 ½ to 2 hours. The idea is to use enough heat to cause the ducks to stick to the bottom of the pan but not cause burning.

Once the ducks are very brown, add the onions, celery, bell pepper, and garlic. Cook, stirring occasionally, until the vegetables are soft and almost caramelized, 20 to 30 minutes.

Add 2 to 3 cups of water and stir with a wooden spoon to loosen any browned bits on the bottom of the pot. (You should have a very dark gravy at this point.)

Add the roux and stir to dissolve. Cover and reduce the heat to very low. Cook until the ducks are very tender. (This may take a few more hours.) Once the ducks are tender, transfer to a platter, cool slightly, and debone.

Transfer the duck meat back to the pot and add the wine and turnips. Simmer, uncovered, for 10 to 15 minutes. Cover the pot and cook over low heat. Check the turnips every 10 minutes or so until a fork pierces the turnips easily. Season with salt and pepper. Remove the turnips with a slotted spoon and arrange in a serving bowl.

Serve the duck with this wonderful gravy over rice and the turnips on the side. You will notice that the turnips pick up the flavor of the duck.

Roast Teal with Jalapeño Sausage

Contributed by **BENJAMIN L. LANDRY**, St. Martinville

Ben says this is not only easy, but also awesome, and doesn't require a whole lot of attention while the ducks are cooking. The sweet potatoes in the cavity will have an incredible flavor as well! Kick back, enjoy a few brews, and discuss your hunt while the ducks cook.

Ben and his buddies hunt in a flooded timber area just outside the Atchafalaya Basin.

MAKES 4 TO 6 SERVINGS

4 to 6 teal, dressed, cleaned, and patted dry
3 tablespoons olive oil
Cajun Injector Creole Butter Marinade
4 to 6 sweet potatoes, whole, uncooked, and unpeeled
3 tablespoons vegetable oil
2 medium-size yellow onions, chopped
2 medium-size green bell peppers, seeded and chopped
2 celery ribs, chopped
1 ½ pounds fresh pork sausage with jalapeños, cut into 3-inch pieces
1 to 1 ½ cups water or chicken broth

Preheat the oven to 350 degrees.

Rub the teals evenly with the olive oil. Inject each bird with several injections of the Creole Butter marinade. Stuff the cavity of each teal with a sweet potato and set aside.

Heat the vegetable oil in a large, heavy oven-proof pot or Dutch oven over medium-high heat. Add the onions, bell peppers, and celery and cook, stirring, until soft and golden, about 8 to 10 minutes. Remove the pot from the heat.

With a spoon, move the vegetables to the sides of the pot and arrange the teals in the center. Arrange the sausage on top of the birds, add the water or broth, cover the pot, and transfer to the oven.

Bake until the teal are fork-tender, about 2 hours. Remove from the oven and let the birds rest for a few minutes.

Serve with rice and hot French bread.

Rocky and Brenda's Goose

Contributed by **ROCKY AND BRENDA LANDRY**, Lafayette

Rocky's family has been operating Don's Seafood & Steakhouse in downtown Lafayette, Louisiana, since 1934. Whenever Rocky can get away from his hectic work, he enjoys fishing at Grand Isle or hunting in the marshes of south Louisiana. This is only one of his delicious goose recipes.

MAKES 4 SERVINGS

1 goose (a specklebelly if possible), dressed, rinsed in cool water, and patted dry
Salt and cayenne pepper or your favorite Cajun seasoning to taste
1 Granny Smith apple, peeled, cored, seeded, and sliced
1 large onion, peeled and sliced
1 orange, peeled, seeded, and cut into sections
3 cups Amaretto
½ cup water

Season the goose, inside and out, with salt and cayenne pepper or Cajun seasoning. Stuff the cavity with the sliced apples, onions, and oranges. Put the goose in a large roasting pan and bake in a 500-degree oven, breast up, for 30 minutes.

Remove from the oven, reduce the oven temperature to 350 degrees, and pour in the Amaretto and water. Cover and bake (basting occasionally with the pan juices) until the goose is tender and the meat is falling off the bone, about 1 ½ to 2 hours.

Remove from oven, debone the goose, return the meat to the pan (discarding the bones), and heat through. Serve hot.

A Wild Gumbo

Contributed by **KENNETH M. HENKE**, Lafayette

This recipe was originally created to use chukar and pheasant, but Kenneth suggests that you can use anything from Cornish hens, to wild ducks or chicken—whatever you have on hand. As with other recipes, you can make it your own, seasoning it to suit your own taste buds.

MAKES 12 SERVINGS

1 cup all-purpose flour

3 quarts water or chicken broth

½ cup vegetable oil

1 roasting chicken (about 4 ½ pounds), cut into serving pieces and skinned

2 Cornish hens (each about 1 ½ pounds), cut into serving pieces, skinned

2 medium-size onions, chopped

1 garlic clove, minced

2 medium-size green bell peppers, seeded and chopped

4 celery ribs, chopped

1 tablespoon filé powder

1 teaspoon Zatarain's Concentrated Shrimp and Crab Boil (or 1 teaspoon cayenne, 1 bay leaf, and 1 teaspoon dried thyme)

1 tablespoon salt

1 ½ teaspoons freshly ground black pepper

½ pound tasso or smoked ham, coarsely chopped

½ cup finely chopped green onions (scallions)

8 sprigs flat-leaf parsley, stemmed and chopped

To make a dry roux, heat a large, cast-iron skillet over medium-high heat. Add the flour and stir constantly with a wooden spoon from the middle of the skillet outward until the color of the roux is the color of cinnamon, about 30 minutes.

Transfer the roux to a bowl and set aside. (The roux can be made in advance and stored in an airtight container in the freezer.)

Bring the water or chicken broth to a boil in a large, heavy pot over medium-high heat. Then reduce the heat to medium-low and simmer.

Heat the vegetable oil in a large, heavy skillet over medium-high heat until it is hot but not smoking. Reduce the heat to medium and brown the poultry, in batches, until golden, about 3 minutes per side. Drain the meat on paper towels and add it to the simmering water or broth.

Drain all but 3 tablespoons of the oil from the skillet. Add the onions, garlic, bell peppers, celery, and filé powder and cook, stirring, until the onions are soft and lightly golden, about 10 minutes. (The filé will become ropy at first, but will liquefy as it cooks.)

Add the vegetables to the broth and meat mixture and bring to a boil over medium-high heat. Put 2 cups of the broth in a bowl and whisk in the dry roux a little at a time, and continue to whisk until it is smooth.

Add the roux mixture, a spoonful at a time, to the simmering broth and meat, stirring until all the roux has dissolved and there are no lumps.

Add the shrimp boil concentrate, salt, pepper, and tasso. Reduce the heat to medium-low and simmer, uncovered, until the meat is tender, about 1 hour.

Serve over white rice and garnish with the chopped green onions and parsley.

Pass filé powder and hot sauce at the table!

A Duck Dinner

Contributed by **MARCELLE BIENVENU**, St. Martinville

My father was also a passionate outdoorsman, and I learned to cook wild game from him when I was a mere teenager. His favorite ducks to cook were teal.

The green-winged teal, at about 14 inches long, is the smallest of all duck species, but is also much loved! When prepared with care, the meat is tender and flavorful. I remember Papa pointing out several teal when we visited the Rockefeller Wildlife Refuge in southwestern Louisiana many years ago. They looked like small mechanical toys bobbing their heads up and down in a pond of bright green duckweed.

Since teal is so small, I usually allow one bird per person, and when I nail Papa's recipes on the head, guests will be sucking the meat from the bones.

Here is a menu that I served one year following the close of duck season.

The first course—grilled duck breasts—is a contribution from Kirk Sieber, another avid sportsman, who had a stash of boneless mallard breasts in his freezer.

Before I get into the recipe, I've noticed something about men who cook—they are always armed with a bottle of Italian salad dressing. I've seen them marinate everything from steaks to chicken and even add some to their boiling pots when cooking crawfish, crabs, or shrimp. Maybe it's a "man" thing. Anyway, this duck breast recipe has Italian dressing, and I can attest to the fact that the taste is pretty darn good. Count on each guest eating two, so you may want to double this recipe.

Grilled Duck Breasts a L'Orange

MAKES 8 SERVINGS

8 mallard duck breasts (removed from the bone), skinned

Cajun seasoning to taste

1 cup Italian dressing

1 large yellow onion, cut into 8 chunks

1 large green bell pepper, seeded and cut into 8 chunks

2 fresh jalapeño peppers, seeded and each cut into 4 chunks

8 thick bacon slices

1 stick butter

1 (10-ounce) can beer

1 cup orange marmalade

Rub the breasts generously with Cajun seasoning. Place the breasts in a glass bowl. Pour in the Italian dressing, cover, and refrigerate for 4 to 6 hours.

Remove the breasts from the marinade and place a chunk of onion, bell pepper, and jalapeño pepper in the center of each breast. Wrap the breast around the vegetables and wrap each with a bacon strip, securing with a toothpick.

Melt the butter in a small saucepan over medium heat. Add the beer and stir to blend. Heat the orange marmalade in another saucepan. Place the breasts on a grill over medium-high heat and baste with the butter-beer mixture. Close the pit and cook for five to eight minutes. Flip the breasts, baste again with the butter-beer mixture, and then brush with the marmalade. Close the pit and cook for about three minutes. The breasts are best cooked medium-rare, but that's a personal opinion. The sugar from the marmalade crystallizes and gives the duck a marvelous flavor.

A fresh pear salad is a nice accompaniment as the sweetness pairs well with the flavors of the roasted teal.

Fresh Pear Salad

MAKES 6 SERVINGS

2 ripe pears, peeled, cored, and coarsely chopped

2 teaspoons plus 2 tablespoons fresh lemon juice

½ cup walnut or olive oil

1 teaspoon Dijon mustard

1 tablespoon chopped shallots

Salt and freshly ground black pepper

5 cups baby salad greens

½ cup pecan pieces, toasted

Toss the pears with two teaspoons of the lemon juice and set aside.

In a small, clean jar, combine the remaining two tablespoons lemon juice, the oil, the mustard, and the shallots. Fit the jar with a lid and shake to blend. Season with salt and pepper. Shake again and set aside.

When ready to serve, put the salad greens in a large bowl and add the pears and the pecans. Pour on the dressing and toss to coat evenly. Serve immediately.

And now on to the *pièce de résistance*—the roasted teal. The *topinambours,* also known as Jerusalem artichokes or sunchokes, were what made this dish so tasty as far as I'm concerned. The white flesh of these root vegetables has a nutty sweet taste—ideal with wild ducks. You can find them during the winter in some supermarkets. If you can't find them, substitute turnips, although the taste will not be quite the same.

Papa's Roasted Teal

MAKES 8 SERVINGS

8 teals (oven ready)

4 garlic cloves, peeled and slivered

Salt

Cayenne pepper

3 cups coarsely chopped green bell peppers

3 cups coarsely chopped onions

1 cup dry sherry

All-purpose flour

8 strips thickly sliced bacon

1 ½ cups chicken broth

1 pound fresh white button mushrooms, wiped clean, stemmed, and sliced

1 ½ pounds tompinambours (Jerusalem artichokes), peeled

3 tablespoons chopped parsley

Make a slit in each of the teal breasts with a sharp, pointed knife. Insert one or two slivers of the garlic in each hole. Rub the outside and the cavities of the ducks generously with salt and cayenne pepper. Place the ducks in a large deep bowl.

Combine the bell peppers and onions in another bowl and mix. Stuff half of the mixture in the duck cavities and put the remaining half around the ducks in the bowl. Add the dry sherry. Cover and refrigerate for at least 4 hours, turning the ducks once or twice in the marinade. Remove the ducks from the refrigerator, drain, and reserve the marinade.

Preheat the oven to 350 degrees. Dust each duck liberally with flour and set aside.

Fry the bacon in a large cast-iron pot or Dutch oven over medium heat until just browned, but not crisp. Remove and drain on paper towels. Set aside.

Add the ducks to the pot and brown them in the bacon grease, turning often to brown evenly. Add the chicken broth and cook for 10 minutes. Add the reserved marinade with the vegetables. Lay a bacon strip over the breast area of each duck.

Cover and bake until the ducks are very tender, 1 to 1 ½ hours. Baste occasionally with pan gravy and add more broth if the gravy becomes dry.

Arrange the mushrooms and the topinambours around the ducks, cover, and cook for 30 minutes, or until the topinambours are fork-tender. Remove from the oven and sprinkle with the parsley.

Let the ducks sit for 10 minutes before carving to serve.

I'm a big fan of wild rice (Uncle Ben is my personal favorite) with game, but you might want to peruse the rice section at your supermarket. There is some flavored packaged rice out there that might suit your taste buds better. The gravy and vegetables in the roasting pan are fabulous to spoon over any kind of rice you choose.

I chose to serve a field pea casserole, the recipe for which came from another hunting pal, the late Henry L. Mayer, Jr., who was by far one of the greatest camp cooks I've come across other than Papa! The combination in the dish may sound a little far-fetched, but I think it's great.

Henry's Field Pea Casserole

MAKES 6 TO 8 SERVINGS

3 (1-pound) cans field peas (undrained)
2 large tomatoes, thinly sliced
3 large white onions, thinly sliced
2 large green or red bell peppers, seeded and thinly sliced
8 bacon slices
Salt and freshly ground black pepper
½ cup freshly grated Parmesan cheese

Preheat the oven to 400 degrees.

Arrange layers of the field peas, tomatoes, onions, and peppers in a large casserole dish. Lay the bacon over the mixture and season with salt and pepper. Sprinkle with the cheese and cover with aluminum foil. Bake until bubbly, about 30 minutes.

Remove the foil and place under the broiler for about 5 minutes. Serve warm.

It was a hard decision about the dessert. I personally like lemon icebox pie with game and fish, but everyone voted for a traditional bread pudding.

Marcelle's Real Bread Pudding

MAKES 6 TO 8 SERVINGS

3 hamburger buns, light toasted and crumbled, or 1/2 loaf day-old French bread, torn into small pieces
1 quart milk
4 large egg yolks, beaten (reserve the egg whites)
½ cup sugar
2 teaspoons pure vanilla extract
4 tablespoons butter, cut into pieces
Meringue (recipe follows)

In a large baking dish, soak the bread in the milk for about 1 hour, then mash well with a fork so that there are no lumpy pieces. Preheat the oven to 300 degrees.

In a mixing bowl, beat together the egg yolks, sugar, and vanilla. Add this mixture to the milk and bread mixture. Stir to mix. Dot the top with the butter. Bake until the pudding firms up, 1 to 1 ½ hours. Remove from the oven and top with meringue. Serve with whiskey sauce.

Meringue

6 egg whites
½ teaspoon cream of tartar
⅓ cup sugar

Preheat the oven to 325 degrees.

Using an electric mixer, beat the egg whites and the cream of tartar in a large bowl until soft peaks form. Gradually add the sugar, beating until stiff and shiny.

Spread the meringue evenly over the bread pudding and bake until the meringue is golden, about 20 minutes.

Whiskey Sauce

4 tablespoons butter
½ cup sugar
4 large egg yolks, beaten
¼ cup bourbon or rum

In the top of a double boiler, melt the butter over low heat. Then gradually add the sugar, stirring constantly with a fork or wire whisk. Do not let the mixture become too hot. Add the beaten eggs in a steady stream, whisking constantly until the mixture thickens.

Remove from the heat and add the bourbon or rum. Spoon the mixture over the bread pudding and serve immediately.

Duck, Oyster, and Andouille Gumbo

Contributed by **MARCELLE BIENVENU**, St. Martinville

A cold front is moving in and the ducks are flying! Put on a gumbo! This one made with teals or mallards, fresh oysters from the bays along the Gulf of Mexico, and smoky andouille is a favorite one of mine. The rich oyster liquor gives the gumbo an extra depth of flavor in my opinion.

MAKES 6 TO 8 SERVINGS

2 mallards, dressed, rinsed in cool water, and patted dry
Salt, black pepper, and cayenne pepper
1 ¼ cups vegetable oil
1 cup all-purpose flour
3 medium-size yellow onions, chopped
2 medium-size green bell peppers, chopped
8 cups (about) water or chicken stock
2 pounds andouille sausage, cut crosswise into ¼-inch slices
2 dozen oysters with their liquor
¼ cup chopped green onions (green part only)

Cut the ducks into serving pieces and season generously with salt, black pepper, and cayenne pepper. Set aside.

Heat ¼ cup of the oil in a large, heavy pot (preferably cast-iron) over medium heat. Add the duck pieces and brown evenly on all sides. Transfer the duck pieces to a platter and set aside.

Drain off the oil in the pot.

In the same pot, over medium heat, combine the remaining 1 cup oil and the flour, and stirring slowly and constantly, make a dark brown roux. Add the onions and bell peppers and cook, stirring occasionally, until the vegetables are soft and golden, 8 to 10 minutes.

Return the ducks to the pot and slowly add enough warm water or stock to cover the ducks completely. Add the andouille and reduce the heat to medium-low. Simmer, uncovered, until the ducks are tender, about 2 hours.

Add the oysters with their liquor and the green onions and cook until the edges of the oysters curl slightly, about 3 to 4 minutes. Serve hot over rice.

Pan-Fried Duck Breasts

Contributed by **MARCELLE BIENVENU**, St. Martinville

This is easy, quick, and delicious. Serve the duck breasts as an appetizer or make it a meal by adding a salad and mashed potatoes.

MAKES 10 SERVINGS

20 boneless duck breasts
Salt, garlic powder, and coarsely ground black pepper to taste
1 ½ cups clarified butter

Rub the breasts generously with the dry seasonings. Pour about 4 tablespoons of clarified butter into a large, heavy skillet, heat the butter, and quickly fry 3 to 4 duck breasts, leaving them a bit rare. Add more butter and repeat the process until all of the breasts are cooked. Keep the duck breasts warm in a covered dish in the oven.

Grilled Duck Breasts

Contributed by **MARCELLE BIENVENU**, St. Martinville

Years ago a duck-hunter friend dropped by my house with a bag of duck breasts and all the ingredients for this delicious dish. Every time I prepare this I think of him. Thanks, Buddy!

MAKES 6 SERVINGS

8 tablespoons (1 stick) butter
1 tablespoon Worcestershire sauce
1 teaspoon chopped garlic
8 ounces fresh mushrooms, sliced
6 duck breasts (preferably mallard), deboned and skinned
Salt, freshly ground black pepper, and cayenne pepper
6 thick bacon strips
6 slices white bread, toasted and buttered

Melt the butter in a saucepan over medium heat. Add the Worcestershire sauce, garlic, and mushrooms. Cook, stirring occasionally, until the mushrooms are just soft, about 3 minutes. Remove from heat and set aside.

Light a fire in the barbecue pit and allow the coals to get glowing red hot. Rub the duck breasts generously with salt, black pepper, and cayenne pepper. Carefully wrap each breast with a strip of bacon, securing it with toothpicks. Let stand at room temperature for 30 minutes.

When the coals are ready, grill the breasts quickly—3 to 4 minutes on each side if you like them juicy with a little blood in the meat, longer if you prefer them well done. Baste with some of the butter sauce.

To serve, place the duck breasts on the toasted, buttered bread and pour the remaining butter and mushroom sauce over each breast.

Accompany the breasts with a tossed green salad dressed with a tangy vinaigrette dressing. A nice red wine would be good as well.

INDEX

Page numbers in boldface type refer to photographs.